WINNING ON THE MARKETING FRONT

WINNING ON THE MARKETING FRONT

The Corporate Manager's Game Plan

WILLIAM A. COHEN

JOHN WILEY & SONS

New York   Chichester   Brisbane   Toronto   Singapore

This publication is designed to provide accurate and
authoritative information in regard to the subject
matter covered. It is sold with the understanding that
the publisher is not engaged in rendering legal, accounting,
or other professional service. If legal advice or other
expert assistance is required, the services of a competent
professional person should be sought. *From a Declaration
of Principles jointly adopted by a Committee of the
American Bar Association and a Committee of Publishers.*

Library of Congress Cataloging in Publication Data:
Cohen, William A., 1937–
   Winning on the marketing front.

   (Wiley series on business strategy)
   Includes index.
   1. Corporate planning.   I. Title.   II. Series.

HD30.28.C63   1985   658.4'012   85-12200
ISBN 0-471-81935-2

Printed in the United States of America

10   9   8   7   6   5   4   3   2   1

This book is dedicated to my teacher,
the master management strategist,
Peter F. Drucker.

OTHER BOOKS BY WILLIAM A. COHEN

The Executive's Guide to Finding a Superior Job, 2nd ed.

Principles of Technical Management

How to Sell to the Government

Successful Marketing for Small Business (with Marshall Reddick)

The Entrepreneur and Small Business Problem Solver

Building a Mail Order Business, 2nd ed.

Direct Response Marketing

Top Executive Performance (with Nurit Cohen)

SERIES PREFACE

Peter Drucker has said, "The future will not just happen if one wishes hard enough. It requires decision—now. It imposes risk—now. It requires action—now. It demands allocation of resources, and above all, of human resources—now." The John Wiley Series on Business Strategy is published to assist managers with the task of creating the future in their organizations.

Creation of the future requires application of the art and science of strategy. *Strategy* comes from the Greek word *strategia*, which means generalship. It has clear military roots, which defined how a general deployed the available forces and resources to achieve military objectives. But business and military strategy, though similar, are not identical. Business strategy is the allocation of resources to achieve a differential advantage at the time and place of decisive importance. *Resources* may be human; they may be financial or promotional, have to do with unique know-how, or have a psychological emphasis. But to be effective, these resources must be concentrated

viiiSERIES PREFACE

so as to be superior where it counts. This achievement is the essence of any successful business strategy and the theme of the series.

The series will investigate strategy in all its many facets in business, including marketing, management, planning, finance, communications, promotional activities, leadership, and corporate culture, to note only those topics under preparation or planned. Its aim is to equip the practicing manager with the techniques and tools he or she will need for the most competitive and exciting period of all time.

WILLIAM A. COHEN
Series Editor

CONTENTS

WINNING ON THE MARKETING FRONT

INTRODUCTION

In a small room in the faculty club at Claremont Graduate School in Claremont, California, Prof. Peter F. Drucker spoke to a special and select group of students back in 1975. These students were all enrolled in a unique doctoral program, unique because all were senior managers and executives of major corporations or nonprofit organizations. In this very first session with this unusual group of students, Peter Drucker emphasized what he felt to be most important for top managers. "The implementation of strategy," he said, "is the manager's prime task."

If it wasn't known or thoroughly understood before the advent of the supercompetitive 1980s, it is clear today that planning and strategy are the keys to winning in business. This fact is being confirmed by more and more articles published in business magazines, such as *Fortune* or *Harvard Business Review,* which stress not only the need for planning but also strategies recommended by today's business

1

theorists. For more than twenty years, slowly at first, and then with greater urgency, colonies of strategy boutiques and consulting firms specializing solely in strategy or planning have been founded and have quickly prospered. Seminars conducted on an almost bewildering assortment of strategy and planning topics have been successful on an international basis, and numerous academic conferences have been devoted solely to these subjects. In 1979, a book by George Steiner, *Strategic Planning,* became perhaps the first strictly business book to become a selection of a major book club. Even throughout the period of intense interest in Japanese management techniques, planning and strategy have remained hot topics in American companies both large and small. And yet another book, *The Mind of the Strategist,* by Kenichi Ohmae, the Japanese director of the Tokyo office of McKinsey and Company, took issue with the notion that Japanese management does not depend heavily on strategy. And this book itself was based on his best-selling book published in Japan, *The Corporate Strategist,* which sold over 100,000 copies in that country.

Nor has this intense interest waned in not-for-profit organizations. Hospitals, universities, and government agencies at federal, state, or local levels have all shown increasing awareness in planning and developing strategies as the keys to success in their endeavors. On several occasions I have been contacted by U.S. Air Force research and development organizations to assist with developing, implementing, and facilitating planning conferences for their organizations. For while planning and strategy both originated in the military, it has been only recently that these important and powerful concepts have been formally harnessed to nonmilitary operations, such as research and development, within the military establishment.

WHY THIS BOOK IS UNIQUE

The Corporate Strategist's Guide to Planning is different from other books that have been published on these topics in recent years. It is the only book that doesn't build strategic concepts out of some quick looks at a few years of operation but is based on strategy evolving over the last 7000 years. This does not mean avoidance of well-known strategy-planning tools, such as those developed by the Boston Consulting Group and others. But what it does mean is this: The development of a strategy is basically an allocation-of-resources problem under risk, uncertainty, and limited resources. For example, the fundamental principle of military strategy is to be stronger at the decisive point of conflict. As noted by famous British military strategist Liddell Hart, "The principles of war, not merely one principle, can be condensed into a single word—concentration."

Some reflection will confirm that this is as true in business as in battle. The resources of any organization or business—profit or non-profit—are always limited. This is accurate whether resources consist of arms, dollars, or people. The opportunities and threats existing in any situation always exceed the resources needed to exploit the opportunity or avoid the threat. Thus strategy in business as in warfare is essentially an allocation-of-resources problem and must involve allocating superior resources against the decisive opportunity. But any tool, technique, or structure must reflect the strategic environment in which the company is engaged. Thus rather than recommending only one tool for strategy development, this book covers each tool with advantages and disadvantages for any situation and goes one step further by showing how to develop a strategy development technique depending on any organization's competitive situation.

Military thinkers have given considerable thought to concepts of strategy. One of the earliest documented was written by Chinese General Sun Tzu in *The Art of War,* more than 2300 years ago. Yet this book is still in print today and even today studied by students of military strategy. In addition there is a tremendous body of knowledge of strategy that did not stop with Sun Tzu 2300 years ago. It has continued with writings that have stood the test of time by such well-known strategists as the Swiss General Jomini, the German General Clausewitz, the previously mentioned Capt. Liddell Hart and General J. F. C. Fuller, both from England, and numerous others and has been amplified in writings by such well-known historical figures as Caesar and Napoleon. Thus there has been a significant body of strategic concepts developed and recorded by military thinkers over several millenniums. In comparison, business strategic thinking over the last few years is a drop in the bucket.

The value of military strategic concepts for business and other nonmilitary interests can be easily demonstrated. For some years firms have recognized that the market for a product or a service is not a mass of look-alike, think-alike, act-alike human beings but rather a number of smaller submarkets, each of which may have certain similar demographic, psychographic, or life-style characteristics which can be measured. Going after a single submarket, instead of attempting to market the same product to everyone, is known today as the strategy of "market segmentation." Using this strategy, a firm's marketing activities are concentrated against that single market segment that offers a greater potential of profitability, as well as customer satisfaction, considering the goals and objectives of the firm and its ability to implement them. It took years and millions of dollars in research and analysis plus wasted effort before business strategy theorists recognized the value of this strategy of market segmentation. Yet it can be clearly derived from the fundamental principle of war strategy: concentration. Al Ries and Jack Trout wrote a valuable book on marketing and advertising called *Positioning—The Battle for Your Mind*. This book developed the notion that a product can be profitably positioned relative to competing products in the mind of prospective customers. A military strategist would immediately recognize that the concept corresponds closely to two so-called principles of war that have evolved in military strategy, that is, "maneuver" and "economy of force." *Maneuver* in battle generally refers to the positioning of physical resources, but it can also mean the manipulation of economic of psychological factors in order to achieve planned objectives. *Economy of force* emphasizes the fact that unless you have overwhelming superiority of resources you can't be strong everywhere, and considering the U.S. military effort in Vietnam, even when general superiority exists, this may not be possible. Accepting this as a fact, this principle admonishes the general to allocate only minimum efforts to secondary or unimportant efforts. Combining these two principles and translating them into the genre of promotion and communication results in a concept of positioning that says pick out the best and most attractive niche in the marketplace for your product and don't try to be everything to everybody.

Similarly, most books on business strategy and planning recommend an analysis of the competition. The products of these analyses are usually a one-for-one comparison of products, pricing, distribution, or supposed strategies. But they do not indicate what the competition is doing or the business battlefield in any overall fashion. Thus the response of a corporate strategist in attempting to take advantage of opportunities and avoid the threats is bound to be tactical and not strategic. In this book I show you exactly how to map competitive actions over time. You won't need a corporate spy to know exactly what your competitors are planning—whether this is revealed in their day-to-day operations or not.

I believe that the book that you have in your hands is different in another way. It does not stop at merely stating a theory but goes on to develop it in detail along with examples to illustrate every aspect. Even further than that, it includes special forms which have been developed to help you both in planning and in strategy development.

WHAT TO EXPECT FROM THIS BOOK

It is true that only a combination of your own inherent talent as a strategist along with experience and training can make you a world-class business strategist. But this book will be of considerable help to you. First, it will show you the basic concept is of strategy as developed by military and academic theorists. Second, it will save you an immeasurable amount of time through use of the forms which have been specially designed to help you in planning and solving your strategic problems by taking advantage of potential opportunities and avoiding potential threats. And finally, it will assist you in developing winning strategies for your organization documented by

clear and logical plans based on strategic rules and principles which
have been proven sound in the past and will prove successful in the
future. As Napoleon Bonaparte said:

> All of the great captains have done great things only by conforming
> to the rules and natural principles . . . that is to say, by the nicety of
> their combinations and their reasoned correlation of their means to
> ends and of efforts to obstacles. Whatever may have been the audac-
> ity of their enterprises and the extent of their success, they have suc-
> ceeded only by conformity to rules and principles.

1

THE PLANNING OF STRATEGY

Many years ago as a young Air Force officer, I was navigating a B-52 jet bomber. It was the middle of the night over the Atlantic Ocean hundreds of miles from land and out of the range of land-based navigational aids. As a consequence, the position of the aircraft and its safe arrival were largely in my hands. I navigated through a combination of airborne electronic gear and celestial navigation, the latter much as the ancient mariners. At one point during a period when most of our electronic navigational aids were useless and before I found our position through celestial means, the pilot called to me over the intercom and asked, "Where are we?" Glancing at the electronic instruments before me, I noted that the one instrument that was still working properly was our Doppler radar. But this instrument gave only ground speed and drift. Of course, I knew our position within a couple of miles through a technique known as "dead reckoning," an estimate based on heading and speed from our last known position. But I jovially answered, "I don't know where we are or where we are going, but according to our Doppler we're getting there very fast."

Since that night over the Atlantic, I have seen a number of managers in major, as well as smaller, companies who could just as easily have given the same answer in seriousness rather than jest. A business project could be rolling along at high speed but with no reference to the whole, to the future, or to reality. Such a project, regardless of funding and the monies invested in it, runs great risk of failure. Without planning and a well-conceived strategy, an organization is trying to achieve its goals and objectives by rolling the dice. It must fail as many times as it will succeed.

Osborne Computers went from zero to $100 million a year in sales and over a thousand employees through good planning and the development of a device which, while it looked ugly and its packaging lacked beauty, sold at a cost of less than 50% of competitive computers. In twelve months, Osborne Computers grabbed huge shares of the market. Yet despite the fact that Osborne Computers had a good product and had made such a major impact in the computer industry, only two years later the company went under. This failure was not because of technical errors but because of the lack of good planning and the ignoring of critical factors in success as the environment changed, such as IBM compatibility. As a result, sales faltered, and the company became strapped for cash.

A STRATEGY PROBLEM

Whereas no planning or poor planning leads to failure, the planning of an excellent strategy can lead to remarkable success. At this time I would like you to stop and consider the illustration of opposing forces in Figure 1.1. Can you solve this strategy problem that actually occurred in warfare? Here are the limitations that existed: You cannot cross the river at your back. You cannot escape parallel to the river in either direction due to hills. You have 20,000 infantry troops and your opponent has 70,000. Each side has 2000 mobile forces. Neither side has air, naval, missile, or any other forces except

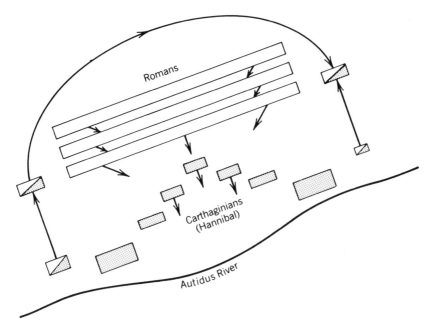

FIGURE 1.1   The Battle of Cannae, phase I.

those noted previously. The enemy can be expected to attack at any moment. The enemy's attack formation and the position of its troops are shown in Figure 1.1. Here is your problem:

How would you position your 20,000 infantry and 2000 mobile troops to meet this attack? Or would you take some other action? Take a few minutes to consider what you as a strategist would actually do.

The Solution to the Strategy Problem

This strategy problem actually occurred at the Battle of Cannae in 216 B.C., in which the Carthagenians opposed the Romans. Hannibal led the Carthagenians and Varro was general of the Roman army. Hannibal won because he developed and executed a well-thought-out plan which incorporated an innovative strategy. His plan was for a defensive-offensive battle in two phases. In phase one,

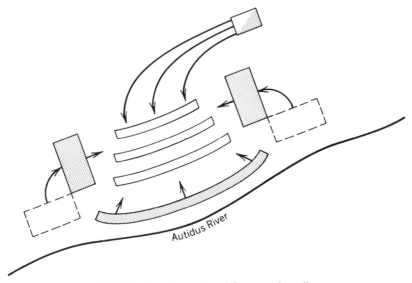

FIGURE 1.2.   The Battle of Cannae, phase II.

Hannibal divided his forces into an advanced weak center and strong flanks, each flank resting on a natural terrain obstacle. His cavalry was posted on both flanks. The mass of cavalry under Hasdrubal was on his left. His center was ordered to withdraw slowly as the Roman's advanced, but his wings were to remain fixed in position. Hasdrubal was to destroy the enemy's right-flank cavalry, then circle the line and destroy the enemy's left-flank cavalry. The enemy cavalry on its left flank was opposed by a small force of Carthagenian cavalry which was to merely hold the Roman force in place. This is as shown in Figure 1.2.

The Action on the Battlefield

Hasdrubal, with his superior cavalry force on the left flank, destroyed and put to flight the cavalry of both the Roman flanks, first one and then the other. Meanwhile, the Carthagenian center withdrew slowly toward the Autidus River. Varro, smelling victory as he saw the Carthagenian center fall back, ordered the mass of Romans to advance, which they did. In ever-increasing numbers and density, they rushed toward the center in order to take advantage of what Varro perceived to be the disintegrating Carthagenian line.

In the second phase of Hannibal's plan, shown in Figure 1.2, Hannibal ordered his center to cease retreating and to join the attack. At the same time, he ordered his two strong wings to wheel in on the Romans as Hasdrubal's cavalry struck unopposed at the enemy's rear to close the trap. So close together were the Roman forces massed that they could not use their famous short swords effectively. The result was the most decisive battle in the history of warfare. Attacked from all sides, the Romans were massacred. Of the original Roman force of 72,000, 60,000 were left dead on the field of battle. The Battle of Cannae went down in history as one of the finest examples of intelligent planning as well as precise execution.

But the advantages of planning are not limited to warfare. *Boardroom Reports,* the bimonthly business magazine, once interviewed an unusual manager. He was not a business executive. Rather, Arthur Resnick was coach of the girls' soccer team at a high school in Scarsdale, New York. Why did *Boardroom* interview a high school girls' soccer team coach? Coach Resnick had led his team to seventy-five consecutive wins and four regional titles in four seasons. Yet all other teams at this high school, both male and female, had just mediocre records during the same period. Further, prior to Resnick's arrival, the girls' soccer team had done no better than the other teams at this school. Resnick was asked about the reason for his success. Among the reasons that he gave for his success was this: "We have a daily, weekly and seasonal plan. Every member of the team gets a letter from me before the season starts stating the goals that the team will be striving to attain."

These successes have have in them lessons which extend beyond their immediate spheres of practice that we can apply to the realm of business. Consider the following:

1. Superior strategy can be more important than superior resources.

2. Planning enabled Hannibal's victory at Cannae; it didn't just happen by his troops "doing their best."

In the words of General George S. Patton, Jr., "Wars are not won by dying for your country, but by getting some other SOB to die for his country."

3. The plan executed by Hannibal's Carthagenians at the Battle of Cannae was a corporate plan. Each separate wing or division of his army or branch, cavalry and infantry, did not act on its own but acted as a part of a cohesive whole in order to achieve victory.

This chapter is about planning and strategy, more specifically, the planning of strategy. Sometimes the words *planning* and *strategy* are used to mean the same thing, but they are not the same.

Strategy. Strategy is how we will achieve company goals and objectives.

Planning. Planning is the formulation of strategy.

These definitions are pretty straightforward, and it would seem only to make sense that every responsible business leader and executive would waste no time in formulating strategy through planning for every important undertaking that was part of his or her responsibility. Yet this is not the case, and some otherwise pretty smart folks sometimes try to do without any type of formal planning whatsoever. The most common reason given when asked about this is: "I have no time to plan. I must react fast and instantaneously. Therefore, I do not need nor have I time to document formal plans and strategies on a piece of paper. I do it all in my head."

Union General Burnside had the same attitude during the American Civil War. He announced publicly that his headquarters were in the saddle, implying that the real planning for any operation was in his head at any given time. On hearing this, General Lee, who defeated General Burnside at Fredericksburg, said, "General Burnside's headquarters are located where his hindquarters should be."

Indeed, planning in your head is good for an emergency only, not for standard operating procedures. It is poor procedure to follow because, since planning in any manager's head is not explicit, it may be incomplete and it also may be misunderstood by others who must execute the plans. Therefore, no matter how good your strategy actually may be, you will still fail unless you have some form of formal documented planning of your strategy.

SUCCESSFUL PLANNING AT FORD MOTOR COMPANY

One of the greatest successes in recent automobile history, which was due to superior planning and execution, started with an environment that included declining sales.

In the late 1950s, several Detroit companies, including Ford Motor Company, attempted to meet the inroads that had been made by foreign cars, principally Volkswagen, by introducing smaller cars of their own. Ford's product was the Falcon. Like contemporary models in other companies, which included the Chevrolet Corvair and Plymouth Valiant, initially the models met with success and captured a respectable share of the market. However, as each succeeding year found greater options and luxuries added and the weight increased, it was clear that the car was becoming simply a scaled-down version of Detroit's larger cars. Sales of the Falcon and the models of Ford's competitors began to decline. At this point, Ford did some in-depth market research and environmental scanning. This effort paid off in the location of an opportunity. While sales of the Falcon had declined every year, sales of certain optional features increased every year. Such options included padded dashes, bucket seats, "four-in-the-floor" gearshifts, and other sports-car features. Redefining its target market and objectives and using prior experience from 1955, 1956, and 1957 with the then two-seat Thunderbird, Ford developed an entirely new concept which it introduced in 1964. It inflicted a Cannae on Ford's competitors. This, of course, was the Mustang, a model type still selling well today but a concept which took several years for its competitors to copy successfully. Such is the result of good planning: clear objectives, knowledge of the marketplace, excellent strategy, and ultimately successful execution.

But no wonder planning works. Several years ago the Conference Board surveyed fifty chief executive officers and asked about their role in planning. Interestingly enough, these fifty chief executive officers felt that planning, as they understood it, was not just a managerial function—it was management.

While earning my Ph.D. at Claremont Graduate School in California, I had the great good fortune to have Peter F. Drucker as my professor and mentor. Peter emphasized again and again the importance of planning as well as the development of strategies. This is emphasized in most of Peter's writings but nowhere perhaps as much as in his classic *Management: Tasks, Responsibilities and Practices,* published by Harper & Row in 1974. According to Peter Drucker, managers must think through and understand their business thoroughly: "This leads to the setting of objectives, the development of strategies and plans and the making of the day's decisions for tomorrow's results."

On April 25, 1975, Col. Harry G. Summers, Jr., U.S. Army, was in Hanoi as chief of negotiations of the U.S. delegation. As reported by Colonel Summers in his book *On Strategy,* during a break in the discussions, he turned to Colonel Tu, chief of North Vietnam delegation, and said, "You know you never once defeated us on the battlefield." Colonel Tu pondered this a moment and then responded, "This may be so, but it is irrelevant."

In fact, a recent Army War College study confirmed that one of the primary reasons for the defeat in Vietnam was a lack of the appreciation of strategy and strategic theory which led to a faulty definition of the nature of the war. According to this study, in which Colonel Summers was involved, the conventional wisdom of the U.S. Army during this period was that "the U.S. Army doesn't make strategy."

If the U.S. Army didn't make strategy and if strategy is how one achieves goals and objectives, it is clear how the Army could never suffer a tactical defeat on the battlefield and yet still fail to achieve goals and objectives necessary "to win the war."

Cleary, planning and strategy are intertwined, and a corporate strategist must not only know the various options but also how to formulate this strategy in the most efficient and effective manner.

Still, planning is a process. It is a process that begins with the definition of a problem and continues on to describe how to solve the problem. The American Management Association has said that planning is a process by which an organization can become what it wants to become. Although as a process, it is always dynamic, always moving and never fixed. This is as it should be and must be because the environment in which a firm is doing business is constantly changing. The process of planning and the plan and objectives must be responsive to these changes, or fail.

Consider this. Winnebago Industries makes motor homes. In 1980 its sales fell 62% in a single year, yet only three years later it had its best year in the entire history of the company and earnings rose 36%. How did Winnebago change defeat to victory? Basically Winnebago won by redefining its market objectives due to a changing environment and zeroing in on a target market of 35 to 45 years old rather than its traditional market set at 45 years and over. This redefinition led to the introduction of new products, advertisements in new media, and so forth. This in turn led to success.

Planning must also be considered a way of life. A couple of years ago a book by a seventeenth-century samurai, who was reputed to have killed sixty men in personal combat by the age of thirty, became a management best-seller and sold over a hundred thousand copies in a single year. This book was *The Book of Five Rings* by Miyamoto Musashi.

Musashi said, "In all forms of strategy, it is necessary to maintain the combat stance in everyday life and to make your everyday stance your combat stance as well."

Musashi was counseling his readers that day-to-day operations should be no different from combat operations. Planning—it means planning, not a once-a-year plan—must be a part of our day-to-day work life. During World War II, Eisenhower, who, as commander in chief, was responsible for the planning and execution of the largest seaborne invasion ever attempted, said "Plans are nothing; planning is everything."

BENEFITS DERIVED FROM PLANS

Planning and plans encompassing a good strategy are essential for the successful strategic operation of any business. But plans also have additional benefits important on a tactical level for daily operations and on a long-range basis for the welfare of the corporation.

Improving Management Style

Those who have the capability of organizing and planning an activity successfully can move up in a corporation because they are able to get things done. Therefore, planning to a considerable extent is a technique which helps to train future top managers.

Assisting in the Most Efficient and Optimum Use of Company Resources

Efficiency and *effectiveness* are not synonymous. Effectiveness has to do with getting the job done; efficiency, how well one gets the job done. You can be successful and still not be efficient. In fact, it is possible to misuse resources to such an extent and in such a wasteful manner that the long-range result is a negative impact on the corporation despite the short-term success. Thus it is extremely important that all corporation resources, including money, capital equipment, and, most importantly, human resources are utilized to the optimum extent and as efficiently as possible. Planning helps to ensure that this will happen.

Integration of the Functions of Different Organizations

Plans provide the broad base and rallying point which all subordinate organizations can use as guidelines to ensure that they are working and continue to work toward the same corporate objective. Thus suboptimization, in which the corporation does an outstanding job and yet the corporation still loses, is avoided. Instead, all organizations work not to the maximization of their individual goals but to the maximization of the goals of the corporation.

The Basis for Good Communication

Plans provide a good basis for communication both up and down the chain of command and among all levels. This does not mean that no other oral, visual, or written communications exist in an organization, but plans provide the opportunity for something special. The development of a good rapport between manager and subordinates at all levels depends not only on a similar interpretation of the organization's goals and objectives but also on the exchange of views between top management and first-line supervision and all levels in between. This is especially critical when you consider that top management has a greater view of the whole, whereas first-line supervisors, who are nose-to-nose with the problem, have the knowledge of the issues which only direct and immediate experience on the firing line can give. Knowledge of both are essential for success. Planning enables this knowledge at all levels to be shared.

Performance Measurement

Plans identify the stages of progress or units of production intended to be accomplished over a given time schedule. It therefore permits both quantitative and qualitative measurements of creativity, innovation, imagination, and knowledge over a given time period. It provides information not only as to how well things are going but also as to what must be done in response to changes in the environment or shortfalls in performance.

Forces Management toward Clear Objectives

Warren Bennis, doing extensive research on executive leadership and management while at the University of Southern California and on the basis of his own experiences not only as a consultant but also as an executive as the president of a major U.S. university, found that individuals will strive harder for explicit and clear objectives. A plan documents these objectives for all to see and makes them explicit so that everyone knows what these objectives are. You can't get "there" if you don't know where "there" is.

If you think having explicit and clear objectives is unimportant, you might considered what happened to *Collier's, Saturday Evening Post, Look* and *Life* magazines. Once the top in their field, each and every one went under. At the same time these magazines failed, magazine sales in total were on the increase. But the objectives, the target markets, of these magazines were unclear because they were too general: human interest and a mass market. To reenter the market successfully, some of these magazines have redefined their target markets with specific, not fuzzy, objectives. Whereas once they went after the entire market, ultimately losing to television, today they practice market segmentation and go after specific groups of readers.

A classic poem, "The Charge of the Light Brigade," would never have been written had it not been for an unclear objective during the Crimean War. Lord Cardigan led some 700 English cavalry against a far-superior Russian force. He not only failed but suffered 75% casualties. Yet these sacrifices were totally unnecessary inasmuch as the objective which he attempted to capture was the wrong one . . . a small error due to the lack of explicitness in his instructions.

THE IMPORTANCE OF PLANNING AND STRATEGY

Some years ago Heidrick and Struggles, the Rolls-Royce of executive search firms, did a survey of chief executives of 500 of the largest industrial companies and 50 of the largest financial, retailing, and transportation companies in the United States. One of the questions it asked was, What is your most important responsibility as chief executive officer?

Interestingly, 100% of those surveyed ranked planning and strategy over other management functions, including management development and selection, capital allocations, profits, policy decisions, and maintaining morale. Further, 62% ranked planning and strategy as their number-one responsibility. This percentage increased as the company size increased. Indeed, 70% of companies over $2 billion ranked planning and strategy as number one.

WHY DO CORPORATIONS PLAN?

During the height of the emphasis on Japanese management in which planning and strategy was downgraded, a book was published in the United States by Kenichi Ohmae called *The Mind of the Strategist*. Kenichi Ohmae is managing director of the Tokyo office of McKinsey and Company. *The Mind of the Strategist* was based on a best-selling book which he had written and published in Japanese, which sold over a hundred thousand copies, called *The Corporate Strategist*. In this book, Ohmae said:

> In Japan, as in the West, it is not unheard of for major companies to fail outright, but I know of no such company that could not have changed direction before it was too late. In each case I have observed, management at a certain point in time simply lost sight of the range of alternatives that were still open and rushed with ever-increasing mental vision to their own destruction.

In 1971, the American Management Association published a book called *Long-Term Profit Planning*, which was written by Ernest H. Weinwurm and George F. Weinwurm. This book described research based on interviews with fifty-nine companies and twenty-three responses to a mail questionnaire. Eighty-two American companies were contacted in the course of this research. What these companies had to say about the reasons for their engaging in what was called "long-term profit planning" may well be applied to all planning.

> The process helps the company's managers reach agreement on the directions in which we should be moving and our basic objectives.

We find that the more effective control of our business that has resulted from our planning process has increased our profitability.

Most noticeable is the increased incentive throughout the company to achieve our objectives.

We find that our program of long-term profit planning forces our divisions to think consciously about the future.

We're just more efficient, that's all.

Our long-term profit plan provides us with a basis for evaluating alternatives.

Having a long-term profit plan forces us to use an orderly planning procedure.

Our management is now forced to think about the future.

Having goals gives us something against which we can compare our progress and alerts us when some corrective action might be necessary.

The different functions of our business are now better coordinated and focused on common objectives.

We are now better disciplined in our thinking about the future.

We have been stimulated to take actions that might otherwise have been deferred.

Our attention is now focused on future opportunities.

Our long-term profit plan is a major communication device between the corporate and divisional levels.

Our planning process helps our management avoid unpleasant surprises.

Planning develops a climate for future thinking.

Now we can make reasonable long-term cash-flow projections.

Success To Those Who Do It Right; Failure To Those Who Don't Do It Or Don't Do It Right.

At one time Volkswagen (VW) swept the world and was the most popular car in history, with sales exceeding 20 million units, including 5 million in the United States. It became Europe's largest auto manufacturer and perhaps the symbol of Germany's resurging industry. Yet though the American auto industry managed to turn a profit in 1982 and 1983 to the tune of some $7 billion for both Ford and Chrysler combined, VW lost $135 million over the same period. What happened? According to a story in the *Los Angeles Times* on February 12, 1984, a Frankfurt banker with close ties to VW stated, "They just rested on their laurels and ignored what was going on in the marketplace."

In other words, VW did not alter its basic strategy to reflect a change in the environment which included not only a change in demand of potential customers but also the addition of strong competition in both the United States and Japan.

In 1982 the Tylenol crisis began when seven deaths occurred in the Chicago area from cyanide-laden extra-strength Tylenol capsules. As a result, millions of bottles of Tylenol were yanked off the shelves. The most successful product in its field disappeared from the marketplace in a few weeks. However, within a year, Tylenol was back—not only was it back on the shelves but it had captured most of the sales that it had lost even though many marketing and advertising experts had pronounced Tylenol down-and-out. This brilliant success was not accomplished in a haphazard manner and was not only due to good advertising, corporate responsibility in removing the potentially hazardous product, and protection of the potential customer through tamper-proof packaging. It resulted from the formulation of a workable strategy through the process known as planning.

Armstrong Rubber Company bounced back from a 1980 deficit of $16.4 million to a record $17.4 million in profits only two years later. This turnaround, masterminded by James A. Walsh, chairman and chief executive officer, and Frank R. O'Keefe, Jr., president, was not an accident but came about through timely planning and a shrewd strategy. As reported by *Fortune* in its September 6, 1982, issue, O'Keefe revamped the entire strategic planning process for Armstrong. In fact, wherever he went he carried with him a 100-plus-page looseleaf notebook which he referred to frequently. "If you've got a plan," he explained, "communicate it. Don't keep it hidden away in a drawer or in the hands of a select few." If everybody in the organization knows the game plan and his or her mission within that plan, you don't have any trouble making judgments and evaluating performance.

It only took nineteen months for Storemaster, a subsidiary of D&E Manufacturing in North Kansas City, Missouri, to go from concept to 20% of the gang box market. Gang boxes are 50- to 600-pound steel tool chests that contractors and industrial shops buy from distributors to store their tools. How was it done? According to Les Nordquist, vice president of the Storemaster subsidiary, and Bob Flowers, president of the parent company, in an interview with Sally Scalon, senior editor of *Sales and Marketing Management* magazine, the process started with a thorough analysis of the gang box market, including a look at such things as competitive products, pricing, terms, physical distribution, costs, and patterns, as well as internal parent company's capabilities. As a result of this environmental scanning, a plan was concocted which included a push strategy. The entire marketing effort was concentrated on reps and distributors, leaving to the distributors the marketing effort to the ultimate buyers.

The crucial message of this chapter is not only that planning and strategy are far from dead and have not disappeared from the corporate scene but that this is the two-element key to success for any business undertaking. In Chapter 2 we are going to look at basic concepts of planning and strategy and their applications to business. Chapter 3 is devoted to one of the most important elements of the environmental variables in which a firm finds itself: the competition. We will learn how to do a competitive analysis in such a fashion that the competition's plans and strategies are revealed, whether the competition likes it or not. Thus actions can be taken to avoid threats and take advantage of opportunities inherent in the competition's strategies. Chapters 4 through 8 all include various methodologies of structuring strategies using the product life-cycle and product portfolio analyses. In particular, Chapter 8 will tell you how to develop your own specialized multifactor portfolio technique which can be optimized according to your company's situation at any given time.

Chapter 9, on the marketing plan, demonstrates by example how to develop and structure a plan incorporating some of the techniques discussed earlier.

Throughout this book, the intent is to provide information so that the corporate strategist can exercise intuition, judgment, and talents in developing creative strategies in the company to better the competition through satisfying the customers' needs in a more complete and expeditious manner. Thus the planning of strategies results in victory not only for the corporation but also for the customer and clientele which it services.

2

THE BASIC CONCEPTS OF STRATEGY

In this chapter we look at the basic concepts of strategy and business strategy as a foundation for all strategic moves that a company might make in beating its competition and satisfying the needs of its customers.

Strategy is simply how we go about achieving the objectives and goals we set. It is hardly a new concept and had its beginning in antiquity. The earliest-recorded military fortifications that have ever been found have been unearthed at Jericho on the west bank of the River Jordan. Most of us are familiar with the Battle of Jericho and the Bible's description of Joshua's victory. Recall that Joshua's objective was to capture the town. His strategy involved a demonstration in which once each day for six days the entire Israelite force marched around the city in a menacing fashion. On the seventh day they not only marched around it seven times but, on command, shouted in unison as the priest blew the ram's horn. According to the Bible, the walls of Jericho immediately fell down and the de-moralized defenders were easily beaten. Clearly, this was no simple contest of might but involved a definite strategy. In fact, even before Joshua led the Israelites to the outskirts of Jericho to lay siege, Joshua had initiated his campaign of attacking the morale and spirit of his enemies. The Bible reports that Rehab, a harlot who lived in Jericho, told him, "The terror of you has fallen on us and all inhabi-tants of the land are losing heart because of you." Recent excava-tions have confirmed that the walls of Jericho were destroyed at a time period corresponding to Joshua's conquest. Whether the walls were destroyed or were not destroyed instantaneously and miracu-lously, the defenders of Jericho were probably beaten even before the first spear was thrown or sword was thrust as a result of Joshua's strategy of psychological warfare, which culminated in daily marches around the city and built up to the final day's activities when the city was actually taken.

As noted earlier, the first book written on strategy was by Chinese General Sun Tzu more than 2300 years ago. Thus serious thinking about strategy, at least military strategy, goes back several thou-sands of years into the past. Yet it is the basis for the most modern strategic actions by General Motors, Procter & Gamble, Boeing, Bendix, in fact, of all major U.S., international, and multinational corporations as well as smaller companies. Truly, the corporate strategists behind the scene are descendants of these ancient practi-tioners of strategic skills and concepts that have been developed over the millennia.

The reason these early military strategic concepts are still applica-ble and are applied in business operations is that strategy is basically an allocation-of-resources problem. Further, resources are always limited, no matter the size of the company, the business, or even the country which is engaging in strategy. The object in business is to allocate these limited resources in such a fashion as to be stronger at a point that will make that company decisive over its competition in satisfying the needs and wants of its customers. The military prob-lem in which a general must allocate superior resources to be stronger at the decisive point of battle is a close analogy. In business, we call this allocation of resources to the decisive point a "differential," or a "competitive," advantage. It means that at the particular point we are speaking of, we are stronger than our competitors. We have strength against their weakness where it counts. Note that this does not mean that we are stronger everywhere. Few companies can be stronger than all their competitors or even their strongest competitor everywhere. It is because of this fact that much smaller companies can take on and win against industrial giants at certain points of contact or niches in the market where superior strength can be achieved by the smaller competitor. In these situations, these are the decisive points. Thus the fundamental concept of strategy, to be stronger at the decisive point, must pervade all our strategic thinking and planning, regardless of what techniques we employ or processes we use to develop and plan our strategy and to implement it.

In this chapter we discuss four fundamental strategic concepts: product differentiation, market segmentation, positioning, and the indirect approach. In addition, we also talk about the twelve principles of strategy for business. These principles must be considered at any time a strategy is evolved. Finally, we talk about the strategic variables (product, price, promotion, and distribution) and when each should receive emphasis under different conditions.

PRODUCT DIFFERENTIATION

Product differentiation is a strategy in which the marketer differentiates its products from those of its competitors and promotes those differences to its customers. The success of a product differentiation strategy is highly dependent on the differences which can be promoted, whether these differences are in the products themselves, the packaging, the price of the distribution, or other aspects by which we make our offering different from that of our competition.

The possibilities of differentiating any product are limitless. Automobiles can be made of higher quality, higher performance, or greater economy in usage. They can also be differentiated by price such that a Rolls-Royce is very expensive and a Volkswagen inexpensive. A typewriter can be made fully portable and lightweight or can be given many additional features that portable typewriters cannot incorporate. A company that provides the service of developing film can develop it quicker than competitors, provide a higher-quality product, or offer it at a lower cost. A book on computers can be differentiated for business, for the serious hobbyist, or for the beginner. Even a commodity like gasoline can be differentiated by the service provided with it, low price, credit card availability, restroom facilities, and so forth. Noted Harvard marketing professor Theodore Levitt believes that everything can be differentiated. To accomplish this, he suggests viewing a product from three different perspectives: generic, expected, and augmented. The "generic" perspective would be simply the product itself. Considering our gasoline example, it would be simply the gasoline itself. Gasoline, segmented by octane or by lead content, may be perceived to be approximately the same as all other brands of gasoline; thus the generic product perspective. An "expected" gasoline product would be the generic product plus a certain number of minimal customer expectations. These might be the price; certain peripheral services or additionals available at the place of purchase, such as water, air, and restrooms; and perhaps the availability of certain basic automobile parts or components, such as tires, batteries, or windshield wipers. Finally, we come to the "augmented" product. This perspective would represent not only the generic and expected product but also something more than is expected by the buyer and that he or she may not have even considered. An example might be gasoline with an additive to reduce engine wear or perhaps gasoline which produces far greater mileage than would ordinarily be the case.

Through product differentiation one can offer products different from those of the competitor to the same market or can increase market share by offering different products to the same market and giving customers a choice.

MARKET SEGMENTATION

A market is not a homogeneous mass of prospects but contains numerous submarkets, each of which may be composed of potential customers that have certain characteristics in common. These characteristics may be demographic or psychographic, or they could have to do with geographic location or buyer behavior. For example, a mass market may be segmented demographically by age, sex, family size, income, occupation, education, religion, race, and nationality. In psychographics we may segment by the introvert versus extrovert, by conservative, liberal or radical, or by life-style. And by buyer behavior, we may segment according to brand loyalty, readiness to purchase, price of benefit sought, or usage rate. Of course, we can always segment by geographics depending on the region of the country, city size, climate, and so forth. The fact is that each segment is different. We usually cannot satisfy the needs of all such segments simultaneously, but we can concentrate superior resources against a particular segment (the decisive point) and satisfy these needs better than our competition.

In order for a company to practice a strategy of market segmentation, the market must be divisible into identifiable and measurable subsets which have some common characteristics. If a submarket cannot be measured, a segmentation strategy cannot be followed. However, even if such a subset is identifiable and measurable, it must also be reachable by the marketer. Maybe we know that a certain segment of the mass market exists in a foreign country for a food product which we are selling here in the United Sates and this market segment can be measured. However, we may still not be able to market to this particular segment because of difficulty in channels of distribution, promotion, transportation, or other problems. Finally, even after we have been able to identify, measure, and reach the market, the market must be of sufficient size in terms of purchasing power in order for us to make it profitable to do so. Whether this is so or not will vary, depending on what we are selling, as well as other environmental and internal variables, including the size of our company and the overhead we are carrying. Thus a smaller company may be able to identify a certain market segment and find it very profitable to sell to that segment, whereas a larger company, because of overhead, cannot do this.

Clearly, following a strategy of market segmentation is highly dependent on the ability to do market research to discover the various factors which make up common characteristics of a particular subset of the overall market. Segmentation bases, which are of a demographic or geographic nature, are relatively easy. For example, in Figure 2.1, a combination of age, income level, and education might be used to segment an overall market into thirty-six different submarkets, or market segments. Each one would then be evaluated in terms of potential, and a strategy could be developed to reach those segments that have the greatest profit potential in the particular situation being analyzed. Using a computer, one can analyze or break down many other subsegments with different combinations of demographics or geographic variables. Although the same can be done with psychographic and behavioral segments, these are somewhat more difficult and less straightforward to measure than geographic and demographic information, which could be obtained by using a simple survey form.

William Wells and Doug Pigert developed the activities, interests,

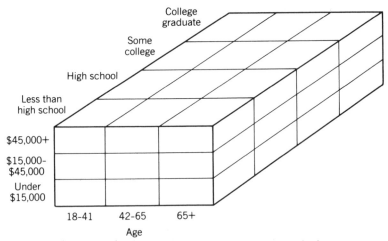

FIGURE 2.1. Market segmentation by age, income, and education.

and opinions concept, in which they attempted to measure people's activities in terms of:

1. How they spend their time
2. Their interests
3. Their opinions in terms of how they view themselves in the world around them

One technique developed in order to assist in buyer behavior segmenting is known as "multidimensional scaling." With this technique, different dimensions of customer perception of various products and customer preference are noted and measured on a scale such as that shown in Figure 2.2. Figure 2.2 is a measurement of only two dimensions of a product, in this case, power and econ-

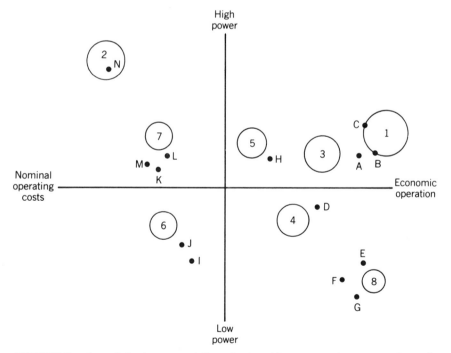

FIGURE 2.2.   Buyer behavior segmentation of automobile power and economy using multidentional scaling. Circles indicate demand; dots indicate automobile brands or models.

omy. However, in real life and with the use of computers, many dimensions can be measured simultaneously. This figure is derived by first asking consumers to rate known brands as to the quality that the market researcher wants to measure, in this case, automobile power and automobile economy. Consumer responses are then averaged and plotted on the perceptual map shown in Figure 2.2. Note that when two different brands are close together, they are perceived as being somewhat the same. One can also survey consumers to find out what their ideal image of the product is for the qualities measured. These points can also be plotted and then clustered by the circles, as indicated in the figure. The largest circles are where the heaviest demand is located according to the survey response.

The multidimensional scaling map also has implications for strategy and objectives in that the product, in this case, automobiles, might be modified so as to move it into the areas of heavier demand. Thus automobile A might be moved into the area of highest demand (circle number one) by increasing power and economic operations slightly.

PRODUCT DIFFERENTIATION VERSUS MARKET SEGMENTATION

While at times both product differentiation and market segmentation strategies can be followed, at other times the two are at odds and one must consider which strategy is best given a certain situation. R. William Kotrba developed a strategy selection chart that follows six factors in deciding which strategy to pursue. These six factors are size of market, consumer sensitivity, product life cycle, type of product, number of competitors, and typical competitor strategies. Let's look at each in turn.

Size of Market

If the total number of potential buyers for a particular product is not great, then clearly a segmentation strategy is less possible in that it violates one of the criteria for implementation of this strategy, that is, that the market be of sufficient size in purchasing power. Therefore, a small market segment implies a product differentiation strategy.

Consumer Sensitivity

In situations where consumers are sensitive to a differentiated product, product differences become more important and a product differentiation strategy should be considered. On the other hand, should the product or its attributes be perceived by its potential buyers as dull and uninteresting, there is less reason to promote these differences and a greater argument for a market segmentation strategy.

Product Life Cycle

During the early part of a product's life cycle, when the market is not familiar with the new product's attributes, a considerable opportunity exists to promote product differentiation. At the same time, during the growth stage, when a company is seeking to establish that product in the marketplace by capturing large market shares, it is less efficient to go after individual market segments. Thus the early stages of a new product introduction into the market generally call for a product differentiation strategy, as opposed to a market segmentation strategy. However, if a product is introduced into a market in which similar products have been around for quite a while, it may be far better to pick off a major segment and to promote to it if other criteria are met, since differences may not be as well perceived by the mass of potential customers in the total target market.

Type of Product

If a product easily lends itself to having significant changes made in its appearance, its design, or its performance, it is possible that the same product can be adapted with few changes to different markets or segments. Clearly, this is not true for all products. Some products, such as those of a commodity nature (salt, gasoline, or steel), cannot be easily adapted to different types of markets through a change in the product itself. In such cases, it is better to adopt a strategy of product differentiation in which these products can be made different through a change of packaging, distribution, or other strategic variables in order to gain a competitive advantage.

Number of Competitors

The greater the number of competitors, the more difficult it is to sell a differentiated product, because it is more difficult to make a product different enough to be perceived as different from numerous other products. That means that if there are a lot of products in the same marketplace, the key to success is usually to find a niche or a market segment and concentrate on dominating it rather than trying to make your product somehow different from many, many other products of the same type. If there are only a few products of your product type in the market, a product differentiation strategy is usually better.

POSITIONING

The concept of positioning differs from that of product differentiation, although the two concepts are related. With positioning, the product, as a mix of attributes, is modified to be perceived in a certain position relative to other similar products in the mind of the consumer. This concept became popularized starting in 1972 when two advertising executives, Al Ries and Jack Trout, initiated a series of articles for *Advertising Age*. Later, they wrote a book called *Positioning—The Battle for Your Mind*. In it they emphasized that "positioning is not what you do to a product; positioning is what you do to the mind of the prospect. That is, you position the product in the mind of the prospect."

Analyzing the competition to decide on positioning may be accomplished with a multidimensional scaling technique, as indicated
previously. Or it could be done with a perceptual map, as shown in
Figure 2.3. The perceptual map in Figure 2.3 is the result of a number of surveys of products existing in the marketplace, in this case,
products A, B, C, D, and E. Let us say that the five products analyzed are different home computers and various market segments
would be identified and asked questions regarding different features
that may be considered important. The closer the dots with the letters representing the different computer products are to one another,

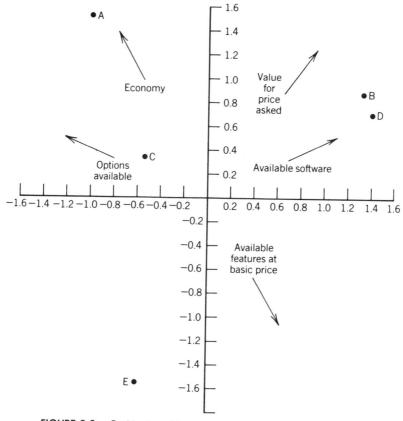

FIGURE 2.3.   Positioning of home computers, using a perceptual map.

the more similar the products are. Thus products B and D, which are fairly close together, are similar and are perceived as being such by their potential customers. Note the five features plotted on this perceptual map that an individual looks for in purchasing a computer: economy, available software, features provided at the basic price, additional options available, and value for the price asked. These are indicated by arrows. The perception for these attributes can be read for each of the five different computers. For example, computer A is the highest on economy as perceived by that market segment surveyed. Computer E is the lowest for value for price asked.

With the use of the perceptual map, as indicated in Figure 2.3, a corporate strategist can decide where to position a new product in the marketplace or where to position her or his firm versus competitive firms or brands versus competitive brands.

Dr. Yoram Wind of the Wharton School at the University of Pennsylvania has identified six different alternative bases for developing a product positioning strategy:

Specific Product Features.   Thus a corporate strategist can position a soap product on the basis of the fact that it floats or on its smell.

Benefits, Problems, Solutions, or Needs.   The soap could be positioned by the fact that it kills more bacteria than another soap and leaves one smelling fresh.

A Specific Use or Occasion.   A soap can be positioned for particular occasions, such as on a date.

User Category.   The soap could be positioned for everyday use or for those who want the very best.

Against Another Product.   A soap could be compared with another product and advertised that more value is given for the same price.

Product Class Disassociation.   Instead of a cleansing agent, a soap can be positioned as a skin softener. This identifies it as an entirely different type of product than one would expect by the title "soap."

INDIRECT APPROACH

The indirect approach was developed by master military strategist Liddell Hart. Captain Hart studied all the great campaigns of history. His basic thesis was that in most campaigns the dislocation of the enemy's psychological and physical balance had been the vital prelude to victory. Further, dislocation was brought about by a strategic indirect approach whereby the successful protagonist never sought to achieve objectives directly. Liddell Hart himself considered the indirect approach the key to practical achievement not only in warfare but also in politics, business, and all forms of human endeavor.

The indirect approach implies that whatever the resources, be they physical, psychological, or other, they should never be used directly or obviously against an objective. In implementing an indirect approach strategy, Liddell Hart, in his book *Strategy*, developed eight maxims, six of which were positive and two negative, as a guide for operationalizing an indirect approach strategy:

Positives

1. Adjust ends to means. This means keeping a cool sense of the art of the possible and recognizing when something is not possible.

2. Keep the object always in mind. Every objective should bear on a final object, and alternative objectives should be considered relative to their possibility of attainment, along with their furtherance of achievement of the objective if attained.

3. Choose the line or course of least expectation. In other words, do the unexpected.

4. Exploit the line of least resistance as long as it leads you to achieve an objective that contributes to the ultimate underlying object.

5. Choose a line of operation which offers an alternative objective. Following this advice allows you to put your opponent

on the horns of dilemma in which one way or the other you attain at least one objective that will lead to the attaining of your final object, since the opponent cannot guard every objective equally.

6. Ensure that both plan and disposition are flexible and adaptable to circumstances as you encounter them. Since, once engaged, things will never go exactly as planned, you must ensure that your disposition of resources will allow you to exploit or adapt as quickly as possible.

Negatives

7. Do not commit yourself while your opponent is ready for you. According to Liddell Hart, the expanse of history shows that except when going against a much inferior competitor, no second stroke is possible until the competitor's power of resistance or invasion has been neutralized or minimized.

8. Do not renew a campaign along the same lines or same ideas as the one that has failed. A mere reinforcement of resources along that line is not sufficient since it is probable that the competitor has also reinforced along this line of defense.

THE PRINCIPLES OF WAR

The principles of war were developed by military thinkers and writers over the millennia. According to Napoleon Bonaparte, the principles of war have regulated the great captains from the beginning of recorded warfare. Unfortunately, while there is some general agreement as to the content of these principles, they have been extensively modified both before, during, and since Napoleon's comment. As a result, there is no one single list, and different lists have been compiled depending on the writer or even the country that has compiled them. For example, the U.S. Army acknowledges nine principles of war, but the Soviet Union only five. The United Kingdom lists nine principles, but three of the nine are not identical with those stated by the U.S. Army. John M. Collins, a specialist in national defense and former director of military strategic studies and chief of the Strategies Research Group of the National War College, developed a comparative chart of several of these lists of the principles of war, as shown in Figure 2.4. Note that ten principles are listed for the United States. This is because when the U.S. Air Force obtained its independence from the Army in 1947, the Army decided to switch one principle, the principle of coordination, and change it to the principle of unity of command, while the U.S. Air Force elected to retain the original principle.

THE PRINCIPLES OF BUSINESS STRATEGY

Using the list of the principles of war developed by Collins, I have developed a listing of twelve principles of business strategy which eliminates duplication and includes only those principles that can be definitely applied to business.[1] Let's look at each of these in turn.

1. *Objective.* The principle of the objective implies that every strategy must have an objective and that the objective of every strategy should be the attainment of a specified and decisive goal. It must be specified and documented so that it is clearly understood by everyone responsible for or participating in the attainment of that objective. You must also be decisive in order to minimize the cost of attainment in resources and time.

2. *Initiative.* Initiative implies action, not reaction. Thus the principle is one of maintenance of an offensive attitude so that the business strategist controls the time and place of action and, in this fashion, dominates both situation and competitors. When a defensive attitude is forced on the business decision maker, it must be considered only as a temporary expedient until a counteroffensive action can regain control and the initiative.

[1]From William A. Cohen, "The Application of Historical Military Strategy Concepts to Marketing Strategy," in John C. Rogers III (ed.), *Developments in Marketing Science,* Vol. 6 (Miami: Academy of Marketing Science, 1983).

Principles Including Alternative Titles	United States	United Kingdom	Soviet Union	Sun Tzu	Clausewitz	Fuller
Purpose						
Aim		X				
Objective	X			X	X	X
Direction						
Initiative						
Offensive	X	X		X	X	X
Concentration		X		X	X	
Mass	X					X
Economy of force	X	X			X	
Maneuver	X					X
Mobility				X	X	
Movement						
Unity of command	X*					
Cooperation	X					
Coordination				X		
Security	X	X				X
Surprise	X	X		X	X†	X
Simplicity	X					
Flexibility		X				
Freedom of action						
Administration		X				
Morale		X	X		X*	
Exploitation					X†	
Pursuit						
Quantity/quality of divisions			X			
Armament			X			
Ability of commanders			X			
Stability of the rear			X			

* U.S. Army only.

† Listed as an "element," rather than a principle.

FIGURE 2.4. Principles of war. (Adapted from *Grand Strategy*, by John M. Collins, Naval Institute Press, 1973.)

3. *Concentration.* The principle of concentration is part of the fundamental concept of all strategy. It means that concentration of resources, whether they be human, dollars, capital equipment, or psychological factors. It was stated amply during the Civil War by Confederate General Nathan Bedford Forrest, who said that winning battles was a matter of "getting there fustest with the mostest."

4. *Economy of Force.* Since resources for any company or for any project are always limited, it goes without saying that no one can be strong everywhere. Once you face this fact, you can avoid trying to do the impossible and focus on being strong where it counts. Economy of force cautions the strategist to allocate minimal resources to secondary efforts but, following the principle of concentration, to be stronger at the decisive point.

5. *Maneuver.* Maneuver has much to do with the positioning of resources to assist and obtain the accomplishment of the objectives that have been set. In military strategy, it implies physical positioning. However, for business, it can also mean the manipulation of the economic or psychological factors in furtherance of plans or in response to unexpected opportunities that arise. Maneuver also incorporates the concept of timing, which is most important in deciding when to do what and in what sequence.

6. *Unity of Command.* This principle requires that for every assigned task or project there is only one responsible manager. This alignment ensures unity of effort, which is absolutely required in order to obtain the maximum power output from the resources that are available.

7. *Coordination.* This principle emphasizes cooperation between other organizations within the company and the integration of tasks and planning the overall strategy as well as implementing it. Through coordination, the dangers of suboptimization, in which a subordinate unit does well but the overall mission fails, are minimized, while such principles as economy of force and concentration are made easier to implement.

8. *Security.* The principle of security demands that you must never allow a competitor to acquire an unpredicted advantage over

you. This is the rationale behind competitive market research. It reduces the vulnerability of the business campaign to competitive action and reaction. Reducing this vulnerability may refer to physical security as well as to guarding information about your own capabilities and intentions from an actual or potential competitor.

9. *Surprise.* Surprise may come from different sources, including perception, secrecy, variation of methods, innovations, audacity, speed of action, or, simply, doing the unexpected. All studies of strategy have shown that surprise can compensate for grossly inferior resources. Further, the principle of surprise does not require that your competitor be totally ignorant of your intentions, only that you can accomplish what you intend before your competitors can effectively react to stop you.

10. *Simplicity.* Simplicity is recognized as an important principle of business strategy because the strategist and planners who put together any plan of action for a campaign must recognize that it is others who must implement the strategy that they concoct. Thus this principle emphasizes that plans must be as simple and direct as possible, since even the most simple plans are usually difficult to execute under operational conditions and pressures in the marketplace. Since implementation of the strategy is the final step in attaining the objective, this implementation must be emphasized even in the early planning stage through application of the principle of simplicity.

11. *Flexibility.* An old maxim says that everything that can go wrong will go wrong. Von Clausewitz called the difference between what was planned and what was actually encountered in combat "battle friction." Every corporate strategist must be prepared for battle friction. This is accomplished by building flexibility into the plan in such a way that risk and uncertainty are allowed for to the maximum extent possible. Thus a change of direction, once engaged in the marketplace, is not only possible but fairly easy to accomplish.

12. *Exploitation.* Exploitation refers to the continuance of the successful campaign. Operationally, it says that when winning, keep going and don't relax the pressure until the success is complete, as

long as sufficient resources are available. When this principle of business strategy is applied, a competitor is kept forever off balance and has minimum opportunities to regroup to initiate a counter-strategy.

In general, there are four ways that we may utilize these principles of business strategy.

1. *For Better Understanding.* We may use them for a better understanding of what happened and why, that is, for postmortems. Thus a campaign where only a partial success occurred can be examined for lessons to be learned in terms of these twelve principles of business strategy.

2. *As a Checklist.* The principles of business strategy can be used as a checklist to ensure that none of these principles is unintentionally violated. This means that while sometimes it may be necessary to violate one or more of these principles for valid operational reasons, we must ensure that these violations are not unintentional and that risks and uncertainties are known and minimized.

3. *Developing New Strategic Concepts.* Some of the strategic concepts stated earlier, such as product differentiation, market segmentation, and positioning, have all been developed from empirical experiences in the marketplace. Naturally, this hard-won knowledge should not be thrown out. But consideration of the principles of strategy may lead us to concepts of strategy which in various combinations may be successful without paying the penalty of experience first.

4. *Comparing Alternative Strategies.* The application of strategy is situational. In certain situations, some principles of business strategy are more important than others. Thus a weighting system for decision making can be developed, as shown in Figure 2.5. Depending on the relative importance in a given situation, a subjective importance value in points would be assigned to each principle. Each alternative strategy option would be compared relative to this weighting system and the extent which that strategy incorporated

	Weighting	Strategy 1	Strategy 2	Strategy 3
1. Objective	.10	.10 × 3 pts. = .3	.10 × 2 pts. = .2	.10 × 1 pt. = .1
2. Initiative	.10	.10 × 5 pts. = .5	.10 × 2 pts. = .2	.10 × 4 pts. = .4
3. Concentration	.30	.30 × 2 pts. = .6	.30 × 3 pts. = .9	.30 × 2 pts. = .6
4. Economy of force	.10	.10 × 2 pts. = .2	.10 × 5 pts. = .5	.10 × 1 pt. = .1
5. Maneuver	.12	.12 × 2 pts. = .24	.12 × 1 pt. = .12	.12 × 3 pts. = .36
6. Unity of command	.03	.03 × 2 pts. = .06	.03 × 5 pts. = .15	.03 × 1 pt. = .03
7. Coordination	.03	.03 × 2 pts. = .06	.03 × 4 pts. = .12	.03 × 3 pts. = .09
8. Security	.03	.03 × 1 pt. = .03	.03 × 1 pt. = .03	.03 × 5 pts. = .15
9. Surprise	.07	.07 × 2 pts. = .14	.07 × 1 pt. = .07	.07 × 2 pts. = .14
10. Simplicity	.04	.04 × 5 pts. = .20	.04 × 3 pts. = .12	.04 × 1 pt. = .04
11. Flexibility	.04	.04 × 1 pt. = .04	.04 × 2 pts. = .08	.04 × 2 pts. = .08
12. Exploitation	.04	.04 × 4 pts. = .16	.04 × 1 pt. = .04	.04 × 1 pt. = .04
	1.00	Total 1.09	Total .91	Total 1.05

FIGURE 2.5.   A weighting system for comparing strategies on the basis of the use of the principles of business strategy (weight × points).

the principle being analyzed. Those strategies with the highest values would be considered candidates most likely for successful implementation.

USE OF THE STRATEGIC VARIABLES

"Strategic variables" are those variables that we control for formulating marketing strategies: product, distribution, price, and promotion. The promotional variable is further subdivided into advertising, personal selling, sales promotion, and publicity.

We will be discussing these in greater detail as they are used in developing a marketing plan for any business situation in Chapter 9. However, it is important early on to recognize that, as no firm has sufficient resources to do everything it may want, in every business situation, resources must be allocated to the decisive point. Professors Stewart H. Rewoldt, James D. Scott, and Martin R. Warshaw, all of the Graduate School of Business Administration at the University of Michigan, have developed a marketing strategy planning matrix to illustrate which of these strategic variables to emphasize in any situation. Let's look at three widely different products for an example. A sample matrix is shown in Figure 2.6. The three products that we look at are home computers, insurance, and soft drinks. Now, once again, the question is, How can we distribute our resources among those variables that are most important for any par-

Strategic Variables	Home Computers	Insurance	Soft Drinks
Product	5	2	2
Distribution	3	4	4
Price	3	2	3
Promotion			
Advertising	4	3	4
Personal selling	3	5	1
Sales promotion	2	1	2
Publicity	4	3	2

FIGURE 2.6.   Matrix for allocating strategic variable resources: Allocations for home computers, insurance, and soft drinks.

ticular situation? If we are marketing home computers, it might be possible to allocate resources equally among development of the product, distribution, pricing, and the various aspects of promotion. However, this would be a very unwise strategy and would be akin to trying to be strong, or at least as strong as we could, everywhere. We would be averaging our resources among all possibilities. A competitor who concentrated resources in maximizing one of these strategic variables would probably do better than we would in satisfying potential customers. By putting more money into product, it could have a better product than we could. Or it could have a better distribution system or a lower price or be able to let more people know about the virtues of its product through promotion. Thus averaging our strength is not a good strategy. Look at the matrix shown in Figure 2.6. Using a rating scale of 0 to 5, assign importance values to each strategic variable for each product. Assign the most important variables for each product a 5, and those of least importance a 0. For the home computer, the product variable would probably be the most important strategic variable. Most consumers will spend a lot of time comparing different models and makes of computers before they purchase. If the product is unsatisfactory, because it has inferior features, it will not be purchased. But distribution is also important for the computer, although perhaps not a "5." The question we must ask ourselves is, If a distribution system is already set up, can we significantly increase sales by adding additional channels of distribution or somehow improving our older channels? Let's assign a 3 for distribution for home computers. How important is the price variable? Well, for a similar model offering similar features, unless the price is dropped drastically, the price is probably not too critical. Certainly a small change of 10% in price will probably not have much effect on the product. Let's give the price variable a 3 also. Advertising is clearly more important, so we'll give it a 4. Personal selling in this instance is important but not critical, so we'll give it a 3. Sales promotion, which includes sweepstakes, contests, special gift offers, and discounts to encourage purchases, is probably not very important, so we'll give it a 2. Finally, we have publicity. Publicity with the home computer, a high-technology product, is probably of some importance. If our computer gets poor publicity despite our advertising, we probably cannot be successful. On the other hand, good publicity can really help sales. We'll assign it a 4. In the same fashion, we should go through insurance and soft drinks.

Life insurance will be assigned the following values: product 2, distribution 4, price 2, advertising 3, personal selling 5, sales promotion 1, and publicity 3. Soft drinks will be assigned product 2, distribution 4, price 3, advertising 4, personal selling 1, sales promotion 2, and publicity 2.

From Figure 2.6, we can see how these different variables are important for different types of products that we may introduce and where the emphasis should be for these strategic variables. For example, if we are going to sell the home computer, the product variable is the most important and it should have a large amount of our resources assigned to it. On the other hand, note that the product variable is not nearly as important with soft drinks or with insurance. With the home computers, personal selling has been given a 2 value, but with life insurance personal selling is a 5. Clearly, insurance requires a different emphasis than either home computers or soft drinks, which has been given a 1 for personal selling.

The way the matrix has been filled out is only for illustration, and in different business situations we might assign different values for the different products listed here. Further, it is unlikely that one company or division would have such different products as home computers, life insurance, and soft drinks. Rather, think of your product line in such a matrix with the products being labeled A, B, C, D, E, and so forth, and the various emphases listed in distributing resources due to different strategic variables. The point is, don't distribute your resources equally or try to be strong everywhere. Be strong where it counts!

In this chapter we've looked at the very beginnings of basic strategic concepts that are required in order to prevail over the competition. The basic idea is that of concentrating your resources at the decisive point to result in a differential advantage or competitive advantage at a position of your choosing. The attainment of this objective is dependent on a thorough analysis. This will be discussed further in the coming chapters, and additional techniques will be provided to assist in the fundamental aim of being decisive and having overwhelming and superior resources at the decisive point.

3

COMPETITIVE ANALYSIS

THE NEED FOR COMPETITIVE ANALYSIS

The analysis of the competitor in any business situation is essential, due to the fact that the competitor constitutes an intelligent obstacle to achieving the goals of the corporation. A competitor will react to our actions or strategies so as to attempt to offset any benefits that would normally accrue and to stop us from achieving our goals and objectives. Contrasted with competitors, other environmental variables lack a hostile intelligence. At times they hinder our strategies, but at other times they help us, since there is no intent to oppose our designs by serving the marketplace better.

THE TRADITIONAL BASES OF COMPETITIVE ANALYSIS

Traditionally, competitors have been analyzed on the basis of certain quantitative and nonquantitative measurements. Such measurements might include sales, market penetration, profits, pricing, product performance comparisons, and numerous financial ratios, which could include measures of liquidity, measurements of stock performance, measures of return on investment, and measures of profitability. A more complete listing and definition of these financial ratios can be found in Appendix II. But the important thing to realize here is that although such comparisons should be made, there are limitations to this type of quantitative analysis. Financial ratios are based on financial position at one particular time and are derived from past performance. They are not in themselves forward-looking or indicative of a company's strategy. Also, businesses are not perfectly comparable. Assets or liabilities can be described in different ways on financial statements. As a result, the financial ratios completed for your business may differ from an industry average or from supposedly identical ratios of your competitors for reasons other than performance. Product comparisons in themselves may not be too enlightening, unless you also know the market segments for which they are intended. Finally, it is difficult to understand what the competitor is up to by simply comparing numbers. Such comparisons of quantitative facts give little indication of what they mean in the sense of the strategy and strategic moves and positioning of your competitors.

Back in 1974 Jerry Wall did a survey on competitive analysis which was published in *Harvard Business Review* in the November–December 1974 issue as "What the Competition Is Doing: Your Need to Know." In this survey Wall sought to discover the kind of information respondents felt management needed to know about competitors. The results of this survey indicated that what was needed was far more extensive than was previously anticipated. Wanted was competitive information on pricing, expansion plans, competitive plans, promotional strategy, cost data, sales statistics, research and development, product styling, manufacturing processes, patent and infringement, financing, and executive compensation. Certainly such competitive information should be collected and compared wherever possible. This data, when plotted, leads to a series of competitive analyses, such as the product comparison shown in Figure 3.1. But these competitive analyses must be presented in some coordinated fashion.

COMPETITOR PROFILE OUTLINE

William L. Sammon, an analyst on the corporate strategic planning staff of Pfizer, Inc., in his book coauthored by Mark A. Kurland and Robert Spitalnic, *Business Competitor Intelligence,* recommends a complete competitor profile outline as follows:

I. Background/History
    Major events, acquisitions, divestitures, mergers
    Overseas investments
    Industry reputation
    Corporate culture: past, present, continuity
II. Business/Product Mix
    Five-year segment analysis: sales/profits/investments
    Major products: market share/market growth
III. Major Corporate Objectives/Strategies
IV. Recent Trends/Business Developments
V.   Financial Analysis: Five-Year Comparison with
     Industry/Business Norm
     Sales growth
     Profit growth
     Return on assets
     Asset turnover
     Operating margin
     Net margin
     Return on equity
     Debt ratio

VI. Strategic Assessment
     Strengths/weaknesses: functional and operational
     Strategic direction/management assumptions
     Expected performance/responsive capability
     Implications to Company Z and Company Y (your company)

However, as pointed out by Sammon, other questions might be
asked if the requirement was to evaluate competitive strengths of a
division of a company or to evaluate the strategic significance of an-
nouncement of a major investment in a new manufacturing facility.
For an analysis of a division of a company, questions might be asked
regarding divisional sales of each product; percentage breakdown of
each product by type; major features; key components; how the
product is used; market served; what has been the division strategy;
how successful has it been; distribution channels; terms of sales and
credit policies; market share by product line; geographic region
served; concentrations; size; competence; organization of sales force;
technical service provided; whether the division is more or less profitable than the other division or the company's other businesses;
whether the segment uses more capital than it generates; how the financial performance of the segment compares with industry norm,
including growth, sales, profits, assets, return on assets, and return
on sales (operating margin); asset turnover; major cost issued in division; key sources of profits; character and productivity manufacturing processes; process, size, capacity, and operating rates of major
facilities; plant locations; capital investments; overseas sources; relationship to marketing staff; competition to this division, including
number and size of rivals; comparative market share and growth
prospects; strategic position and performance; comparative financial
statistics; management competence, including age, length of service,
and depth; dominant professional background, that is, whether
marketing, tactical, financial, and so forth; company reputation; industry reputation; organizational and functional ability; recruit-
ment sources; advancement past; flexibility; and adaptability. In the
case of a major investment in a new manufacturing facility, investi-
gations might include the configuration, that is, the production

Type & Manufacturer	Weight (Size Medium), lb	Protection	Material	Cost (Small Quantities), $
American Body Armor & Equipment Co. Model 310	10	.44 magnum	Nylon & steel	120
Centurion Mark II	4½	.44 magnum	18 plies nylon	60
Burlington S/7840	6¼	.41 magnum	20 plies of 1050 nylon	70
David Clark	3	.357 magnum	Kevlar	130
Protective Materials PA-120	9	.357 magnum	Fiberglass	135
Second Chance	9	.44 magnum	Nylon	60

FIGURE 3.1. Body armor: competitive products in the police market.

53

Type & Manufacturer	Weight (Size Medium), lb	Protection	Material	Cost (Small Quantities), $
Armor of America (Rolls-Royce) Grade 36	10	.44 magnum	Fiberglass	135
Life Shield	4½	.44 magnum	Nylon	60
Transcon	14	.357 magnum	Doron (fiberglass) aluminum	70
Federal Laboratories	4	.44 magnum	Kevlar	160
GOEC (Smith & Wesson)	9	.357 magnum	Nylon & steel	120

FIGURE 3.1. (continued)

54

components layout of the facility; the comparative competitive position in terms of scale of manufacturing costs, determining which key elements of production equipment are subscale; the major reasons for the announced investment; the identified production bottlenecks that this facility will address; how it will affect total and variable manufacturing costs and how customers will view this investment; in what way the facility improvement expansion furthers the competitor's corporate and/or product line strategies; and what the competitor's significance of the investment is to our strategic position.

In every case, Sammon says the information about the competitor that should be analyzed is situational and, borrowing from the military, calls this, the information that should be collected, "essential elements of information" (EEI). The EEI contains the critical items of information regarding the competitor and the competitive environment needed by the business strategist in order to make a decision and develop a strategy.

Michael E. Porter, in his book *Competitive Strategy*, recommends analyzing each competitor's future goals, current strategy, assumptions held about itself in the industry, and its capabilities. In short, all the competitor's strengths and weaknesses. This, Porter said, is accomplished in order to find the answers to the following questions:

1. Is the competitor satisfied with its current position?
2. What likely moves or strategies will the competitor make?
3. Where is the competitor vulnerable?
4. What will provoke the greatest and most effective retaliation by the competitor?

The acquisition of all this information will tell us what the capabilities of the competitor are and also its likely intentions. Of course, while looking closely at intentions, we must always be prepared for what a competitor is capable of doing.

While each of these elements can be analyzed independently, they lack a cohesive structure to enable us to analyze the situation as a whole and to see what the competitor has been doing and where its future actions will lead. To do this, what is needed is a competitive battle map.

THE BATTLE MAP

Consider again the warfare analogy. Since ancient times a pictorial representation of the ground over which a battle is fought has been used with great effect. This pictorial representation, of course, is the battle map. The battle map shows the location and the strength of friendly forces as well as the location and strength of the forces of the enemy. In addition, it shows the major environmental factor with which fighting armies are concerned: terrain. Over a period of time the map can show movement of both enemy and friendly forces; it can show enemy reactions to strategies that have been implemented, revealing enemy movement and strategy in the past as well as potential enemy movement strategy in the future. Through the use of the pictorial representation called a "battle map," a military strategist can spot the strengths and weaknesses of his or her own as well as of the opposing forces. Plainly seen is a graphic representation of both the threats and the opportunities inherent in future strategies that may be undertaken.

BUSINESS BATTLE MAPS

In the same fashion as the battle map for military forces, business battle maps can be used to assist in planning strategy and conducting meaningful competitive analyses. One such business battle map is the "Du Pont Profitability Matrix." With the Du Pont Profitability Matrix, a financial quantitative frame of reference is established using the Du Pont financial ratio analysis formula. This formula, or equation, states that operating margin *times* asset turnover *equals* return on assets (ROA). Via this formula, the Du Pont Profitability Matrix is constructed as shown in Figure 3.2. On the horizontal axis, operating margin is shown; on the vertical axis, operating asset turn-over. The curved lines plotted on the matrix are lines of equal return on asset percentages, which are calculated by multiplying operating margin percentages *times* operating asset turnover. The direction of the arrow shows profitability as ROA increases in this direction. Also plotted on the Du Pont Profitability Matrix are dashed lines. These lines indicate the industry average for operating asset turn-over and for return on operation assets.

In the example in Figure 3.2, competitor A and competitor B both have an identical ROA of 20%. However, clearly, these firms obtained this equal ROA using different strategies. Competitor A's operating margin was far lower than that of competitor B. Further,

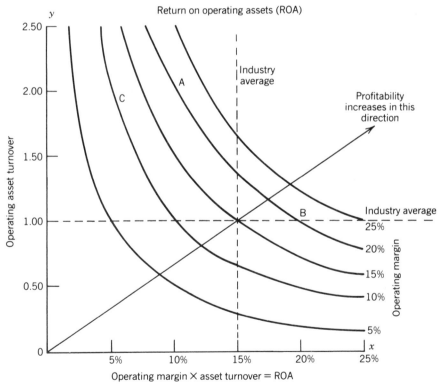

FIGURE 3.2.   The Du Pont Profitability Matrix. Adapted from William L. Sammon, Mark A. Kurland, and Robert Spitalnic, Business Competitor Intelligence, Wiley, New York, 1984.

competitor B's business is probably more capital intensive since the margin is higher than the turnover. Note that competitor C has a lower ROA of 10%, although operating asset turnover is identical with that of competitor A.

As shown in Figure 3.3, the Du Pont Profitability Matrix can be used to plot the firm's ROA over a period of time. From these movements we can see that these firms are following strategies, either intentionally or unintentionally, which reposition their ROA as a result of operating asset turnover and operating margin. Although the Du Pont Profitability Matrix does not in itself provide the answers or describe the strategies that are employed by the companies, it does point out the results in such a fashion as to allow us to ask questions which, under analysis, may lead to the answers of what these strategies might be.

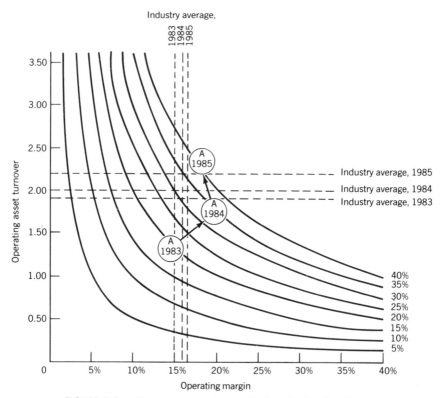

FIGURE 3.3.   Movement over time on Du Pont Profitability Matrix.

Other Business Battle Maps

The Du Pont Profitability Matrix is only one type of battle map
that can be used. Others can be even more descriptive, like the military battle map showing locations of both competitors' and your
own resources and how they are arrayed for any given business situation and location. Further, additional dimensions can be given to
such maps above the two-dimensional matrix available in the Du
Pont Profitability Matrix. William E. Rothschild, in his book *How to
Gain (and Maintain) the Competitive Advantage in Business*, recommends
two such battle maps: (1) the competitive arena map and (2) the
segmentation matrix map. With the competitive arena map, you
first define your business in terms of the need that you fill. This
might be an educational need, a food need, a transportation need, a
communication need, and so forth. You then develop a competitive
arena map of the business arena you serve. The vertical axis is used
to document products and services that fill this arena. The horizontal axis is used to document the various types of customers in the
arena. Choose categories for this axis that help you understand your
customers best. Thus the horizontal axis may be categorized by
land, sea, air, and space customers; by Army, Navy, Air Force,
NASA, DOE for government marketers; from conduit to content for
the information business; and so forth. You then plot the current
providers of these products and services as shown in Figure 3.4.

Segmentation Matrix Business Battle Maps

Once you have completed a competitive arena business battle map,
Rothschild recommends a segmentation matrix battle map for local
or regional plotting of competitors. You begin by selecting the products and services to be analyzed and then determine how they can
best be described. In other words, you segment them according to
the most convenient description for your situation, be it pricing, size,
quality, complexity, function, or whatever is most important. This
description goes on the vertical axis. You then segment your market
into customer groups. This segmentation can be geographical; dem-
ographical, including age, size, family size, family life cycle, income,

Products

A—Ground–air; short range Ground–air; medium range Ground–air/space; Long range Ground–ground; short–med. range	B—Sea–ground; long range Air–ground; short range Air–air Sea–sea; short–medium range	B—Ground–ground; long range Air–ground; long range Space–ground; long range Air–ground; intermed range Air–ground; short range Air–air Space–space	Air–ground short range Air–air Ground–air; short range A—Ground–air; medium range Ground–ground; short–medium range

Services

Consulting A—Feasibility studies Trade-off studies Applied research B—Pure research Development B—Testing	Consulting A—Feasibility studies Trade-off studies Applied research B—Pure research Development Testing	Consulting Feasibility studies Trade-off studies Applied research B—Pure research Development Testing	Consulting B—Feasibility studies Trade-off studies Applied research A—Development Testing

	U.S. Army	U.S. Navy	U.S. Air Force	U.S. Marine Corps
Components	Warhead A—Guidance B—Air frame/space frame Propulsion Defense Launch	Warhead Guidance Air frame B—Propulsion Defense Launch	Warhead A—Guidance Air frame/space frame B—Propulsion Defense Launch	Warhead Guidance Air frame Propulsion Defense Launch
Parts	Electrical Mechanical Hydraulic Fuels Armor Explosive	Electrical Mechanical Hydraulic Fuels Armor Explosive	Electrical Mechanical Hydraulic Fuels Armor Explosive	Electrical Mechanical Hydraulic Fuels Armor Explosive

FIGURE 3.4. A business battle map for missiles, with two companies' activities annotated: Company A and Company B.

61

occupation, education, religion, race, or nationality; psychographical, including social class, life-style, or personality; and behavioral, including use of the product, frequency of use, benefits sought, user's status, usage rate, loyalty status, readiness-to-buy stage, or attitude toward product.

Plot competitors, as well as your own position, on this segmentation matrix business battle map as shown in Figure 3.5.

In both cases, the positions of competitors and their movement will indicate strategies that these competitors are following in concentrating their resources and seeking to dominate various markets or positions on the battle maps that you have constructed. Interestingly, even if a competitor is moving in the marketplace by bumping and blundering along, the business battle map will show this. With such maps, you will know what a competitor is doing in reality— even if the competitor does not.

Making the Business Battle Maps Three-Dimensional

So far these business battle maps are useful. However, they do not indicate all the information that they might because of their two-dimensional aspect. Therefore, it is necessary to add a third dimension in order to make them more useful in planning and analyzing the strategies of our competitors and in noting the opportunities and threats in every business situation. The third dimension in military battle maps is terrain, and terrain features are shown by various colorings of the map and by contour lines of equal terrain elevation. The major terrain feature that we are interested in on a business battle map is the size of each segment that we have depicted in total market. Note that this is not just annual sales in this segment but rather the total market that is potentially available. The *total potential market* is calculated by multiplying the number of potential customers in the segment by the average price of the products sold. Thus if the segment has a potential 2 million customers and the average product price is $2, the segment would be $4 million. Each segment is indicated by a different code. A segment containing less than $5 million in potential sales is left blank; $5 to $10 million in

	Children/Teens	Age 19–35	Age 36+
Plain toothpaste	Colgate-Palmolive Procter & Gamble	Colgate-Palmolive Procter & Gamble	Colgate-Palmolive Procter & Gamble
Toothpaste with fluoride	Colgate-Palmolive Procter & Gamble	Colgate-Palmolive Procter & Gamble	Colgate-Palmolive Procter & Gamble
Gel	Colgate-Palmolive Procter & Gamble Lever Bros.	Colgate-Palmolive Procter & Gamble Lever Bros.	Colgate-Palmolive Procter & Gamble Lever Bros.
Striped	Beecham	Beecham	
Smoker's toothpaste		Topol	Topol

Product segmentation

Customer segmentation

FIGURE 3.5. Segmentation matrix business battle map for toothpaste.

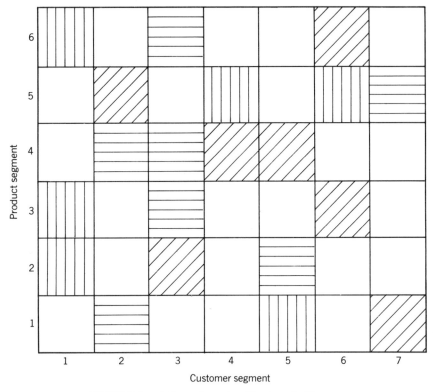

FIGURE 3.6.   A three-dimensional business battle map.

potential sales is indicated by a series of 45 ° lines; $11 to $20 million, by a series of horizontal lines; and $21 to $30 million, by vertical lines. Naturally you can develop your own code for the various segments that may be served in the arena you are analyzing. An example of the three-dimensional map with the information just described is contained in Figure 3.6.

PLOTTING ACTIVITIES ON THE BUSINESS BATTLE MAP

Plotting activities and movement of your firm and of competitors on the business battle map can make the map even more useful to the corporate strategist. Additional information is important, including how much of the share of the market all competitors have and the resources possessed by each competitor. This can be done as illustrated in Figure 3.7. A small rectangle indicates a competitor's or your own activity in a particular segment. This rectangle is divided by a line going from the lower-left corner of the rectangle to the upper right. The upper division of this shows a percentage. This percentage is the market share of that segment of that competitor. The figure shown in the lower-right part of the rectangle, separated by the diagonal, is a quantitative representation of the assets committed to doing business in this segment. If assets cannot be ascertained, use some other measurement of strengths common to all competitors which is known or can be estimated, such as annual profits or sales.

Showing Additional Information on Business Battle Maps

Additional information can be shown on business battle maps through overlays. Overlays, as used with military battle maps, indicate such things as weather, escape and evasion areas, and other factors which, if shown on the basic map, would make it too difficult to read. Through the use of overlays, additional information can be shown without cluttering a map that is already burdened with much essential information. For example, various profitability measurements might be compared for each segment and placed on an overlay, or a measurement of whether the segment is growing or declining could go on an overlay.

Reading the Business Battle Map

A study of the business battle map, especially one plotted over a period of time, will show your own and your competitors' strategies, movements, probable intentions, successes, and failures. For example, if a competitor has initiated a strategy of vertical integration, this will be clearly shown by a competitive arena battle map, which has services through components and finalized products plotted on the vertical axis. Geographical expansion and its direction and intent can be seen on the horizontal axis of a segmentation matrix business battle map segmented by geographical location. The maps

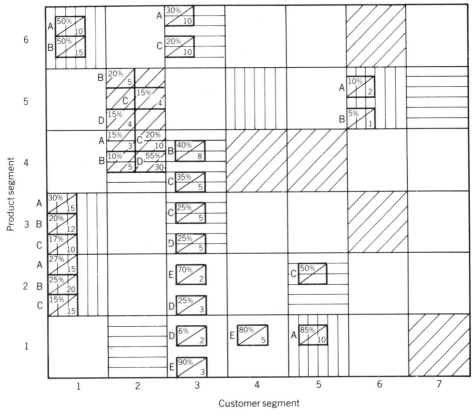

Notes:

1 Companies A, B, C, D, E only plotted.

2 In some cases smaller companies which are
  not plotted have the remaining market
  shares in a segment.

3 Sales estimated in millions of dollars.

FIGURE 3.7. **Three-dimensional business battle map with activities plotted. Notes: (1) Only companies A, B, C, D, and E are plotted; (2) in some cases smaller companies that are not plotted have the remaining market shares in a segment; and (3) sales are estimated in millions of dollars.**

can be used in noting customer segments that are going unserved and areas where resources should be concentrated to realize an opportunity.

Competitive analysis is crucial since competition is the only intelligent element of the environment that can react to cause your plans to fail. But if a complete analysis is accomplished on the competition, including both positioning and strategy, you will be in a position to avoid the threats posed by its strategy while taking advantage of the opportunities in any business situation.

4

THE PRODUCT LIFE CYCLE CONCEPT AND ITS USE

THE PRODUCT LIFE CYCLE CONCEPT

The product life cycle concept was born when it was observed that products go through cycles of life very similar to those of human beings. The different stages of a product life cycle were charted by researchers and separated into different phases with common characteristics. A typical categorization of the different phases for a product life cycle includes introduction, growth, maturity, and decline.

A representative product life cycle is shown in Figure 4.1. The upper curve represents sales, the lower curve profits; the horizontal axis is time, the vertical axis dollars. In the first phase of this idealized product life cycle, the product is introduced. In this phase sales are low, and due to the high expenses of introducing the product,

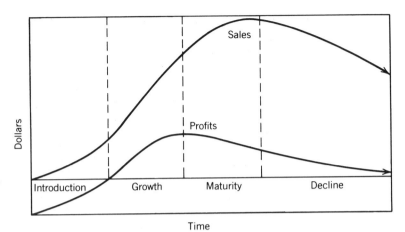

FIGURE 4.1.   Representative product life cycle curve.

profits are low also. In addition, since most products fail in the marketplace, market acceptance of the product is not certain. Clearly, it is in our interest to keep this phase as short as possible.

If the product successfully negotiates its way through the introduction stage, it next enters a period which is termed the "growth phase." Note that in this phase sales grow rapidly. Profits also grow rapidly initially, but then they tend to reach a peak and level out. The reason for this is that the rapid growth attracts competition, which tends to drive prices down even while sales continue to rise.

The next stage is termed the "maturity phase." In the maturity phase, sales peak and then begin to decline also. Profits are declining more rapidly. During this phase the weaker competitors are squeezed out of the marketplace and only the stronger survive.

The final stage of the product's life cycle is the "decline phase." In this phase, sales and profits are falling fairly rapidly. This may be due to new technology, which has resulted in a replacement or better product; social trends; or other environmental factors. Profits, of course, are also still continuing to fall during the decline stage. And in this stage, only the strongest of the original competitors that once marketed this product still remain.

In general, it should be noted that the total time span of the product life cycle is tending to decrease for all products. A hundred years ago a product may have taken fifty years or more to progress from introduction to decline. Back in the late 1930s the DC–3 became a popular airliner and remained so for fifteen years. But several years later, the DC–7 was used by the world's airlines for less than five years. The life cycle for unmodified aircraft remains short. Hand-held calculators, which came on the market in 1972, also have exhibited increasingly rapid life cycles. In 1973 I purchased a calculator for eighty-five dollars which offered little more than the four mathematical functions of addition, subtraction, multiplication, and division; it had no memory and only with difficulty could it be inserted inside my jacket pocket for easy access, although it gave me the appearance of being armed. It came with a ten-year warranty. A year later I allowed my kids to play with this calculator until breakage. For less than one-third of the price, a calculator much lighter, much smaller, complete with functions, including percentages and memory, was available. It, of course, was followed by smaller calculators the size of credit cards, calculators with alarms, chronographs, and so forth. A generally similar pattern has been followed with watches, video games, and other high-technology products. But it is also true of less sophisticated items.

WHY YOU SHOULD USE THE CURVE FOR ANALYSIS

The product life cycle curve can be extremely important in generating strategies, and it should be monitored and controlled by the corporate strategist. This is necessary due primarily to five reasons:

1. Rapid Maturity of Products

As noted earlier, products are maturing faster and progressing through their life cycles more quickly all the time. This is notably true in the higher-technology industries. Therefore if you do not manage the product life cycle and allow for the fact that products that are currently your staples will eventually be obsolete, you can be at a serious disadvantage against an aggressive competitor.

2. Life Cycle Product Mix

An audit of your current product line will reveal products in various stages of the life cycle. This mix may be favorable or unfavorable. If all your products are in one stage, it is analogous to having all your eggs in one basket. If all your products are in the decline phase, you'd better take some sort of remedial action at once. Very shortly you may not have a market for any of your products.

3. Strategic Implications

As we will see shortly, there are different strategic implications and strategies for different stages of the product life cycle. The current strategy that you're following may have been a good one for your product six months or a year or more ago when the product was in a different stage of the life cycle. But now that it's not in this stage, it is imperative to apply strategies that are more likely to cause you to be successful.

4. Product Planning

Strategists are always involved with future planning in order to answer the questions: What will we be doing tomorrow? and What products will we offer tomorrow? This product planning is impossible without a clear analysis and understanding of where your current products are and where they are likely to be next year.

5. Changing the Life Cycle Curve

It has been proved that it is possible to change the shape of the life cycle curve by understanding the principles involved and allocating resources at the right time at the right place. For example, the life cycle curve can be extended through finding a new use for a product. One well-known example is Arm & Hammer baking soda, which originally was used primarily in cooking but today is also marketed as an odor absorbent in refrigerators.

Managing the product life cycle is one major help in avoiding

frightening fires tomorrow and in preparing for the future successfully.

THE PRODUCT LIFE CYCLE CURVE NOT ALWAYS THE SAME

Some strategists have failed in their strategic planning and product
planning when using and developing strategies based on product life
cycle because they assume that the curve is always as shown in Figure 4.1. However, this is not true. One study found nine different
variants of product life cycles. Another extensive study by the Management Science Institute of over a hundred different product categories noted that only seventeen product classes and 20% of
individual brands had the typical shape shown in Figure 4.1. Why
do the shapes vary from that which was originally thought to be typical? Let's look at a few shapes and see why they vary from the so-
called standard.

Figure 4.2 shows a product life cycle curve when new technology

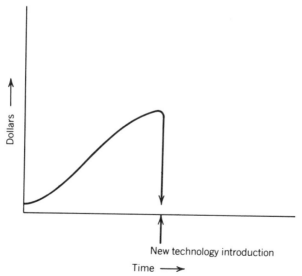

FIGURE 4.2. Product life cycle when new technology is introduced.

is introduced which is so advanced that it immediately obsoletes the product for all but the museum. A relatively recent example of this occurred when hand-held calculators replaced slide rules in the early seventies. Engineers who had habitually carried a miniature slide rule in a pocket and kept a more comprehensive slide rule on the desktop stopped purchasing the product. So did engineering schools and all others who had been accustomed to using the familiar wooden, bamboo, plastic, or metal invention that had been used for more than fifty years. Note that the new technology may obsolete the product in any stage, even though in the case of slide rules this occurred during the maturity stage of the product.

Figure 4.3 shows what happens when one plots the product life cycle of a fashion product. The market for the product continually rises and falls as the product goes in and out of fashion. Men's clothing is an obvious example here. Men's clothing, while changing from year to year, has gone through cycles of fashion: broad ties, narrow ties; broad lapels, narrow lapels. Hair worn either long or short also demonstrates the fashion cycle.

Figure 4.4. shows a fad product. With a fad product, the life cycle really consists of only two stages. The first stage is combined intro-

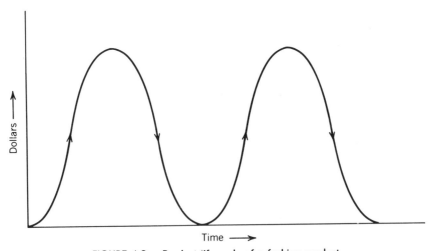

FIGURE 4.3. Product life cycle of a fashion product.

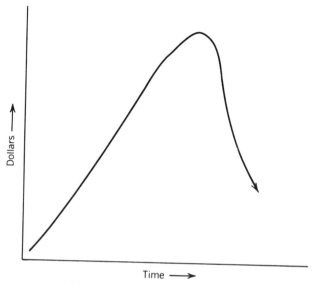

FIGURE 4.4   A fad product life cycle.

duction and growth; the second, rapid decline. There really is no maturity stage unless, as shown by the dotted line in Figure 4.4, the fad has a significant residual market. An example of this might be a book which is a best-seller, enjoys a period on the best-seller list, and then is continually sold over a number of years on the publisher's backlist of books still in print even though it is no longer promoted.

Some products, as shown in Figure 4.5, have an unusually long introduction phase. This occurs when a product is not an instant success and when it may be difficult to get the consumer to accept and adopt the product. Both automobiles and airplanes would fall into this type of product life cycle.

From looking at these curves, it is clear that it would be extremely dangerous to assume a standard shape for any product in any industry and attempt to use it to assist in strategy generation. In fact, the only thing that makes any sense at all is to recognize and understand the concept and then plot your own curve depending on the situation. We will discuss how to plot your own curve in the next chapter.

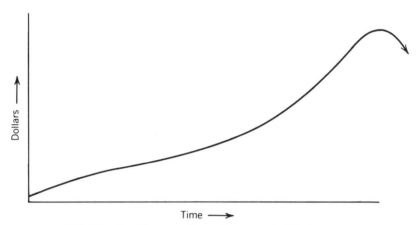

FIGURE 4.5. Life cycle of a product which is difficult to get accepted.

DETERMINING STRATEGIES FOR THE INTRODUCTION STAGE OF A PRODUCT LIFE CYCLE

Regardless of the ultimate shape of the product life cycle you are analyzing, there are certain common strategies that tend to make sense simply on the basis of the fact that the product is in a certain stage. Let's review again the situation in the introduction stage. Here we have few or no competitors of any importance. Of course, the profits we are generating in the introduction stage are slight or nonexistent, due to high production, research and development, and marketing costs. The pricing during this stage of the new product is usually high so that we might start to recover the cost of developing and introducing it, although it could be set low under certain circumstances. There is also a distinct problem in the marketplace: The buyer is not yet convinced about the product and is still buying whatever product or service we hope to replace. There is a high production cost since we have short production runs and must use highly skilled labor and have not yet gone through an experience, or learning, curve. The opportunity for exporting the product at this point is probably limited.

There will also be other situational variables unique to your particular product, industry, business, company, and other factors. As you use the product life cycle concept in developing your strategies, you may want to add these variables to the list to describe the situation of your product in this or any other stage.

In general, for this stage of the product life cycle, we want to establish *market share*. We must do this by persuading what is known in consumer behavior theory as "the early adopters" to buy our product. Clearly, research and development and engineering, as well as production, are all key functions during this phase, and various combinations of product, price, promotion, and distribution channels must all be considered to achieve whatever market share goal we have established.

It is very desirable that the introduction period be as short as possible so that we minimize the tremendous output of resources. Thus we will minimize the negative impact on both earnings and cash flow.

The duration of the introduction stage is determined by both the product characteristics and the amount and nature of the resources we commit. Remember, it takes money to make money.

The newer and more innovative the idea, the harder it generally is to get the concept accepted by the early adopters. The Wright brothers invented the airplane and made the first flight in 1903. Yet it wasn't until 1907 that they were able to persuade the U.S. Army to buy its first airplane.

We can sometimes minimize this psychological newness and differentness by product design. This has been done in calculators which have a beep and make other noises, although they can be built to make no noise at all. The beep and the other noises accustom individuals who are used to associating calculations with noisy machinery. The noisy machinery told them that the machine worked. A silent calculator would not. It was tried and rejected by customers. It was just too different from what had been used previously. An odorless insecticide probably would not sell, even though its advantages would seem to be obvious. Similarly, it was necessary for microwave ovens to have a browning feature which would allow cooked meat to have an artificial brown color, even though the browning itself was unrelated to the cooking of the meat.

Why so? Because people are used to the fact that cooked meat is a brown color and uncooked meat is not. Therefore, no matter how well cooked by their microwave, if meat wasn't brown, psychologically it wasn't cooked.

Overcoming this newness and persuading the early adopters to buy may also necessitate additional resources to disseminate the information to dispel the newness. This may involve promotions, demonstrations, tests, and the gathering of testimonials. Several years ago a new armor material based on a development of plastic never sold due to the unwillingness of the developer to spend additional monies for promotion after research and development. Contrast this with Du Pont which developed Kevlar at no small cost, yet spent an equal amount promoting this new material which, though different, had a significant advantage in several industries over previous materials used. As a result, Kevlar tires have replaced many belted steel radials, and in the armor industry Kevlar cloth displaced a multi-million-dollar ballistic nylon industry.

Complex Products

The more complex the product, the slower the rate of adoption and therefore the longer the introduction stage. This should be planned for ahead of time so that unrealistic sales will not be forecast. Computers, which have achieved tremendous growth, have slowed in one segment: personal computers. Analysts have determined that complexity for home buyers is a major factor. Therefore, if you are introducing a product that is highly complex, anticipate problems ahead of time, develop strategies to solve the problems, and keep the introduction stage as short as possible.

Environmental Factors

Various environmental factors can also slow the introduction stage of new products. I mentioned the introduction of the automobile. The actual introduction stage took approximately twenty years. One reason was the environmental factor of not having paved highways. Government internal politics may also be an important environmental factor for various industries. Firms depending on the government for funding may find difficulty in obtaining this funding because the agency may already be committed to another concept or another product. Or the government may drag its feet in approving a certain product. Some years ago a company invented a product for both inhibiting diaper odor and inhibiting diaper rash on babies. It took four years to gain approval for the introduction of the product to inhibit the diaper odor alone. During the Vietnam conflict the old U.S. Army steel helmet actually had been obsoleted by a titanium helmet that weighed half as much as the steel helmet at the same protective level or could offer twice the protection at the same weight. Although cost was an important factor, another was the fact that the Army was already committed to purchase steel helmets.

Product Characteristics

The duration of the introductory stage may also be lengthened due to certain product characteristics or the lack of complementary products. Color television was developed in the early 1950s but was not adopted or in general usage for almost ten years because color television required color transmission and thus color programming. In the aerospace business, a weapons system may be held up because it is dependent on a critical subsystem.

Differential Advantage

A clear and significant differential advantage over the product which is being replaced can shorten the introduction stage if the need is great and the advantage can be clearly shown and demonstrated in performance, quality, lower price, and so forth. The advantages of the digital watch over the old mechanical watch were crystal clear to all buyers; as a result, the introduction stage was quite short. In general, the more sophisticated and the more expensive the product, the bigger the advantage must be. If you are going to introduce a product which is a different and better type of land transportation than the automobile, the differential advantage must be great. Remember that despite the critical oil shortage in the first half of the seventies, the introduction of battery-powered cars was not successful, despite the fact that several working models were tried. A sufficient differential advantage, considering the expense and size of the product simply was not perceived by the potential customer.

Critical Importance of Marketing

Many companies, both large and small, especially those which are highly technical-oriented, routinely commit the classical mistake of allocating 90% of their resources to the development and engineering of a product and only 10% to the marketing. The fact of the matter is that in many cases the exact opposite allocation of resources may be required. A preponderance of resources must be devoted to the marketing of the product in order to survive the introduction stage. Otherwise, the product fails. Sufficient resources for new product introduction is a must . . . and it is far better to err on the side of planning to allocate more financial resources than are actually required.

DEVELOPING STRATEGIES FOR THE GROWTH STAGE

In the growth stage of the new product, the situation has changed. There are many competitors now, and they are entering the market quickly. During this stage it can be anticipated that profitability and profits will reach peak levels due to the high prices that can be charged and the growing demand for the product. Pricing will generally be high because of the heavy demand, but at some point it may have to be lowered in order to meet and be competitive with the increasing competition. During this period additional buyers will be interested in purchasing the product. Because of the increased demand, they may accept less-than-top quality and will put up with delays and other inconveniences simply to acquire the product. It can also be anticipated that manufacturing will have an undercapacity and that a shift will occur toward mass production of the product. The possibilities for exporting the product are greatly increased during this stage, and distribution tends to be intensive with as many channels of distribution as possible being employed. Sales are growing faster in this stage, and herein lies a great danger since some will forecast this level of sales indefinitely without regard to the life cycle concept.

Strategies for the Growth Stage

This is the stage for capturing what you can in the marketplace. What can be captured now during the growth stage can be held—in many cases—due to the experience curve, which says that as you produce more products, the product costs tend to decrease. This allows you to have additional resources available for use in promoting the product, lowering the price, continuing to improve the product, and so forth.

Product improvement is another strategy that should be considered during the growth stage of the product. Product improvement will allow you to keep ahead of the competition while introducing new products, but it is important to make certain that you are indeed in the growth stage and not in the introduction stage when you make the decision to introduce improvements. If the product fails, you want it to fail with a minimum investment of business and financial resources.

As pointed out earlier, this is the time to use intensive distribution and to use all the channels that you possibly can to distribute your project. However, this generalized rule should not be automatically followed, and you must understand there is something to interchannel competition. To wit: Each channel would like an exclusive on distributing the product and will sometimes exhibit its displeasure by less-than-optimum handling of your product. The decision in developing new channels should be made on a rational basis considering the potential problems.

There are additional opportunities in the growth stage involved in price and quality manipulation: Price can usually be traded off for quality and vice versa while you satisfy the needs of your customers and meet the competition. Price and quality manipulation does not always mean decreasing the price. It is possible to raise the price to meet the competition. Twenty years ago, entrepreneur Joe Cossman introduced a garden sprinkler constructed of a single long tube of plastic with holes in it. When the water was turned on, the tube filled with water, which was then forced through the holes at high speed. For various reasons, this product could not be patented, and because the plastic tubing was inexpensive to manufacture, Cossman knew that after the first season numerous competitors would enter the market. Cossman followed a unique price-quality manipulation strategy. He maintained quality, and rather than reducing price, he increased the retail price to customers while keeping the price charged to the retailer the same as the first season. The result was that Cossman was able to hold on to a good part of his market because of the greater margin offered to merchants who had already successfully handled his product the previous season.

DETERMINING STRATEGIES FOR THE MATURITY STAGE

In the maturity stage, many competitors are competing for a smaller share of the market. There will be a shakeout and, usually, increased price competition. In this stage total profits are lower with lower margins per product. Prices are falling, although buyers are continuing to buy the product. Repeat buying of the product is more prevalent. In production, there is some overcapacity. Now, lower labor skills are needed, and longer production runs are possible with fairly stable and less innovative techniques. Distribution is still intensive, although some channels may be dropped during the latter part of this stage in order to attempt to improve the profit margin. Again, marketing must be continued with increased efforts to broaden the product line and to utilize such techniques as market segmentation and differentiating the product from others in order to increase sales. In most cases, it can be anticipated that sales will be leveling off during this stage and may even begin to decline.

Strategies for the Maturity Stage

In this stage your basic strategy is to defend the position that you've established in the growth stage against inroads made or attempted by competitors. Since you are there already, you have the advantage as far as new competitors attempting to break into the market with a similar product. It is extremely important that you differentiate your product from other products and, of course, that yours is perceived to be better for the particular market segment you choose to go after. Remember that concentrating your resources against a smaller market segment here can be extremely effective, since your overall sales and profits will be greater if you sell more in this smaller segment than if you sell less in a much larger segment or attempt to go for some sort of mass market.

If you are the market leader in this stage, you may attempt to go for low price against weaker competition. This goes along with maintaining your position and share in the marketplace and perhaps forcing the weaker competition from the market altogether through your pricing and the overall value that you offer to your customer.

At the same time you should begin to search for new markets and new uses for your product. Either can extend the time in this stage of the life cycle as Arm & Hammer baking soda did when it suggested the use of its product as an odor inhibitor, as Boeing did when its 707 aircraft was modified to become the military AWACS aircraft, or as McDonnell-Douglas did when its DC–10 was used as a missile launcher or tanker aircraft.

Product extension goes along with product modification and product differentiation. One study of 121 companies applying to two capital goods industries noted 555 innovations, two-thirds of which cost less than $100,000 for a successfully modified product. Such an innovation can be a better strategy than sinking additional money into promotion of the unmodified product. For example, Du

Pont, a company that had invested heavily during World War II in production of nylon parachutes, switched not only to women's hosiery but also to nylon tires, nylon bearings, and nylon composites. It has been estimated that had Du Pont not used this product extension technique through product modification, by 1962 the annual use of nylon would have been 50 million pounds a year. In actuality, 500 million pounds were used that year.

The biggest threat to companies holding large market shares in mature industries in the maturity stage is that of the introduction of a new technology. Strangely, this frequently happens not by a firm in the same industry but by an outsider. Pickett slide rules were not obsoleted by a slide rule company that suddenly went into the hand-held calculator business. An established watch company did not obsolete Swiss watches, whose manufacturers only recently recovered from a failure to introduce electronic watches. Even jet engines were not developed or introduced by old-line engine companies like Pratt and Whitney or Wright, the leaders in reciprocating engines, but rather by outsiders like General Electric and Westinghouse.

DETERMINING STRATEGIES FOR THE DECLINE STAGE

In the decline stage, the marketing situation is always critical for any company. The weaker competition has dropped out. There are few competitors left. Sales are down; profits are declining further as declining volumes cause cost to increase significantly. At the same time prices are continuing to fall. They may get low enough that quick liquidation of inventory may be the best strategy. The buyers have changed also; only the sophisticated buyers that know the product are left. And there is a substantial overcapacity in manufacturing. At this point a smart company has already pared down distribution channels and only those clearly profitable remain. The opportunity for export has also dried up, and marketing at this stage must be watched very closely because minimum expenditures should be made lest they further decrease profits.

Strategies for the Decline Stage

Once a company realizes a product is in the decline stage, preparation for product removal is essential. This removal can be either slow or fast, but it must be planned for ahead of time. What preparing for this removal, a company should milk and harvest all possible benefits. Sometimes advertising can be cut to zero in this milking with no effect. Camel cigarettes were introduced in 1913. Advertising ceased before the government ban on cigarette advertising, and today Camel competes with 170 brands which still do such advertising as is possible. Yet it wasn't too long ago that Camel was the seventh-best seller with sales at $250 million a year despite no advertising. Strict cost control is a major factor in winning in the decline stage.

This is really the time to concentrate and to focus on certain select market segments and markets. Those that are not profitable should be ruthlessly dropped.

At the same time, when the time comes for killing off a weaker product, this should not be avoided either. Remember that there are two major reasons for dropping weak products: (1) Better profits are possible elsewhere and (2) there are better uses for corporate resources, including everything from manufacturing time and space to financial resources to executive time.

However, there are occasionally reasons for maintaining products in the marketplace that are not profitable during the decline stage. These include company image to fill out a product line or to prevent a competitor from access to a market. These must be weighed against the advantages of dropping the product.

STRATEGY IMPLICATIONS FOR A TECHNOLOGY-BASED BUSINESS DEPENDING ON LENGTH OF CYCLE

High-technology products have special problems concerning the life cycle. Accordingly, certain strategy implications should be recognized. If the high-technology product has a short life cycle and we define the life cycle in a period of months rather than years, the key strategy implications are to be first in the marketplace and to be fast. Frequently, approximation is better than absolute precision in meeting technical objectives. Atari was first in the marketplace with its computer games and established an enviable position with its new product. This position was successfully defended for many years despite strong challenges from several major competitors. True, initially joysticks broke, transformers failed—many consumers went through several of these subsystems in a period of a few months. The important thing was that the product was successful because it was recognized that the life cycle was short and Atari got there "firstest with the mostest" in the marketplace.

On the other hand, some high-technology products have longer life cycles. Such products as missiles and satellites are measured in years, not months. Here, efficiency and economic production are usually more important than speed. Performance in technical objectives is clearly critical. Detailed developmental planning dominates and must dominate the situation. in fact, planning in dealing with such products is probably more important than in any other high-tech industry.

WHY CHANGES OCCUR IN THE PRODUCT LIFE CYCLE

Sometimes the product life cycle may change from what was planned without action on our part.

1. *A Need May Disappear.* If the need for a product disappears, the product will tend to disappear too. Whatever happened to orange juice squeezers which were in every home prior to World War II? They were replaced by a product called "frozen orange juice," which obsoleted the need for fresh oranges and juice squeezers in most American homes.

2. *A Need May Return.* The same orange juice squeezers are

making somewhat of a limited comeback due to the current emphasis on natural and health foods.

3. *A Better, Cheaper, or More Convenient Product May Be Developed to Fill the Same Need.* Look again at the hand-held calculator versus the slide rule or the digital watch versus the mechanical watch. But a competitive product may also gain an advantage through superior marketing strategy that will affect the product life cycle. Colgate was the American champion toothpaste for years. How did Crest make serious inroads into Colgate's turf? Gaining the support of the American Dental Association was part of a successful strategy which convinced many consumers that use of Crest would result in fewer cavities.

When any of these three things happen, the life cycle curve will change. You as a corporate strategist must take immediate action not only to defend your position but to retain your initiative in the marketplace.

A BUSINESS AS A LIFE CYCLE

Sears, Roebuck and Company can be considered a business which has clearly and accurately used the life cycle concept in developing strategies to allow the business to prosper. Around the turn of the century and up until World War II, Sears was basically a mail-order business which supplied products to customers in rural America who could not otherwise obtain the variety and choice that Sears could provide. Every farmhouse and rural home had the Sears *Wish Book,* and it and the family Bible both held places of prominence in America's households.

After World War II, Sears shifted its strategy to become the nation's buyer, no longer emphasizing the mail-order aspect but selling at convenient locations in each city around the country. Sears recognized that the demographics of the country had changed and that the rural farmers were no longer so far away that they could not conveniently purchase products in town. Sears aimed at selling general products more conveniently than anyone else.

More recently, Sears again shifted emphasis into the mail-order business as change in buying patterns, the energy crisis, and other factors caused nonstore retailing to increase at 10–16% per year and to reach $140 billion. Sears is aiming to lead in this market by the developing of a floppy-disk catalog and other innovations. Only history can demonstrate whether Sears's analysis was correct and whether its strategy will give it a dominant share of a future market. But clearly Sears is using life cycle analysis of its business to help in charting future direction of the company.

But Sears, Roebuck and Company isn't the only major firm to demonstrate ability to manage the product life cycle. Grumman Aircraft was near bankruptcy; it was the ninth-largest aerospace contractor producing highly complex aircraft, while everyone else was trying to produce and sell military aircraft as inexpensively as possible. Grumman did this because its analysts found that highly complex aircraft were not yet in the decline stage of the life cycle. Grumman therefore invested in developing and producing such sophisticated aircraft as the Navy's F–14 fighter and the E2C Hawkeye, which sold for $35 million each. Then two major conflicts occurred which confirmed that Grumman was correct: the Falkland Islands War, between the United Kingdom and Argentina, and Israel's invasion of Lebanon. In both cases Grumman products were used with great effect, proving that highly complex aircraft and weapon systems were not in the decline stage. The result was that Grumman sales increased significantly compared with the sales of its competitors.

Or consider Du Pont de Nemours, the same company that developed Kevlar. Du Pont de Nemours totally dominated the cellophane market up until the end of World War II. However, at this point, polyethylene film was introduced. It is less sensitive to cold and costs less. Cellophane's days were numbered, and it began losing market share to polyethylene. What did Du Pont de Nemours do? Du Pont introduced product modification, including new coatings which actually increased the size of the cellophane market. The larger market for cellophane resulted in increased profits while the product was extended in the maturity stage. Du Pont then took the profits from this market and bought big shares of the polyethylene business. The result was it dominated both markets.

Or how about IBM? IBM controlled three-quarters of the computer market in the early 1960s. But again, through the use of life cycle analysis, it saw that the product was in the mature stage while competition intensified. Before the product could even enter the decline stage, IBM did a very strange thing. It obsoleted its own product with a more advanced computer while its other products continued to sell well. These new products had a special feature. Once the initial purchase of IBM's new computer was made, it just wasn't economical to switch to anything else.

However, failure to manage the life cycle can be deadly. Entrepreneur Joe Engelberger single-handedly developed a robotics market over a fifteen-year period. After fifteen years and finally in the black with $70 million in sales a year in an estimated $155 million market, he was simultaneously attacked by IBM, General Motors, United Technology, and Bendix. The outcome at this point is uncertain but clearly could be anticipated by the product life cycle concept.

WHAT A STRATEGIST CAN DO WITH THE PRODUCT LIFE CYCLE

As corporate strategist, you can do several things with the product life cycle to the benefit of your company. You can control the mix of your products in different stages of the life cycle by:

1. New product development planning
2. Product line planning
3. Planned allocation of resources and personnel among existing products and product groups according to product opportunity represented by the life cycle positions

You can also control the life cycle of your product to generate additional products.

Perhaps, most importantly, you can develop strategies once you know the shape of the life cycle and your position in it. We will go into this procedure step by step in the next chapter.

5

LOCATING PRODUCTS IN THEIR LIFE CYCLES AND DEVELOPING STRATEGIES FOR THEM

DEVELOPING STRATEGIES USING PRODUCT LIFE CYCLES

To develop strategies using the product life cycle, it is necessary for us to determine the shape of the life cycle curve for the product or service. Once this is done, you can locate the product in the life cycle curve that you have plotted. Then you can develop a desired life cycle profile and determine the position that you wish your product to be on in that life cycle profile. The next important step is to develop strategies in order to obtain the desired position that you have decided on. Finally, you must incorporate these strategies into a marketing action plan. In this chapter, we consider the actions necessary from determining the shape of the life cycle through developing a desired life cycle profile and the position that we wish to be on in the life cycle profile we have developed. From this process we will not only gain the material which must be inputted into our marketing plan but also learn where our products must be for the most profitable mix. The output will also alert us if there is a likelihood of a sudden decine in demand for one or more of our products or services. Finally we will gain strategic insights which will permit us to take advantage of the opportunities in the future while avoiding the threats.

LOCATING PRODUCTS IN THEIR LIFE CYCLES

There are seven basic steps in locating products in their life cycles:

1. Analyze historical trend information.
2. Analyze recent trends.
3. Analyze development of short-term competitive tactics.
4. Analyze historical information on the life cycles of similar and related products.
5. Project sales.
6. Estimate probable years remaining.
7. Fix position in the product life cycle.

Before we begin, you should know that while analyses are dependent on quantitative information, the results are highly subjective in nature as well. This is because of the interpretation, emphasis, and estimates that are a part of the process. Therefore, your managerial intuition and judgment are of no small importance.

STEP 1.   ANALYZING HISTORICAL TREND INFORMATION ON THE PRODUCT YOU ARE ANALYZING

In analyzing historical trend information, look for all information available since the product's introduction. Specifically, you are looking for information on sales, profits, margins, market share, and prices. Each year since introduction should be examined separately. For products with extremely short life cycles, a monthly analysis is appropriate. In analyzing prices, an adjustment should be made for inflation.

What about products that were introduced years ago? How far back do you have to go? This is a question that must be answered by judgment. Some products need to be analyzed only over the past three to five years. This is especially true with products that have relatively shorter life cycles. For high-technology products that are changing in the marketplace and the market environment even more rapidly, the life cycle may be for even shorter periods. But other products must be analyzed over much longer periods.

The Use of Product Life Cycle Analysis Forms

A special form has been constructed to assist you in analyzing the historical trend of a product. This form is called the "Historical Trend Analysis Matrix" and is depicted in Figure 5.1. As you complete the form, use your intuition and judgment based on your experience in the industry and product knowledge. This will play a major role in the quality of your analysis.

Let's go over the sample form in 5.1 together. This example shows the trend analysis for "Micro Satellite." Information is provided for the date, and this is important since you may do other analyses on historical trends at a later date based on changes in your situation. In this case the analysis was done on 10 February 1990. Along the vertical axis of the matrix you will note sales, profits, margins, market share, and prices. Across the horizontal axis of the matrix are periods 1, 2, 3, and 4 and the final notation, "trend." In this case the

Product Micro Satellite	Date 10 Feb. 1990			
	Period 1 (1987)	Period 2 (1988)	Period 3 (1989)	Period 4	Trend
Sales	VL	A	H		←
Profits	L	L	H		←
Margins	L	A	H		↖
Market share	L	L	L		↑
Prices	VH	VH	H		↗

Complete matrix with following information:

Very low or very small
Low or small
Average
High or large
Very high or very large

Characterize trends as:

Declining steeply →
Declining ↗
Plateau ↑
Ascending ↖
Ascending steeply ←

FIGURE 5.1. Historical Trend Analysis Matrix. (Copyright © 1983 by Dr. William A. Cohen.)

analyst has documented three periods: period 1, 1987; period 2, 1988; period 3, 1989. No fourth period was analyzed. If you want to analyze more than four periods, it's easy to split each period into two halves. Therefore, using this matrix and the forms in the book, either periods can be analyzed. The matrix is completed, as noted on the form, with the following information for each period and for each category that's being analyzed: very low, low, average, high, or very high. Note that for the Micro Satellite in the first period of 1987, sales were described as very low. In period 2, 1988, sales were average. And in period 3, 1989, sales were high. In a similar fashion, profits during the first and second periods were low; then during the third period profits were high. Every category—sales, profits, margins, market share, and prices—is analyzed, and descriptors of how they fared in the marketplace during this period, annotated. After this initial analysis is complete, look at the trend column, which is the final column on the form. Look back at the three periods and the descriptors given for each variable. Note that the trends are categorized in Figure 5.1 as declining steeply, represented by an arrow pointed straight down; declining at a nominal rate, represented by an arrow pointed downward at a 45° slope; no change, represented by an arrow pointed horizontally to the right; ascending, represented by an arrow ascending upward at a 45° angle; and ascending steeply, represented by an arrow pointed straight up. Look at the sales category. You will note that the general trend has been straight up; profits have been straight up, also. Margins have been ascending but not quite as rapidly. Market share was low with no change through all three periods. Finally, prices, which started out as very high, have decreased to high and are noted as declining. If a life cycle curve were to be sketched out on the basis of this information, it would look something like the information shown in Figure 5.2. The blank figures, Figures 5.3 through 5.6, of the Historical Trend Analysis Matrix are for your own use in analyzing various products.

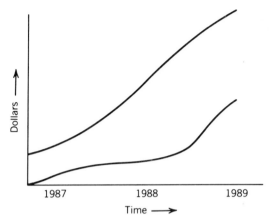

FIGURE 5.2.   Life cycle for Micro Satellites.

STEP 2.   ANALYZING RECENT TRENDS

Now that we have analyzed the historical trends, it is necessary to analyze recent trends in the marketplace for the product or service that we are looking at. Recent trends can be last year or even the last few months or few weeks. We want to analyze recent trends regarding the number and strength of competitors; the number and strength rankings of these competitors; the quality, performance, and advantages of competing products; shifts in distribution channels if they have occurred; and relative advantage enjoyed by the product in the marketplace. Let's look first at Figure 5.7, which is a form for recent trends of competitors, market share, and strength.

A strength code is used on this form, with VW standing for very weak, W for weak, M for medium, S for strong, and VS for very strong. Across the top of the form you will notice four columns: first, "competitor"; second, "market share"; third, "strength"; and, finally, "products." Three aerospace firms have been listed as competitors. In the second column, the market share of each—5, 25, and 50 percentage points—is listed. The strength of each of the three competitors for the products indicated is weak, medium, and strong, respectively. The products indicated are the Mini Satellite I, the Ironi–5A, and the SPD Satellite and Hi-SAT.

Product _____ Date _____

	Period 1	Period 2	Period 3	Period 4	Trend
Sales					
Profits					
Margins					
Market share					
Prices					

Complete matrix with following information:
Very low or very small
Low or small
Average
High or large
Very high or very large

Characterize trends as:
Declining steeply ↓
Declining ↘
Plateau →
Ascending ↗
Ascending steeply ↑

FIGURE 5.3. Historical Trend Analysis Matrix. (Copyright © 1983 by Dr. William A. Cohen.)

Product _____	Date _____				
	Period 1	Period 2	Period 3	Period 4	Trend
Sales					
Profits					
Margins					
Market share					
Prices					

Complete matrix with following information:

Very low or very small
Low or small
Average
High or large
Very high or very large

Characterize trends as:

Declining steeply	→
Declining	↗
Plateau	↑
Ascending	↖
Ascending steeply	←

FIGURE 5.4.   Historical Trend Analysis Matrix. (Copyright © 1983 by Dr. William A. Cohen.)

Product _____ Date _____

	Period 1	Period 2	Period 3	Period 4	Trend
Sales					
Profits					
Margins					
Market share					
Prices					

Complete matrix with following information:
Very low or very small
Low or small
Average
High or large
Very high or very large

Characterize trends as:
Declining steeply →
Declining ↗
Plateau ↑
Ascending ↖
Ascending steeply ←

FIGURE 5.5. Historical Trend Analysis Matrix. (Copyright © 1983 by Dr. William A. Cohen.)

Product _____ Date _____

	Period 1	Period 2	Period 3	Period 4	Trend
Sales					
Profits					
Margins					
Market share					
Prices					

Complete matrix with following information:

Very low or very small
Low or small
Average
High or large
Very high or very large

Characterize trends as:

Declining steeply →
Declining ↗
Plateau ↑
Ascending ↖
Ascending steeply ←

FIGURE 5.6.   Historical Trend Analysis Matrix. (Copyright © 1983 by Dr. William A. Cohen.)

Your Product <u>Micro Satellites</u>   Date <u>10 Feb. 1990</u>

Strength code: VW = very weak   M = medium   VS = very strong
            W = weak   S = strong

Competitor	Market Share	Strength	Products
Zeus Aerospace	5%	W	Mini Satellite I
Rockets, Inc.	25%	M	Ironi-5A
Advanced Space Systems	50%	S	SPD Satellite and Hi-SAT

FIGURE 5.7.   Recent trends of competitor's products, share, and strength. (Copyright © 1983 by Dr. William A. Cohen.)

With this form, we are analyzing our competitor's strength based on market share rather than on the competitor's product itself.

Figures 5.8 through 5.11 are for your use in analyzing your competitor's product, market share, and strength.

Figure 5.12, the next form for aid in analysis, shows recent trends in competitive products. This particular form has columns to indicate company, product, quality and performance characteristics, shifts in distribution channels, and, finally, relative advantage of each competitive product. Whereas in the previous form we were analyzing companies, in this form we're looking directly at the products themselves. What we're looking for is a comparative outline of all products that are competing with our product. Figures 5.13 through 5.16 are for you to use in analyzing recent trends in products that are competitive to your product.

STEP 3. ANALYZING DEVELOPMENT OF SHORT-TERM COMPETITIVE TACTICS

Now it's time to analyze the short-term competitive actions that are occurring in the marketplace and that you must counter. These actions may include announcements of new products, modifications of older products, expansion of production capacity, and, if you are dealing in the industrial or government market, an unexpected bid on a request for proposal (RFP). It may also include any other competitive action which may be important and which could be a flashing red warning light regarding your product and product strategy. To assist in your analysis, use Figure 5.17, showing an analysis of competitor short-term tactics. On this form, you will find a column for listing the competitor, a column for the actions that are taken, a column for the probable meaning of this action, and a final column in which you can check the most likely of the probable meanings of the action. Note how the same is completed in Figure 5.17, and use Figures 5.18 through 5.21 for your own purposes in your analysis of competitor short-term tactics.

STEP 4. ANALYZING HISTORICAL INFORMATION ON PRODUCT LIFE CYCLES OF SIMILAR OR RELATED PRODUCTS

In order to accomplish this analysis, it is necessary to pick a product similar to your product. This similar product should already have completed its life cycle. If the similar product has not completed its life cycle, then choose a subsystem or some other product which is closely related to the product under analysis. Use Figure 5.22 for this purpose, which shows the developing life cycle of a similar or related product. Leaving satellites, let's look at a diet aid.

This form has five columns. The first column, "analysis variables," lists the variables to be analyzed: competition, profits/sales, pricing, strategy used, and, finally, the length of time in each stage of the life cycle. The next four columns are the four stages of the product life cycle: introduction, growth, maturity, and decline.

To complete this analysis form, divide the total life cycle of the similar or related products which you are looking at into the four life cycle stages. Analyze the product over time to describe the situation with each of the analysis variables. For example, in Figure 5.22, during the introduction stage the product had one competitor; profits were almost nonexistent; pricing was $10 per unit; and the strategy was a penetration strategy in order to capture the maximum market share. As indicated, this introduction stage lasted for approximately ten months. During the growth stage of this similar or related product the number of competitors grew to five; the profit margin grew to approximately $3 per unit, although pricing was reduced in the face of competition to $8 per unit. The strategy in this stage was product differentiation. The growth stage lasted for another ten months. In the maturity stage, the number of competitors dropped to three. The profits decreased, and the margin was less than $1 per unit. Pricing was further reduced to $6 per unit. The strategy used by the company for this product at this stage was one of market segmentation; that is, resources were concentrated against a particular segment of the overall market. The product was in this stage for approximately twenty-four months.

Your Product _____ Date _____

Strength code: VW = very weak   M = medium   VS = very strong
               W = weak   S = strong

Competitor	Market Share					Strength	Products

FIGURE 5.8. Recent trends of competitor's products, share, and strength. (Copyright © 1983 by Dr. William A. Cohen.)

104

Your Product _____ Date _____

Strength code: VW = very weak   M = medium   VS = very strong
            W = weak   S = strong

Competitor	Market Share	Strength	Products

FIGURE 5.9. Recent trends of competitor's products, share, and strength. (Copyright © 1983 by Dr. William A. Cohen.)

Your Product _____ Date _____

Strength code: VW = very weak   M = medium   VS = very strong
                W = weak   S = strong

Competitor	Market Share	Strength	Products

FIGURE 5.10. Recent trends of competitor's products, share, and strength. (Copyright © 1983 by Dr. William A. Cohen.)

Your Product _____ Date _____

Strength code: VW = very weak   M = medium   VS = very strong
               W = weak   S = strong

Competitor	Market Share	Strength	Products

FIGURE 5.11. Recent trends of competitor's products, share, and strength. (Copyright © 1983 by Dr. William A. Cohen.)

Your Product Micro Satellites   Date 10 Feb. 1990

Company	Product	Quality and Performance Characteristics	Shifts in Distribution Channels	Relative Advantages of Each Competitive Product
Zeus Aerospace	Mini Satellite I	Extremely high quality and top performance	Attempted sales to U.S. Air Force in 1989; foreign sales in 1990	Top quality and performance. Reliable. Very high cost
Rockets, Inc.	Ironi-5A	Smallest and lightest in weight of competitive products. Good quality	Has been in use by NASA since 1986. No change in customer on distribution	Product. Some limitations as to functions due to size. Smallest in general use
Advanced Space Systems	Hi-SAT	Unknown—prototype still under development	—	Supposed to be almost as small as Ironi-5A but more functions and low cost
Advanced Space Systems	SPD-Satellite	Good quality, reliable. Medium cost. Performs acceptably for current tasks	—	"Work horse" product used by NASA, U.S. Air Force, Navy, foreign governments. Reliability and cost greatest advantages

FIGURE 5.12.   Recent trends in competitive products. (Copyright © 1983 by Dr. William A. Cohen.)

Your Product _____ Date _____

Company	Product	Quality and Performance Characteristics	Shifts in Distribution Channels	Relative Advantages of Each Competitive Product

110

FIGURE 5.13.   Recent trends in competitive products. (Copyright © 1983 by Dr. William A. Cohen.)

Your Product _____ Date _____

Company	Product	Quality and Performance Characteristics	Shifts in Distribution Channels	Relative Advantages of Each Competitive Product

FIGURE 5.14. Recent trends in competitive products. (Copyright © 1983 by Dr. William A. Cohen.)

113

Your Product _____ Date _____

Company	Product	Quality and Performance Characteristics	Shifts in Distribution Channels	Relative Advantages of Each Competitive Product

114

FIGURE 5.15.   Recent trends in competitive products. (Copyright © 1983 by Dr. William A. Cohen.)

Your Product _____ Date _____

Company	Product	Quality and Performance Characteristics	Shifts in Distribution Channels	Relative Advantages of Each Competitive Product

FIGURE 5.16.   Recent trends in competitive products. (Copyright © 1983 by Dr. William A. Cohen.)

117

Your Product __Micro Satellites__   Date __16 Feb. 1990__

Competitor	Actions		Probable Meaning of Action	Check Most Likely
Zeus Aerospace	Attempted sales to Air Force in 1989; foreign sales in 1990	1.	Looking for customer with mission to justify cost	√
		2.	Air Force looking for this type of product	
	"No bid" NASA's Advanced satellite project	1.	Wants to get out of large satellite business	
		2.	Resources currently fully involved with Mini Satellite	√
Rockets, Inc.	Satellite project, has bid every U.S. and Foreign last year	1.	Seeking to expand market share	√
		2.	Needs the business due to high overhead	

Advanced Space Systems	Hiring large numbers of Ph.D. scientists	
1. Hi-SAT program in trouble		√
2. Additional new R&D programs		
3. Planning on new programs outside of satellites		

FIGURE 5.17. Analysis of competitor short-term tactics. (Copyright © 1983 by Dr. William A. Cohen.)

119

Your Product _____ Date _____

Competitor	Actions	Probable Meaning of Action	Check Most Likely

FIGURE 5.18. Analysis of competitor short-term tactics. (Copyright © 1983 by Dr. William A. Cohen.)

121

Your Product _____ Date _____

Competitor	Actions	Probable Meaning of Action	Check Most Likely

122

FIGURE 5.19. Analysis of competitor short-term tactics. (Copyright © 1983 by Dr. William A. Cohen.)

Your Product _____ Date _____

Competitor	Actions	Probable Meaning of Action	Check Most Likely

124

FIGURE 5.20. Analysis of competitor short-term tactics. (Copyright © 1983 by Dr. William A. Cohen.)

Your Product _____ Date _____

Competitor	Actions	Probable Meaning of Action	Check Most Likely

FIGURE 5.21. Analysis of competitor short-term tactics. (Copyright © 1983 by Dr. William A. Cohen.)

Product Diet Aid Similar or Related Product Pounds-Off

Product stage	Introduction	Growth	Maturity	Decline
Competition	One competitor	5 competitors	3 competitors	1 competitor
Profits	0	$3/unit	$1/unit	$0.30/unit
Sales (units)	10,000	30,000	50,000	10,000
Pricing	$10/unit	$8/unit	$6/unit	$4–$1/unit
Strategy Used	Penetration	Product differentiation	Market segmentation	Harvesting/closeout
Length of Time in Each Stage	10 months	10 months	24 months	11 months

FIGURE 5.22. Developing life cycle of similar or related product. (Copyright © 1983 by Dr. William A. Cohen.)

In the final column, Figure 5.22 shows the decline stage of the life cycle of the product. During this stage only one competitor remained. Profit margins were very slim, down to $0.30 per unit, and the pricing had been further reduced to $4 per unit and, finally, to $1 per unit. At this time, the product was discontinued. The strategy used was first a harvesting strategy, then a closeout at a rock-bottom price. The product was in the decline stage for eleven months. Use Figures 5.23 through 5.26 for developing the life cycle of a similar or related product through analysis of the variables, as indicated in Figure 5.22.

Life Cycle Curve of Similar or Related Products Sketch

Now we have the information to sketch a rough curve of the sales and the profits for the similar or related product. Don't try for perfection in doing this. Just consider your facts, the characteristics of each stage of the product life cycle curve, the general shape of the life cycle curve, and the time during which the description of what happened occurred. Note how this has been accomplished in Figure 5.27. Sales and profits on the vertical axis are plotted against time on the horizontal axis. Draw your own curves using Figures 5.28 through 5.31.

STEP 5.   PROJECTING SALES FOR YOUR PRODUCT

Sales should be projected for a period of the next three to five years on the basis of prior analysis and your estimates and forecasts. The only exception is if your product is a fad or known to be of a shorter life cycle. Other information will also be estimated, including total direct costs, indirect costs, pretax profits, and the profit ratio of estimated total direct costs to pretax profits.

The ratio of total estimated direct costs to pretax profits measures the dollars required to generate each additional dollar of profit. The ratio typically improves (becomes lower) as the product enters its growth period, begins to deteriorate (rise) as the product approaches maturity, and climbs more sharply as it enters the decline stage.

Product _____ Similar or Related Product _____

Product stage	Introduction	Growth	Maturity	Decline
Competition				
Profits				
Sales (units)				
Pricing				
Strategy Used				
Length of Time in Each Stage				

FIGURE 5.23. Developing life cycle of similar or related product. (Copyright © 1983 by Dr. William A. Cohen.)

Product _____ Similar or Related Product _____

Product stage	Introduction	Growth	Maturity	Decline
Competition				
Profits				
Sales (units)				
Pricing				
Strategy Used				
Length of Time in Each Stage				

FIGURE 5.24. Developing life cycle of similar or related product. (Copyright © 1983 by Dr. William A. Cohen.)

131

Product _____ Similar or Related Product _____

Product stage	Introduction	Growth	Maturity	Decline
Competition				
Profits				
Sales (units)				
Pricing				
Strategy Used				
Length of Time in Each Stage				

FIGURE 5.25. Developing life cycle of similar or related product. (Copyright © 1983 by Dr. William A. Cohen.)

132

Product _____ Similar or Related Product _____

Product stage	Introduction	Growth	Maturity	Decline
Competition				
Profits				
Sales (units)				
Pricing				
Strategy Used				
Length of Time in Each Stage				

FIGURE 5.26. Developing life cycle of similar or related product. (Copyright © 1983 by Dr. William A. Cohen.)

133

Product _DIET AID_   Similar or related product _"POUND-OFF"_

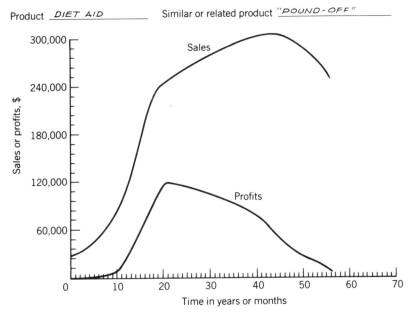

FIGURE 5.27. Life cycle curve of similar or related product; comparing Diet Aid to "Pounds-off." (Copyright © 1983 by Dr. William A. Cohen.).

Product _____   Similar or related product _____

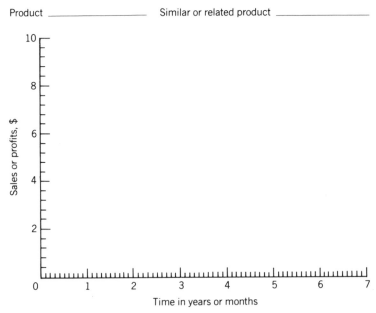

FIGURE 5.28. Life cycle curve of similar or related product; Sketch a rough sales curve and a rough profit curve for a similar or related product. (Copyright © 1983 by Dr. William A. Cohen.)

134

Product _____ Similar or related product _____

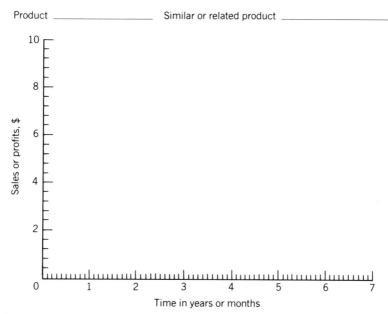

FIGURE 5.29.   Life cycle curve of similar or related product; Sketch a rough sales curve and a rough profit curve for a similar or related product. (Copyright © 1983 by Dr. William A. Cohen.)

Product _____ Similar or related product _____

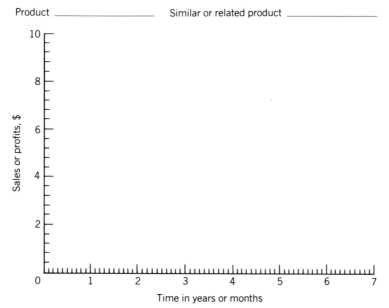

FIGURE 5.30.   Life cycle curve of similar or related product; Sketch a rough sales curve and a rough profit curve for a similar or related product. (Copyright © 1983 by Dr. William A. Cohen.)

135

Product _____ Similar or related product _____

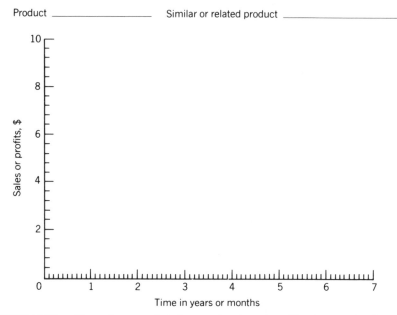

FIGURE 5.31. Life cycle curve of similar or related product; Sketch a rough sales curve and a rough profit curve for a similar or related product. (Copyright © 1983 by Dr. William A. Cohen.)

An example of the information required is shown in Figure 5.32, a sales and profit projection. Note that this form has a number of years across the top, 1 through 5, and you are then asked to estimate and to calculate, in turn, sales, total direct costs, indirect costs, pretax profits, and the profit ratio of total direct cost to pretax profits. Use Figures 5.33 through 5.36 to do this for the product you are analyzing.

STEP 6. ESTIMATING PROFITABLE YEARS REMAINING FOR EACH PRODUCT

We are now ready to estimate the profitable years remaining for each product you are analyzing. A great deal of judgment is used in this work, and the estimate should include not only official forecast inputs from those who furnish this material in your firm but also

Product <u>Vinyl Purse</u> Date <u>August 5, 1985</u>

Year	1	2	3	4	5
Estimated sales	$200,000	$175,000	$175,000	$100,000	$50,000
Estimated total direct costs	$ 25,000	$ 15,000	$ 13,000	$ 8,000	$ 4,000
Estimated indirect costs	$ 75,000	$ 75,000	$ 80,000	$ 60,000	$35,000
Estimated pretax profits	$100,000	$ 85,000	$ 82,000	$ 32,000	$11,000
Profit ratio (est. total direct costs to pretax profits)	1/4	1/5.57	1/6.3	1/4	1/2.75

FIGURE 5.32. Sales and profit projections. (Copyright © 1983 by Dr. William A. Cohen.)

137

Product _____ Date _____

Year	1	2	3	4	5
Estimated sales					
Estimated total direct costs					
Estimated indirect costs					
Estimated pretax profits					
Profit ratio (est. total direct costs to pretax profits)					

FIGURE 5.33. Sales and profit projections. (Copyright © 1983 by Dr. William A. Cohen.)

138

Product _____ Date _____

Year	1	2	3	4	5
Estimated sales					
Estimated total direct costs					
Estimated indirect costs					
Estimated pretax profits					
Profit ratio (est. total direct costs to pretax profits)					

FIGURE 5.34. Sales and profit projections. (Copyright © 1983 by Dr. William A. Cohen.)

139

Product _____ Date _____

Year	1	2	3	4	5
Estimated sales					
Estimated total direct costs					
Estimated indirect costs					
Estimated pretax profits					
Profit ratio (est. total direct costs to pretax profits)					

FIGURE 5.35. Sales and profit projections. (Copyright © 1983 by Dr. William A. Cohen.)

140

Product _____ Date _____

Year	1	2	3	4	5
Estimated sales					
Estimated total direct costs					
Estimated indirect costs					
Estimated pretax profits					
Profit ratio (est. total direct costs to pretax profits)					

FIGURE 5.36. Sales and profit projections. (Copyright © 1983 by Dr. William A. Cohen.)

141

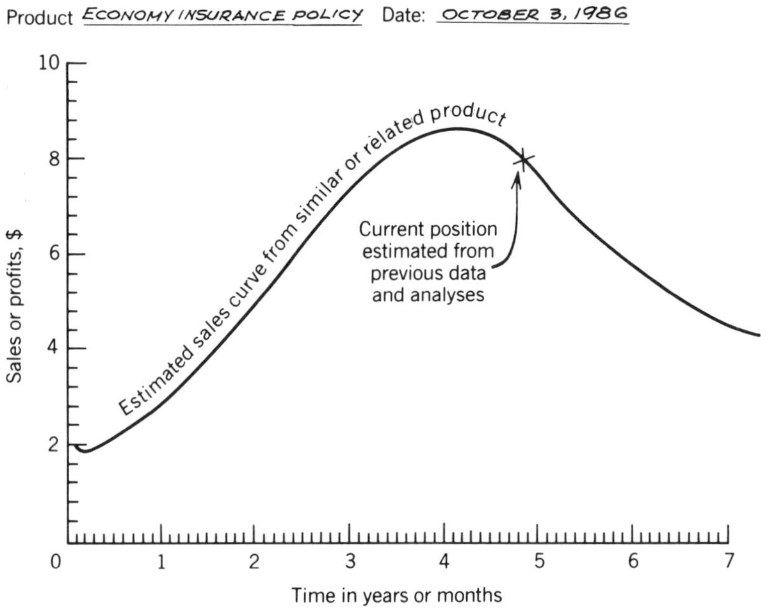

Product *ECONOMY INSURANCE POLICY*   Date: *OCTOBER 3, 1986*

FIGURE 5.37.   Position in product life cycle curve. Copyright © 1983 by Dr. William A. Cohen.

your own work based on your judgment and the analysis that you completed earlier on the similar product life cycle. Where the data are inconsistent for any reason, you must make a judgmental decision as to what data to use.

STEP 7.   FIXING THE POSITION IN THE PRODUCT LIFE CYCLE

Now, take the life cycle curve you developed in Figures 5.28 through 5.32. Using all the information that you have available from your previous analyses, estimate where the new product is in its life cycle and plot it on Figures 5.28 through 5.32, as I have done in Figure 5.37.

To recapitulate, we have developed as realistic a life cycle curve as we possibly can and have positioned our product or products as accurately as possible on this life cycle. We can now use this information:

1.   If we plot all the product in our product line on the life cycle curve simultaneously, we will have a good idea as to the total balance of our product line. For example, if all our products are in the decline or maturity stage, this is an indication that our product line is weak in growth and introduction products.

2.   We can develop strategies for products depending on the stage of the life cycle. To do this, we need information on our current sales and profits, as well as the target sales and profits for each stage of the life cycle for each forecast year in the future. Note how this is accomplished in Figure 5.38, showing the percentage of sales in your business area. Use Figures 5.39 through 5.42 to do this for your products.

In allocating resources and developing strategies using the product life cycle (study the summary matrix in Figure 5.43), consider the following: industry obsolescence trends, pace of new product introduction, average length of product life cycles in your product line, growth objectives, profit objectives, and the stage the product is in at the time you are doing the analysis.

In this chapter we have learned that product life cycles can be used to help generate strategies and, in addition, that we can also accomplish strategic planning for products we may want to introduce in the future, referencing the current locations of products in our product line plotted on a life cycle chart for a single product.

Product <u>Crunchies cereal</u>   Date <u>May 3, 1986</u>

		Introduction	Growth	Maturity	Decline
Current	Sales %	3%	8%	?	?
	Profits	0	$3 Mil/yr	?	?
Target	Sales %	2.8%	8%	10%	5%
	Profits	0	$3 Mil/yr	$2 Mil/yr	$1 Mil/yr

FIGURE 5.38.   Percentages of sales in your business area. (Copyright © 1983 by Dr. William A. Cohen.)

144

Product _____ Date _____

		Introduction	Growth	Maturity	Decline
Current	Sales %				
	Profits				
Target	Sales %				
	Profits				

FIGURE 5.39. Percentages of sales in your business area. (Copyright © 1983 by Dr. William A. Cohen.)

145

Product _____ Date _____

	Introduction	Growth	Maturity	Decline
Current				
Sales %				
Profits				
Target				
Sales %				
Profits				

FIGURE 5.40. Percentages of sales in your business area. (Copyright © 1983 by Dr. William A. Cohen.)

146

Product _____ Date _____

	Introduction	Growth	Maturity	Decline
Current Sales %				
Profits				
Target Sales %				
Profits				

FIGURE 5.41. Percentages of sales in your business area. (Copyright © 1983 by Dr. William A. Cohen.)

147

Product _____ Date _____

	Introduction	Growth	Maturity	Decline
Current	Sales %			
	Profits			
Target	Sales %			
	Profits			

FIGURE 5.42. Percentages of sales in your business area. (Copyright © 1983 by Dr. William A. Cohen.)

	Introduction	Growth	Maturity	Decline
Competition	Few or no competitors of importance	Many new competitors entering rapidly	Many competitors for small shares; shakeout; increasing price	Fewer competitors
Profits	Negligible, due to high production and marketing costs	Peak levels, due to high prices and growing demand	Lower profits; lower margins	Declining volumes resulting in increased costs and lower profits
Pricing	Usually high to recover costs of introduction	High, to take advantage of heavy demand	Falling prices	Continues to fall; eventually low enough for quick liquidation
Buyer behavior	Buyer inertia must convince customers to buy	Increasing number may accept delays and lower quality	Repeat buying	Sophisticated buyers
Marketing	Very high marketing costs	High, but less as % of sales than during introduction	Increasing efforts to broaden lines; using market segmentation and product differentiation	Minimum expenditures

FIGURE 5.43. Product life cycle situation, stage, and strategy summary.

	Introduction	Growth	Maturity	Decline
Manufacturing	Overcapacity; short production runs; highly skilled labor required	Undercapacity; shift toward mass production	Some overcapacity; longer runs with standard methods	Substantial overcapacity
International trade	Some exports	Significant exports; a few imports	Declining exports; significant imports	No exports; significant imports
Distribution	Selective, specialized channels	Intensive; multichannels if possible	Some channels pared	Specialty channels; unprofitable channels phased out
Strategy	Establishing market share; persuading early adopters to buy; engineering and R&D important	Market penetration; new segments and channels	Position defense; competitive costs; new markets	Preparation for product removal; harvesting; divestment

FIGURE 5.43. (continued)

150

6

SOLVING STRATEGY AND PLANNING PROBLEMS

Every corporate strategist will be faced with situations that require the use of problem-solving techniques in order to arrive at winning strategic solutions. These situations do not merely require you to develop effective business strategies but also to do so as efficiently as possible and in a time period which permits the strategy to be executed expeditiously and to its maximum effectiveness. The basic process you will use has been called the "Harvard Case Method," but it has also been used in various armies since the nineteenth century to accomplish staff studies on a wide range of problems and to analyze situations, solve problems, and present solutions in a logical manner.

However, before we discuss this process and put it to use, it is necessary to know something about decision making and problem solving in general. Social scientists have divided problem-solving approaches into four basic categories. Each category is used in a

151

somewhat different problem-solving situation. Some categories lead to methods of solution that are almost instinctive, and the solution is arrived at automatically and with very little structure. Other categories require a very structured approach. Most strategic and planning problems fall into this latter group. The four basic categories of decision making are:

1. *Instinctive.* As implied by the name, with instinctive problem solving or decision making, one follows one's own instinct and merely reacts to an external stimulus. If you put your finger on a hot stove, you don't have to think and consider the alternatives to alleviate the pain. You'll move your finger instantly without thinking about it at all!

2. *Following Past Procedures.* With this approach to problem solving, you just think of what you did before and what worked successfully. You do the exact same thing. This procedure works well for some routine operational problems. It does not work well in solving strategic problems, because the environment is constantly changing and the competition is taking new and different actions. As a consequence, you never find precisely the same environment as you found in the past. Therefore, what worked successfully in the past may lead to total chaos and failure in the future.

3. *Use of Common Sense and Logic.* With the commonsense and logic approach to problem solving, the problem solver gathers the important data together mentally and makes as logical a decision as possible. While a structured method is not followed per se, the decision maker is frequently able to indicate the reasons for a particular decision or chosen solution. This method is sometimes used to develop business strategy, but it has a serious weakness. Since the process and relevant factors are not documented, they are difficult to analyze dispassionately. The decision can actually be made on an emotional basis, with reasons gathered to support it after the fact. It is difficult for the unaided mind to tell the difference.

4. *Structured Decision Making.* With structured problem-solving methods, you follow a planned routine to arrive at the best decision

after considering all the factors and doing an analysis. These techniques and methods may be highly sophisticated and may even require the use of a computer. Or structured problem-solving methods can rely more heavily on psychological factors in order to help the problem solver arrive at the optimum solution to his or her problem. Various types of structured methods are definitely required for the corporate strategist.

FOUR IMPORTANT FACTS ABOUT YOUR PROBLEM-SOLVING ACTIVITIES

Before beginning to cope with a structured method of problem solving for strategy and planning, it is necessary to understand four facts regarding any problem-solving process:

1.   Personal and unconscious factors that you may not be aware of definitely influence the decisions that you make, and such influences can be decisive. Consumer behavior psychologists have used this particular fact to assist in the sales of products. For example, consider an advertisement which depicts a multicolored, warmly romantic scene: a handsome man, a beautiful woman, perhaps a fire in the background, an eloquently set table and glasses, and the man and woman looking at each other lovingly while the man pours wine, with the bottle to the side conspicuously displaying the logo of the brand of wine used. Clearly, this advertisement is not simply selling a liquid to be swallowed to quench the thirst. This advertisement attempts to tie in romance with the particular brand of wine advertised. If done well, the brand of wine advertised will be equated with romance in the minds of potential buyers. When the prospective buyers go to purchase wine, they do not think "wine" as much as they do "romance." After a while the decision no longer involves problem solving but rather a habitual brand choice, and the purchase becomes almost instinctive.

2.   Even though logic should be employed to reason to the best-possible solution in any given business situation, logic, without other

considerations, can be extremely deceptive and can result in a less-than-optimal decision. For example, a strictly logical problem-solving approach for a strategic choice which assumes that the competitor will act in a logical fashion may fail if the competitor does not respond "logically" or what we assume to be logically. Therefore logic, while important in the reasoning process, must not be allowed to exclude environmental and psychological factors that may impact on the correct strategy or solution.

3.   No single one of the four basic problem-solving methods may be correct for all situations. Thus in response to a competitor's action, it may be necessary to use a problem-solving method based partially on one or more of the four methods outlined previously.

4.   In any approach to problem solving, the formalized steps tend to overlap one another. Further, these steps must frequently be retraced as additional information becomes available or additional insight is gained during the problem-solving process.

FIVE KEYS THAT WILL ASSIST YOU WITH YOUR STRATEGIC PROBLEM SOLVING

The following five keys can have a tremendous effect on the quality of your strategic problem solving:

1.   *Challenge Everything.*   You should always challenge all information, statements, and assumptions given to you from whatever the source. Do not accept any information immediately on face value. This is especially true for procedures that have been followed in your corporation over a period of time. Frequently assumptions, as well as procedures, may be totally in error; simply asking the question "Why?" can give an entirely new perspective to the problem and may allow for a far more effective strategic solution. An agent of the U.S. government once found that for more than twenty-five years the Air Force had maintained a specification on escape hatches on transport aircraft which had emanated from a World War II study. Modification of hatch dimensions from civilian aircraft to correspond with these military specifications, when civil-

ian aircraft were adopted for military use, had cost the government millions of dollars over the intervening years. Yet these modifications were totally unnecessary since the production of the first jet transport aircraft. Similarly, a major aerospace company made an assumption regarding bidding practice and interpretation of government contracting regulations. This erroneous assumption was followed for more than ten years before the error was detected. Hundreds of government contracts had been bid over this period. A significant number were lost to competitors because a misinterpretation of less than ten words resulting in a company policy had never been challenged by those responsible for bidding within the company.

2. *Make Complicated Problems Less Complicated.*   Without question, some strategic problems that a corporation faces are tremendously complex. The number of environmental, as well as internal, variables that must be weighed and juggled, along with coordination with other divisions of the company, competition, and the government, is mind-boggling. Volatile and changing factors can be overwhelming in number and in magnitude. Some of these factors may be relevant, and some may be totally irrelevant to the best strategic solution. The only way to handle a complicated problem of this sort is to break it down to less complicated component parts. This may be done in several different ways. Perhaps you are faced with a corporate strategy problem that is complicated primarily because of many different markets in which the company deals. In this case it is better to segment the market in some fashion and to solve each market-segment problem separately. The same may be true if you are dealing with a number of different products or a number of different customers or any other aspect in which you must consider multiples of the same class of items. If a complex problem exists in which one solution for all classes will be extremely difficult to arrive at and which may be unworkable, attempt to break the major and complex problem into less complex, smaller problems.

3. *Increase, Do Not Decrease, the Number of Alternatives.*   The prime mistake made by many strategic planners is to eliminate alternatives too early in the problem-solving process. Never eliminate alterna-

tives until they have been thoroughly investigated and analyzed. The more alternatives available initially, the better. Even impractical alternatives are useful for stimulating other alternatives which you may not have thought of earlier but which are workable and can lead to an effective strategic solution.

4. *Don't Try to Work Totally in Your Head When You Are Solving Strategic Problems.* Writing the facts down and using graphic drawings to help you will frequently be of assistance in understanding how various elements relate to one another and in structuring the strategic issue for a resolution. Figures 6.1, 6.2, and 6.3 show some examples of this. In Figure 6.1 you may be seeking a strategy to increase the sales of a product. The lines drawn between the five key factors show the major relationships. Figure 6.2 attempts to solve the same problem with a different approach. The problem is placed at the center of an imaginary circle, and the factors that may affect the problem are placed around the periphery. In Figure 6.3 a "Pert"

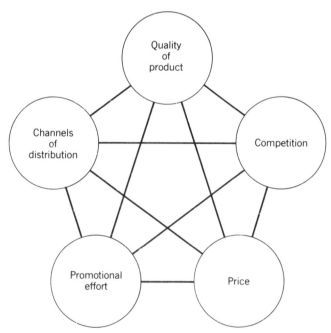

FIGURE 6.1.   Line relationships between factors.

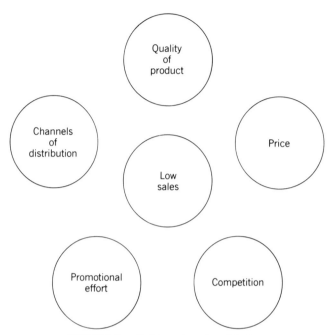

FIGURE 6.2. Problem at center of factors.

type of approach is used, which illustrates the relationship between the major factors in task sequence. As the major relationships in the process are identified, they are positioned on a network associated with the task necessary to result in a favorable result. Thus, in the figure, this begins with the marketing effort. It ends with what is felt to be the major factor in reaching the strategic objective, or solving the problem.

5. *The Use of Psychological Techniques to Assist in Strategic Planning and Problem Solving.* Certain psychological techniques may be employed by the corporate strategist to assist in arriving at quality strategic solutions. Sometimes one technique is best, sometimes another. Sometimes all three techniques can be used.

Brainstorming. The first technique is "brainstorming," and it is pretty well known. But it is frequently not used properly or as much as it could be. With this particular technique, two or more strategists get together and discuss ideas. Allow a free flow of ideas, and do not attempt to block any idea as it is presented. It is generally helpful to have a chalkboard available so that ideas can be written down. I want to repeat: It is very important not to eliminate any idea too early, no matter how wild or impractical or unworkable the idea may at first appear. Instead, it should be written down and discussed. Brainstorming is usually most effective with individuals who get along fairly well together, among whom a free, open interchange of ideas can be accomplished. For corporate strategists who work better alone, the technique is not much good.

The Patience Technique. The "patience technique" is another technique that is not much used. It requires that the strategist "passively wait" for a solution. This goes against much of what has been taught to American managers about action and decision

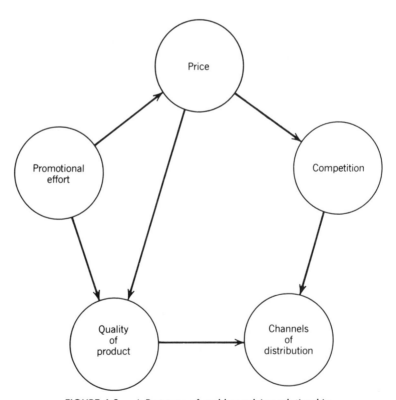

FIGURE 6.3.   A Pert type of problem-solving relationship.

making. The technique may be simple, but it is very powerful when done properly. It is important that the individual who is "waiting" for the solution while using this technique not put a great deal of pressure on himself or herself but simply gather together all the facts, go someplace where it is quiet, relax, sit down, and wait. You have to try this and experience it to appreciate just how well it works. Perhaps the most well-known advocate of this technique was the inventor Thomas Edison, whose ability to solve unique problems is documented by his numerous famous inventions. His methodology was simply to go into a dark room and sit down. This waiting could take him hours and, on rare occasions, days. But considering the magnitude of the inventions that Edison came up with, his solutions were well worth waiting for. If you want to use this technique, you probably should do so with some discretion, lest you be labeled as an incurable eccentric. In the corporate world, this could interfere with your ability to get your recommendations adopted. Still, this technique is psychologically sound, and if you have not tried it, it is worthwhie giving it a shot.

Use of the Subconscious Mind.   Many psychologists have conducted experiments for using the subconscious mind to arrive at solutions. The sometimes astounding results are well documented. An article in the *Wall Street Journal* in 1982 refers to psychologist Dr. Charles A. Garfield of the University of California at San Francisco who, in his research, explored differences of effective and noneffective executives. It turns out that one difference is that effective executives tend to be those who may have used the subconscious mind to assist them in their problem solving and in other aspects of their corporate responsibilities. You may have already used subconscious mind techniques without realizing it. Have you ever gone to bed with a problem that worried you and then awoke in the morning having "miraculously" received the solution without having thought of the problem once since going to bed the night before? This solution was made possible by your subconscious mind which, while your conscious mind slept, continued to work. Using the subconscious mind for decision making depends heavily on a relaxed state of mind. Therefore, you must be totally relaxed and not under pressure, or you must be asleep to make it work.

TRAINING YOURSELF FOR FAST RESOLUTION OF STRATEGIC PROBLEMS

There are some situations where, due to the competitive nature of the business environment, a decision must be made immediately. Some managers and strategists have a great deal of trouble with this. However, it is easy to train yourself to make fast decisions. The key is to practice rapid problem solving and decision making in noncritical, even nonwork environments. You can do this in a restaurant. If you cannot make a decision between several possible choices on the menu, quickly review the advantages and disadvantages of each choice. Practice making your selection in as short a period of time as possible. You can do the same exercise in making a decision for different shows, movies, or television channels to watch. Consider all such decisions as training sessions in rapid problem solving and decision making. With minimal practice, you will carry over this training into your work environment. However, it does not mean that every decision, in every situation, should be accomplished off the top of your head. Some decisions need the time for a thorough analysis or additional information. Other situations simply do not require an immediate decision. If some delay will result in a better decision, take the time to get it right. But if a decision must be made rapidly, you can learn to make your decision with little information and few facts and yet have a surprisingly high batting average of success.

INTUITION

While a structured problem-solving procedure is best for most strategic problems, "intuition" can be successfully applied, especially by the manager who must implement strategic plans. Intuition can be an important asset in your ability to arrive at workable strategic solutions, because your intuition integrates not only education and your work experience but all the factors in the strategic situation of which you are aware, both conscious and unconscious. Researchers have found that intuition has been used successfully to arrive at effective strategic solutions and strategies in many companies. Thomas J. Peters and Robert H. Waterman, Jr., after their study of sixty-two American companies in *In Search of Excellence,* concluded that rationality by itself did not explain what made the excellent companies work. Intuition played a significant part.

RISK TAKING

"Risk taking" is a part of any executive's life-style. This is particularly true of the corporate strategist. As a strategist, you plan and, in some cases, implement the best job that you can. But then, ultimately, history and the bottom line will decide whether your strategy was correct. This book should go a long way in assisting you to come up with more correct solutions than incorrect ones. Nevertheless, it is the lot of every strategist to occasionally "blow one." However, you cannot avoid the risk. It is your duty as a corporate strategist. Also, failure to take a risk can sometimes result in a greater loss to your organization. Finally, the sheer audacity of the strategic decision which assumes high risk may sometimes win the day. Therefore, accept risk as the constant companion of your profession and only pause to calculate the risk so that you can decide when risks should be taken and when they should not.

HARVARD CASE STUDY METHOD FOR STRATEGIC PROBLEM SOLVING

The following is the structured method I spoke of earlier in the chapter. It will greatly assist you in solving many of the operational problems that will confront you as a corporate strategist. This structure is used in many fields. It is used at Harvard to analyze business problems; it is used by attorneys to analyze cases in court; and it has been used by the military for many years for conducting staff studies on a variety of different operational problems. Extremely effective, it will enable you to consider all major and relevant factors in any strategic situation and to arrive at a decision based on logic but, at the same time, will allow you to consider nonlogical and psychological factors. Its very structure represents an outstanding method of presenting your findings either in written form or in a formal oral presentation.

The steps of this basic strategic problem-solving structure are six:

1. Define the central strategic problem.
2. List the relevant factors.
3. List the alternative courses of action, with the advantages and disadvantages of each.
4. Analyze and discuss the relative merits of each alternative.
5. Draw conclusions.
6. Make your decision or recommendation as to which strategic alternative or strategy to follow.

Let's look at each element of this structure in turn.

Defining the Central Strategic Problem

Defining the "central strategic problem" is probably the most important and difficult part of the whole procedure. In almost every situation in which a single strategy must be involved, you will be confronted with many different problems, large and small, primary and secondary. These will greatly confuse the issue and your ability to discover the most important element. What first appears to be a major problem may simply be a symptom of a more basic problem. Most strategic problem-solving situations in business will involve money and have to do with profits, sales, costs, or market share.

These are frequently symptoms of a more serious strategic issue. Therefore, before simply defining the central problem as "profits being down" or "sales falling off," you should ask yourself why these symptoms are present. This answer will help you uncover the main issue. Even after you have spent some time in identifying and wording the central strategic problem, you will need to return to it during your analysis for further refinement. This is because as you proceed, you will acquire additional insights that you did not have when you first defined the central strategic problem. In some cases, the problem is so complex that a single strategy may not work for each problem. In fact, there may be several different central strategic problems or issues to be analyzed. If so, identify each separately and perform the same six-part analysis on it.

Listing the Relevant Factors

The words *relevant factors* contain two elements, both of which are extremely important to this particular part of the analysis. First, every factor must be *relevant*. That means that it must have bearing on the central problem, as you have identified it. It is not necessary—nor should you waste your time or confuse yourself by trying—to list every single factor which may be involved in the situation. List only those that are relevant to the central problem, as you have defined it. Second, the reason that the term includes the word *factor* and not *fact* is that you must include assumptions, calculations, and estimates, as well as facts that are derived or made available to you. You will never have complete facts for any given analysis. Some will always be missing, and assumptions and estimates must be made.

Listing Alternative Courses of Action, with the Advantages and Disadvantages of Each

The third part of this structure is to find alternative solutions and to list them. Naturally, every single course of action that you list will have advantages and disadvantages. If a solution is available that has all advantages and no disadvantages, probably the process is unnecessary. The strategic solution sought will probably be obvious. Each alternative should be one of action and should solve the strategic problem, as you have defined it. If a "solution" is identified which does not solve the problem, this generally means that the central problem must be reworded and redefined. One possible course of action is what you are doing now. It should always be included as an alternative, since even if what you are doing may not be profitable or meet sales, market share, or other expectations, it may be the best-possible alternative under the circumstances. Other courses of action may be much worse and may result in a much more negative impact on your company. After you have completed all the alternatives, check to make sure that each alternative solution does in fact solve the problem you have set.

Analyzing the Relative Merits of Each Alternative

This is the main portion of the analysis. This is where you do your thinking and you document your thinking in a discussion of the relative importance of each of the advantages and disadvantages of each alternative course of action. However, the process is not simply free thought, and you should attempt to organize your discussion and to write it down so that it proceeds in an organized fashion. Analyze one alternative and then another in turn. As you proceed, you may think of additional alternatives to be considered. If so, you should go back and include them. If you do this, you should again go back and proceed through the analysis once again.

Developing Conclusions

The conclusions you develop should be the result of the analysis you have just completed. It is best to state them simply, without additional discussion or explanation. If additional discussion or explanation is necessary, it should be done in the previous section of analysis. This will make your conclusions stronger and will aid you in eliminating or rewording faulty conclusions. It will also encourage you to return to your analysis if insufficient support exists for a tentative conclusion, since every conclusion that you list must have support from the previous sections. An important test of whether you have done this correctly is to show your analysis section and all the preceding sections to someone else without showing the person your conclusions. Ask this individual what conclusions he or she arrives at. If your conclusions and his or hers are identical, then you have done this correctly. If not, there is an error somewhere in the logic process of your structure, and you have insufficient support for the conclusions that you have listed.

Selecting the Correct Strategic Alternative

In this last section, you should use the conclusions you have drawn from your analysis to select the strategic alternative you have decided on. Again, this should be accomplished without explanation. If done correctly, no explanation will be necessary, and lack of explanation here will again assist you in eliminating a faulty decision. In fact, it is best to state your decisions or recommendations in the imperative form, with action words stating exactly what you want done. This method of statement will also be useful if it is necessary to present this recommendation and the reasons for it to higher authority within the company. In fact, the whole outline—that is, the central strategic problem, relevant factors, alternative solutions with their advantages and disadvantages, discussion/analysis, conclusions, and, finally, decision (which can be presented as recommendations)—can be used in presenting your analysis on any strategic issue to top corporate management if required.

To assist you in strategic analysis and planning, forms are presented in Figure 6.4.

CENTRAL PROBLEM: _____
_____
_____
_____

Relevant factors (list): _____
1. _____
2. _____
3. _____
4. _____
5. _____
6. _____
7. _____
8. _____
9. _____
10. _____
11. _____
12. _____
13. _____
14. _____
15. _____
16. _____
17. _____
18. _____
19. _____
20. _____

Alternative solutions:
1. _____
_____

Advantages:
    A. _____
    B. _____
    C. _____
Disadvantages:
    A. _____
    B. _____
    C. _____

2. _____
_____

Advantages:
    A. _____
    B. _____
    C. _____

FIGURE 6.4.   Strategic analysis and planning forms. (Copyright © 1982 by Dr. William A. Cohen.)

Disadvantages:

   A._____

   B._____

   C._____

3._____

_____

Advantages:

   A._____

   B._____

   C._____

Disadvantages:

   A._____

   B._____

   C._____

4._____

_____

Advantages:

   A._____

   B._____

   C._____

Disadvantages:

   A._____

   B._____

   C._____

5._____

_____

Advantages:

   A._____

   B._____

   C._____

Disadvantages:

   A._____

   B._____

   C._____

Discussion/analysis:_____

_____

_____

_____

_____

_____

_____

_____

FIGURE 6.4.   (*continued*)

_____
_____
_____
_____
_____
_____
_____
_____
_____
_____
_____
_____
_____
_____
_____
_____

Conclusions (list):

1._____
2._____
3._____
4._____
5._____
6._____
7._____
8._____
9._____
10._____

Recommendations or decisions (list):

1._____
2._____
3._____
4._____
5._____
6._____
7._____
8._____
9._____
10._____

FIGURE 6.4.   (continued)

168

7

STRATEGIC ANALYSIS METHODS

In this chapter we cover methods of strategic analysis for portfolios of products or businesses. Portfolio analysis is necessary for the following reasons:

To Determine the Potential Value of a Specific Product or Business. A product, on the surface, may seemingly be of great value to your company or of very little value. Until you can analyze and compare it with other competing products or businesses, its real value compared with alternatives is not known.

To Determine a Balance Between Products Generating Cash and Products Using Cash. Products or businesses can be categorized by those requiring cash and thus resulting in a negative cash flow and those generating a positive cash flow. But the strategic implications are not that simple. In some cases products generating a positive cash flow will require harvesting without further investments, whereas those currently requiring a significant outlay every month should receive top priority for continued investments. Until this analysis is made, it is impossible from a simple computation to tell which way the cash is running.

Risk Balance. Some products, projects, and businesses are highly risky; others, less so. It is important for you as a corporate strategist to understand not only which are more risky than others but also how your portfolio of risk balances with other factors.

Growth Balance. As we learned in Chapter 5, products have different stages of life: introduction, growth, maturity, and decline. Here it's important to know not only what's happening to this product or this business but how the overall balance is aligned so that we do not have all products grouped in one stage or in another of its life cycle.

Goal Setting. Our portfolio of businesses or products must be aligned to facilitate the determination of the right goals and objectives.

Strategy Development. Until we can see the overall big picture and our alignment of our products or businesses within our corporation, a true corporate strategy is not possible.

A portfolio analysis can be done using the product life cycle curve discussed in Chapter 4, and some of the answers will be forthcoming from this analysis. However, as we will see in this chapter, much more information can be obtained and a more complete analysis made by additional analytical techniques. Further, these techniques, combined with the product life cycle analysis, can help us in generating strong corporate strategies that lead to overall success and attainment of our goals and objectives.

PETER DRUCKER'S PRODUCT PORTFOLIO CLASSIFICATION SYSTEM

Methods of classifying products or businesses into certain areas are not recent. Bruce Henderson's Boston Consulting Group developed its well-known four-cell matrix back in 1960. Even earlier, Peter Drucker developed a product portfolio classification system. Drucker categorized all products into six different areas which he felt represented the entire spectrum of possibilities in different strategies depending on the category. These categories are as follows:

1. Tomorrow's breadwinners
2. Today's breadwinners
3. Products capable of becoming net contributors if something drastic is done
4. Yesterday's breadwinners
5. The also-rans
6. The failures

MICHAEL PORTER'S THREE GENERIC STRATEGIES

In more recent times, Michael Porter, well-known Harvard business professor, developed what he called "generic strategies," which he felt were applicable to any business or industry. These three generic strategies are:

1. Overall cost leadership
2. Differentiation, which involves producing something your customers will view as unique
3. Focus, which involves concentrating on a specific market, channel of distribution, or geographic area

Michael Porter's three generic strategies are somewhat similar to strategies developed by marketing theorists and known, respectively, as market segmentation and product differentiation. Market segmentation refers to the fact that a packet, instead of being made up of a mass of look-alike, act-alike, buy-alike customers, is in reality made up of a number of segments, members of which act similarly in their buyer behavior but differently from other segments. Product differentiation involves differentiation of some of a product's features, its appearance, or its performance from those of other similar products sold to the same market. Both of these concepts are similar to a principle of strategy evolved over thousands of years of warfare which simply states that superior resources should be allocated to the decisive point of the situation.

PROFIT IMPACT MARKETING STRATEGIES

The profit impact marketing strategies (PIMS) program was initiated in the early 1970s at a nonprofit organization, the Marketing Science Institute, which was and still is associated with the Harvard Business School, and was intended to determine the profit impact of marketing strategies, through utilization data empirically gathered from a number of different practicing businesses. It is computer-based, integrates available factors, and attempts to identify for a given situation the major factors responsible for profit.

Through its early work the PIMS program identified 37 profit influences after analyzing 602 businesses over a three-year period. For example, outputs of the PIMS program determined that (1) there was a relationship between return on investment (ROI) and market share, (2) market share was the most important factor for profit and, in fact, counted for some 15% of the results for those companies and businesses analyzed, and (3) higher quality generally equaled higher profitability.

Despite the very important insights that are still being generated from the PIMS and other such computer-data–generated programs, there are several problems and limitations with applying the PIMS output operationally.

First, the PIMS output consists of generalized conclusions; consequently, these conclusions may or may not always be true, depending on your business, your industry, and your unique business situation. For example, one PIMS study indicated that high research and development plus high marketing depressed ROI. But many companies have found the opposite effect. Further, even if a

PIMS study indicated that results over a wide number of industries and situations were true in 85% of the situations, a corporation finding itself within the remaining 15% that applied a PIMS conclusion blindly would suffer a 100% failure.

Second, another limitation of PIMS is that the focus is not on the future or on future developments but must by its very nature be on what has happened and occurred empirically in the past. While this in itself is not an overwhelming limitation, automatic adherence to PIMS conclusions could conceivably lead a company to fail to anticipate threats or opportunities which may occur in the future.

Third, PIMS and similar methods are not by themselves methodologies for analysis. They provide conclusions after analyzing other data. These conclusions can be used for strategic guidance, but they are not methodologies enabling a strategist to evolve corporate strategies without additional analysis.

THE BOSTON CONSULTING GROUP'S PRODUCT PORTFOLIO MATRIX

In 1960, Bruce Henderson of the Boston Consulting Group developed the first product portfolio matrix that permitted simultaneous comparison of different products in an external environment. The objective of this matrix was to develop the best mix of products to maximize long-term growth earnings of the firm.

The "four-cell product portfolio matrix" developed by the Boston Consulting Group also involved a concept known as the "strategic business unit" (SBU). In the SBU concept, a number of businesses of a corporation (all of which were found to have characteristics that would cause it to perform similarly or react similarly to factors in its external environment) were classed or grouped together in order to make the analysis manageable and to develop corporate strategies which were coordinated for a manageable number of SBUs.

This four-cell portfolio matrix was first adopted by the Norton Company in the late 1960s, which used it with a considerable degree of success.

The original concept is as shown in Figure 7.1. Note that there are only two significant variables that are analyzed. Along the horizontal axis are today's earnings, represented by the current market share along the horizontal axis. Along the vertical axis is the potential for market growth, which is represented by the growth rate of the market segment in which the business competes.

The thinking behind the construction of this matrix was that the greater share of the market you own, the farther along you are on the experience curve. The experience curve itself was not a new idea, being kin to the concept that has been around since World War II known as "the learning curve." In the learning curve concept, the labor costs of producing any item become cheaper as you produce more and as management and labor learn how to produce this item more efficiently. Thus to produce the hundredth item is cheaper in cost than to produce the first item, and to produce the thousandth item is cheaper than the hundredth, and so forth. Henderson took this concept and made the assumption that not only learning benefited but also experience. Thus it was not only the cost of labor itself which should decrease but also efficiency in buying raw material for the product, in sales, in marketing, and so forth. In other words, not only labor enjoyed the benefit of longer-run production but also all

Relative Market Share

	High	Low
High	Stars	Question marks (also called "problem children")
Low	Cash cows	Dogs

Product sales growth rate

FIGURE 7.1.   Boston Consulting Group's four-cell product portfolio matrix.

aspects of costs associated with producing or manufacturing a product.

Henderson divided his matrix into four cells. SBUs that fell into the upper-left cell, those which had high relative market share as well as high potential market growth, he considered "stars." A star had high performance but also could have negative cash flow, since the needs might be great and it might require sinking more money into this SBU in order to keep up with its growth. In the lower-left quadrant were SBUs in which the relative market shares were high but in which the potential for growth was low; these were called "cash cows." A cash cow was the mainstay of corporate funding and always had a positive cash flow. The upper-right quadrant of the four-cell matrix was for SBUs which currently had a low relative market share but which had a high potential. These were known as "problem children," or "question marks." They were most definitely cash drains. As to whether they would eventually become "stars," with relatively high market share as well as potential growth, or become "dogs" remained to be seen. In the lower-right quadrant were SBUs in which the corporation had both a low market share and a low potential for growth. Clearly, SBUs in this quadrant required careful attention and a decision as to whether to maintain the SBU or to drop it from the portfolio.

In order to assist its clients in deciding on growth strategies, the Boston Consulting Group (BCG) came up with a formula which it called "the formula for maximum sustainable growth":

$$G = D/E \; (R-i) \; p + Rp$$

This formula assumed no equity financing, and the letters stood for the following:

G = maximum sustainable growth
D/E = debt/equity ratio
  R = after-tax return on assets assuming constant dollars
  p = rate of retained earnings
  i = current cost of debt after taxes

CHARACTERISTICS AND STRATEGIES USING THE FOUR-CELL BCG MATRIX

Each of the four cells of the matrix has certain characteristics that imply various strategies for the firm having those products.

Stars

Stars require continual expenditures for capacity expansion and a continual stream of cash flow. Earning characteristics are low to high; however, the cash flow is negative, not positive. Thus the strategic implication for products falling in this quadrant is to continue to do things to increase market share, even at the expense of short-term earnings and profits.

Cash Cows

Cash cows, in contrast with stars, require very small cash expenditures for maintenance purposes. The earning characteristics of products in this category are high, the cash flow positive. The strategy recommended and implied by this condition is to maintain the share of the market and cost leadership through additional investment until such time as investment results in only marginal return.

Question Marks

Question marks, like stars, require heavy expenditures, at least initially, and generally high research and development costs. The earning characteristics of question marks, however, unlike those of stars, are negative to low; but the net result is identical—a negative cash flow. Here, the strategy implied is one of assessment. Primarily, the big question for the question mark SBUs is to determine whether the company can dominate this segment of the market with the SBU. If the chances of domination are good, the indication is that further investment is warranted. If the chances are poor, the implication is that the SBU should be withdrawn from this market in order to utilize the resources elsewhere.

Dogs

Dogs have earning capacities ranging from high to low. However, investment characteristics gradually deplete capacity. Therefore, though there may be positive cash flow, alternative investments for other SBUs are such that strong consideration must be given to dropping the dog SBU. How to do this and to plan orderly withdrawal, so as to maximize the cash flow, is a major challenge to the corporate strategist.

Balanced Portfolios

The BCG four-cell matrix does not necessarily recommend situations in which one has all stars or all cash cows. Rather, a balanced portfolio is sought in which cash cows are well positioned with stars to provide growth and yield high cash returns in the future. Questions marks are supported as required. Dogs are either dropped or managed, dropped for straight cash purposes or managed generally for political reasons, in which customers of other corporate SBUs might be affected—the two are so related that we decide to accept the low ROI from our dogs in order to retain much greater ROIs or SBUs in other categories of the matrix.

Unbalanced Portfolios

The corporate strategist using the BCG four-cell matrix must be alert to the danger of "unbalanced portfolios." This includes situations in which:

1. There are too many losers due to inadequate cash flow, inadequate products, and/or inadequate growth.
2. There are too many question marks due to the inadequate cash flow and inadequate profits.

3. There are too many profit producers due to inadequate growth and excessive cash flow. You may ask why this is bad. The answer is, it may be bad not so much for today but for the future—when the cash cows have become dogs and there are no new cash cows.

4. There are too many developing winners. This will result in excessive demands on finances, excessive demands on our management of our products, and on unstable growth and profits. It implies an unbalanced and overly risky corporate strategy.

If you choose to use the BCG matrix, you should recognize that there are limitations and problems associated with it. For example, not all products are sold on the basis of low price. Thus overall cost leadership in itself is only half the secret of victory.

Also, big profits are possible with a diminutive market share. This is especially true if either the market is so large that a tiny share may in itself be profitable and allow firms to do other things in other markets or the margin on each product is such that a small market share will be exceptionally profitable.

Cost reduction according to the experience curve which, of course, the four-cell matrix is based on, is not automatic. Actions must be taken by the firm in order to achieve these cost reductions. The actions and resources required may not be possible or advisable for other reasons.

Other situations exist in some industries and markets in which profit margins are not related to market share or in which the experience curve does not yield a cost advantage, for example, making only one of an item, as is the case with some products in the aerospace industry or in some large capital goods industrial markets.

The four-cell matrix does not require direct consideration of other environmental factors, such as the competition, government regulations, the firm's own resources that it may or may not have, and other important environmental factors.

THE GE-McKINSEY MULTIFACTOR PORTFOLIO MATRIX

The GE-McKinsey multifactor portfolio matrix was designed to overcome some of the limitations of considering only the two factors of market share and market growth as a starting point for developing corporate strategies. The idea was to consider all important factors and analyses and yet to have a matrix with SBUs falling in each cell representing common characteristics and common strategy implications. Also, by developing a matrix containing nine cells, instead of four, finer gradations of actions and situations were permissible.

All the above was enabled by the construction of a nine-cell matrix, with industry attractiveness being the descriptive factor along the horizontal axis and business strengths along the vertical axis, both increasing toward the upper-left quadrant of the matrix. This is as shown in Figure 7.2.

When General Electric (GE) first developed the matrix, it indicated only four factors for industry attractiveness:

Size

Market growth and pricing

Market diversity

Competitive structure

General Electric also listed eleven business strength factors to be considered in the matrix:

Size	Technology Position
Growth	Strengths/weaknesses
Share	Image
Position	Pollution
Profitability	People
Margins	

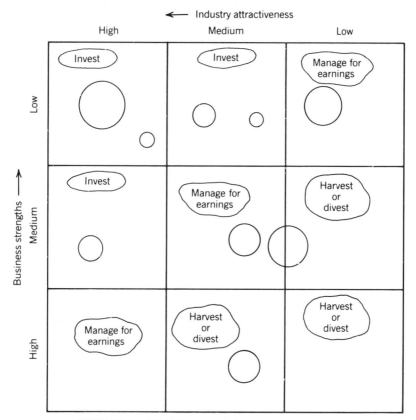

FIGURE 7.2.   GE-McKinsey Multifactor Portfolio Matrix.

Thus although the matrix was still a structure in only two dimensions, horizontal and vertical, the multiplicity of factors could be considered simultaneously. In this case, fifteen factors in all—four industry attractiveness factors and eleven business strength factors.

As shown in Figure 7.2, three cells in the upper-left-hand quadrant contain SBUs in which the company is advised to utilize strategies involving investment or growth. The lower-right-hand three-cell quadrants contain SBUs that the company is advised to harvest or divest itself of. The three quadrants in the center, moving diagonally from the lower left of the figure to the upper right, are those in which SBUs are to be selectively managed for earnings. The size of the circles in the figure represents annual sales of the SBU.

Further refinement of the nine-cell matrix has been accomplished by others. One example is the directional policy matrix, shown in Figure 7.3. Here, along the horizontal axis, we have business-sector prospects instead of industry attractiveness, and along the vertical axis, we have company's competitive capabilities instead of business strengths. Also, with this matrix, business-sector prospects increase from left to right, and company's competitive capabilities increase from the top to the bottom of the matrix. Again, each quadrant implies certain strategies. For example, in the extreme upper-left quadrant the instructions are "disinvest," and in the lower-left quadrant the product, or SBU, is called a "cash generator."

In all cases, designing numerical factors, as well as selecting which to use, is highly judgmental. Further, different products or product

	Business-sector prospects		
	Unattractive	Average	Attractive
Weak	Disinvest	Phased withdrawal Proceed with care	Double or quit
Average	Phased withdrawal	Proceed with care	Try harder
Strong	Cash generator	Growth Leader	Leader

FIGURE 7.3.   Directional policy matrix.

groups, that is, different SBUs, may involve different factors. And, finally, though the instructions appear precise, cell performances are not precise. Thus multifactor analyses, even as an improvement over a two-factor matrix, such as the Boston Consulting Group matrix, also suffer from limitations.

Many strategists have used product groupings (sometimes called "strategic product units," or SPUs) instead of SBUs. The principles of strategy development using SPUs are the same as with SBUs.

In the next chapter we're going to develop a multifactor analysis matrix in more detail and show you how to assign weightings and how to develop your own structured methodology for strategy development. Though there are limitations, the methods presented are by far better than a "by guess and by golly" means for understanding the problems, opportunities, threats, and major influences affecting strategy generation and development, and they assist greatly in providing a formalized means for the development and planning of corporate strategies.

8

DEVELOPING YOUR OWN STRATEGY ANALYSIS STRUCTURE

For many companies the strategy analysis structures discussed earlier are unwieldy and less than optimal. There are either too many factors or too few, making the process more difficult than it need be or less sensitive than it has to be, or the factors themselves are not those primary for developing competitive strategies considering the marketplace in which the company is engaged. In this chapter we look at developing a complete methodology and adapting it to your particular company-industry-market situation.

STEPS AND COMPLETE STRATEGY STRUCTURE DEVELOPMENT AND ANALYSIS

Nine steps are used in accomplishing your own structure development and analysis:

1. A fit analysis of current products and potential market segments

2. Preparation of competitive profiles

3. Development of strategic product units (SPUs)

4. Calculation of SPU value for business strength

5. Calculation of SPU value for market attractiveness

6. Plotting SPUs on a multicelled, multifactored matrix

7. Strengths, weaknesses, opportunities, threats, and sales analysis

8. Planning strategic moves of the SPUs on the multifactored analysis matrix

9. Strategy development for each SPU

STEP 1.   A FIT ANALYSIS OF CURRENT PRODUCTS AND POTENTIAL MARKET SEGMENTS

The objective of a fit analysis of your current products and potential market segments is to discover where gaps exist between your current products and potential markets and the products needed to close these gaps. In order to do this we will use Figure 8.1, in which your products are documented opposite potential market segments. First, list the products on this form along the vertical axis. Next, note the potential market segments along the horizontal axis. Use numerical descriptors within this matrix as follows:

1 = currently meets needs fully

2 = minor changes in product needed

3 = significant changes in product needed

4 = major changes in product needed

5 = totally new product required

In accomplishing this analysis, you should group similar products together. Also note here that the definition of a "market segment" is a subset of a larger market described by demographics, psychographics, life-style, or geographic location; in the case of industrial markets, by industry, company, SIC, size of company, and so forth; or, in the case of a government market, by a specific agency, department, or geographic location.

Note that a market segment may exist for which you currently have no product and which you do not service.

Complete Figure 8.1 for all the products you plan or currently market. Use the blank forms (Figures 8.2. through 8.5) as required.

STEP 2. PREPARATION OF COMPETITIVE PROFILES

The next step is the preparation of competitive profiles on other companies that compete in the product areas which we have indicated. For this purpose, use Figure 8.6. List your company's products and those of your company's competition along the vertical axis of this figure. Along the horizontal axis list the major product attributes and/or performance characteristics. Blank forms are available (Figures 8.7 through 8.10) for your use. You should complete a separate form for each product that you either plan to introduce or currently manufacture.

STEP 3. DEVELOPMENT OF STRATEGIC PRODUCT UNITS

A strategic product unit (SPU) is like the strategic business unit (SBU) discussed in Chapter 7. However, it differs in that the unit is not a business grouping but a product or product-line grouping with a distinct market focus for which a strategy and a plan can be developed. Please note also, however, that an SPU can be for a single product; if you are grouping businesses, you can use the SBU designation instead of the SPU.

The development of SPUs is in itself an important task, and certain implicit assumptions are made during this development:

DATE February 13, 1983

Potential Market Segments

Products: Seminars	Small business	Medium and large business	Nursing professionals	Engineering professionals	Psychology/ sociology professionals	Noncollege female	Noncollege male	College-educated female	College-educated male	Management professionals	Education professionals
1. Accounting	1	2	4	4	4	2	2	2	2	2	N/A
2. American culture and language program	N/A	N/A	N/A	N/A	5	1	1	1	1	N/A	N/A
3. Art	N/A	N/A	N/A	5	N/A	1	1	1	1	N/A	N/A
4. Business	1	1	5	5	5	1	1	1	1	1	N/A
5. Business management	1	1	4	4	4	1	1	1	1	1	N/A
6. Career/life planning	N/A	N/A	4	4	4	1	1	1	1	4	N/A

186

Product	1	2	3	4	5	6	7	8	9	10	11	12	13
7. Communications	1	2	3	3	3	1	1	1	1	1	1	1	N/A
8. Data processing	2	2	3	3	3	1	1	1	1	1	2	2	N/A
9. Education	N/A	N/A	N/A	N/A	N/A	N/A	N/A	N/A	N/A	N/A	N/A	N/A	1
10. Educational test prep.	2	2	1	1	2	1	1	1	1	1	2	2	2

Numerical code:

1 = Currently meets needs fully
2 = Minor changes in product needed
3 = Significant changes in product needed
4 = Major changes in product needed
5 = Totally new product required

FIGURE 8.1. Products vs. potential market segments.

DATE _____

Potential Market Segments

Products

Numerical code:

1 = Currently meets needs fully
2 = Minor changes in product needed
3 = Significant changes in product needed
4 = Major changes in product needed
5 = Totally new product required

FIGURE 8.2. Products vs. potential market segments. (Copyright © 1983 by Dr. William A. Cohen.)

189

DATE _____

Potential Market Segments

Products

Numerical code:

1 = Currently meets needs fully
2 = Minor changes in product needed
3 = Significant changes in product needed
4 = Major changes in product needed
5 = Totally new product required

FIGURE 8.3. Products vs. potential market segments. (Copyright © 1983 by Dr. William A. Cohen.)

DATE _____

Potential Market Segments

Products

192

Numerical code:

1 = Currently meets needs fully

2 = Minor changes in product needed

3 = Significant changes in product needed

4 = Major changes in product needed

5 = Totally new product required

FIGURE 8.4. Products vs. potential market segments. (Copyright © 1983 by Dr. William A. Cohen.)

DATE _____

Potential Market Segments

Products

Numerical code:

1 = Currently meets needs fully

2 = Minor changes in product needed

3 = Significant changes in product needed

4 = Major changes in product needed

5 = Totally new product required

FIGURE 8.5. Products vs. potential market segments. (Copyright © 1983 by Dr. William A. Cohen.)

Date ___						
	Attributes/Performance Characteristics					
Products: Accounting seminars	CSULA	UCLA	USC	External Cos.	CSU	Community Colleges
Fee	$35–475	$65–235	$75–245	$100–2200	$35–475	Free–$120
Credit or Non-credit	C & NC	C & NC	C & NC	NC	C & NC	NC
Location	S	S	H & S	H	H & S	S
Enrollment	H	H	H	H	H	H
Promotion	brochure	catalog	catalog	brochure	catalog	catalog

FIGURE 8.6. Competitive profiles.

S = School; H = Hotel or other location   H = high; L = low; M = medium

Date _____   Attributes/Performance Characteristics

Products

197

FIGURE 8.7.   Competitive profiles. (Copyright © 1983 by Dr. William A. Cohen.)

Date _____

Products

Attributes/Performance Characteristics

FIGURE 8.8. Competitive profiles. (Copyright © 1983 by Dr. William A. Cohen.)

Date _____

Attributes/Performance Characteristics

Products

FIGURE 8.9. Competitive profiles. (Copyright © 1983 by Dr. William A. Cohen.)

Date _____

Attributes/Performance Characteristics

Products

FIGURE 8.10. Competitive profiles. (Copyright © 1983 by Dr. William A. Cohen.)

1. *Grouping.* All products grouped under a single SPU will perform similarly under a competitive environment. Thus a single grand strategy is applicable to the generalized class of products under this designation.

2. *Control.* Simply developing a strategy is insufficient. A strategy must be executed. Therefore, the principle of strategy known as "unity of command" is most relevant here. That is, the strategist or planner who is doing this work must ask herself or himself whether the control of all the elements of the SPU anticipated is possible or even likely on the firing line of actual implementation.

3. *Competition.* Any strategy planned and then implemented will, in turn, affect the operations of competitors in the same marketplace. The implicit assumption is that the competitors for all elements of the SPU are identical.

In summary, for guidelines in the construction of SPUs or SBUs, look for similarity in customer servicing or product line under a single manager having the same or nearly the same competitors.

Remember that the objective in establishing SPUs or SBUs is to avoid having to analyze in detail and to develop separate strategic plans for each individual product of a much larger portfolio when the process can be simplified by grouping and analyzing together simultaneously.

To assist you in the establishment of SPUs or SBUs, use the form provided in Figure 8.11. This form asks you to indicate the basis of your grouping, as well as the products grouped under this area, and to develop a short statement as to current performance of that SPU or SBU.

STEP 4.   CALCULATION OF SPU VALUE FOR BUSINESS STRENGTH

In order to allow for a two-dimensional matrix with many factors to be analyzed, we will use two descriptors, business strength and market attractiveness. It is first necessary to calculate an SPU value for

Date _____

SPU 1   Basis of grouping _____

Product _____
Product _____
Product _____
Product _____
Product _____
Product _____

How is SPU 1 currently performing? _____

SPU 2   Basis of grouping _____

Product _____
Product _____
Product _____
Product _____
Product _____
Product _____

How is SPU 2 currently performing? _____

SPU 3   Basis of grouping _____

Product _____
Product _____
Product _____
Product _____
Product _____
Product _____

How is SPU 3 currently performing? _____

SPU 4   Basis of grouping _____

Product _____
Product _____
Product _____
Product _____
Product _____
Product _____

FIGURE 8.11.   Development of SPUs or SBUs. (Copyright © 1983 by Dr. William A. Cohen.)

How is SPU 4 currently performing?

SPU 5   Basis of grouping _____

Product _____
Product _____
Product _____
Product _____
Product _____
Product _____

How is SPU 5 currently performing? _____

SPU 6   Basis of grouping _____

Product _____
Product _____
Product _____
Product _____
Product _____
Product _____

How is SPU 6 currently performing? _____

FIGURE 8.11.   (*continued*)

every SPU for business strength. In order to do this, perform the following substeps:

1. List the business strength criteria important to the SPU being analyzed. This may be based on your judgment, research in the market, or recent performance.

2. Establish relative importance weightings so that the total of these weightings equals 1.00.

Consider the following example: Assume that for the particular SPU or SBU being analyzed, only four business strength criteria are considered of significant importance. Clearly, this is somewhat unusual, and normally one would expect to find many additional business strength criteria worth noting. However, in this case, we will assume that there are only the four listed:

Engineering know-how

Size of the organization

Organizational image

Productivity

Now the question is, What is the relative importance of each of these four? After some thought you decide that the size of the organization and its productivity are about of equal weight but that organizational image is twice as important as either of these two factors. Finally, you decide that engineering know-how is probably one-third more important than even organizational image. From this information you could establish numerical weights. Note that they total 1.00.

	Weight
Engineering know-how	.40
Size of the organization	.15
Organizational image	.30
Productivity	.15
Total	1.00

Now we have completed the first two substeps. The final substep in calculating SPU value for business strength is to rate each of the business strength criteria for the SPU or SBU being analyzed. We can accomplish this very simply by using a numerical system of rating:

Very weak = 1 pt

Weak = 2 pts

Neither weak nor strong = 3 pts

Strong = 4 pts

Very strong = 5 pts

All we do to compute weight or rank for each business strength criterion is to multipy this weight by the rating of strength we gave it and to total these figures. Thus the calculation is as follows:

	Weight × Rating
Engineering know-how	.40 × 5 pts = 2.00
Size of the organization	.15 × 2 pts = 0.30
Organizational image	.30 × 4 pts = 1.20
Productivity	.15 × 3 pts = 0.45
	Total 3.95

Naturally, there are many different business strength criteria that might be incorporated into your analysis. Some are more relevant than others for your particular situation. Consider them all in working out the weighted rank for the SPU. Here is a list of typical relevant business strength criteria that might be considered for your analysis:

Current market share	Raw materials cost
SPU growth rate	Image
Sales effectiveness	Product quality
Proprietary nature of product	R & D/technology advantages
Price competitiveness	Engineering know-how
Advertising promotion effectiveness	Personnel resources
	Product synergies
Facilities location or newness	Profitability
Productivity	ROI
Experience curve effects	Distribution
Value added	

In order to accomplish this analysis, use the business strength computation sheets presented in Figures 8.12 through 8.16. The form is self-explanatory and asks you to list the business strength criteria while performing the multiplication of the weights and rankings and the calculation of the weighted rank as indicated previously. Do not forget to total this weighted rank in order to come up with a single figure for the specific SPU or SBU.

SPU # _____ Date _____

Business Strength Criteria	Weights	×	Rankings	=	Weighted Rank

206

1.00   Rank   =

FIGURE 8.12. Business strength computation sheet. (Copyright © 1983 by Dr. William A. Cohen.)

SPU # _____   Date _____

Business Strength Criteria	Weights	X	Rankings	=	Weighted Rank

FIGURE 8.13.   Business strength computation sheet. (Copyright © 1983 by Dr. William A. Cohen.)

Rank   =

1.00

SPU # _____ Date _____

Business Strength Criteria	Weights	X	Rankings	=	Weighted Rank

210

FIGURE 8.14. Business strength computation sheet. (Copyright © 1983 by Dr. William A. Cohen.)

Rank   =

1.00

SPU # _____ Date _____

Business Strength Criteria	Weights	×	Rankings	=	Weighted Rank

Rank =

1.00

FIGURE 8.15. Business strength computation sheet. (Copyright © 1983 by Dr. William A. Cohen.)

213

SPU # _____ Date _____

Business Strength Criteria	Weights	×	Rankings	=	Weighted Rank

1.00   Rank   =

FIGURE 8.16. Business strength computation sheet. (Copyright © 1983 by Dr. William A. Cohen.)

215

STEP 5.   CALCULATION OF SPU VALUE FOR MARKET ATTRACTIVENESS

In the same manner that we calculated business strength, we must now calculate market attractiveness in order to compute a weighted rank value for the SPU for the other axis of our strategy analysis structure.

Again, we must (1) list those market attractiveness criteria important to the SPU or SBU being analyzed and (2) establish relative importance weightings, the total of which must equal 1.00.

For example, if only the following four market attractiveness criteria were considered important within a specific case, relative importances might be assigned as indicated:

	Weight
Size of market	.30
Growth of market	.30
Ease of entry	.25
Life cycle position	.15
Total	1.00

In this example, the size of market and growth of market are both considered of major and of approximately equal importance and are therefore assigned the same value of .30. Ease of entry is considered of somewhat lesser importance, life cycle position, of even lesser importance.

Once again you must rate each market attractiveness criterion for the SPU or SBU being analyzed as follows:

Very unattractive = 1 pt

Unattractive = 2 pts

Neither attractive nor unattractive = 3 pts

Attractive = 4 pts

Very attractive = 5 pts

Now compute the weight or rank for each market attractiveness criterion by multiplying this weight by the rating you gave to it, as in the following example:

	Weight × Rating
Size of market	.30 × 4 pts = 1.20
Growth of market	.30 × 4 pts = 1.20
Ease of entry	.25 × 1 pt = 0.25
Life cycle position	.15 × 5 pts = 0.75
	Total 3.40

In this example, size of market for this SPU or SBU was given a rating of 4 points because it was considered attractive, as was growth of market, which was given the same rating. Ease of entry, however, was considered very unattractive and therefore was given the low rating of 1 point. Finally, life cycle position was considered very attractive and was therefore awarded 5 points.

Again, you must select and develop your own list of market attractiveness criteria that are of significant importance in your particular situation. However, a typical relevant market attractiveness criteria list follows. Add or subtract from this list as appropriate for your situation.

Size of market segment	Raw materials availability
Growth of market segment	Energy impact
Market pricing	Ease of entry
Customer's financial condition	Life cycle position
Cyclicity of demand	Competitive structure
Vulnerability to inflation	Product liability
Vulnerability to depression	Political considerations
Need for product	Distribution structure
Government regulation	

Use the market attractiveness computation sheets in Figures 8.17 through 8.21, for your analysis and computation of weighted ranks.

SPU No. _____ Date _____

Market Attractiveness Criteria	Weights	×	Rankings	=	Weighted Rank

218

1.00

Rank =

FIGURE 8.17. Market attractiveness computation sheet. (Copyright © 1983 by Dr. William A. Cohen.)

SPU No. _____ Date _____

Market Attractiveness Criteria	Weights	×	Rankings	=	Weighted Rank

220

1.00

Rank

=

FIGURE 8.18. Market attractiveness computation sheet. (Copyright © 1983 by Dr. William A. Cohen.)

SPU No. _____   Date _____

Market Attractiveness Criteria	Weights	X	Rankings	=	Weighted Rank

1.00   Rank   =

FIGURE 8.19.   Market attractiveness computation sheet. (Copyright © 1983 by Dr. William A. Cohen.)

223

SPU No. _____ Date _____

Market Attractiveness Criteria	Weights	X	Rankings	=	Weighted Rank

Rank   =

1.00

FIGURE 8.20.   Market attractiveness computation sheet. (Copyright © 1983 by Dr. William A. Cohen.)

225

SPU No. _____   Date _____

Market Attractiveness Criteria	Weights	×	Rankings	=	Weighted Rank

226

Rank =

1.00

FIGURE 8.21.   Market attractiveness computation sheet. (Copyright © 1983 by Dr. William A. Cohen.)

227

List the market attractiveness criteria that you have selected along with the importance weights and multiply these by the ranking assigned to develop the weighted rank for each market attractiveness criterion. Add the total weighted rank to come up with a weighted rank for each SPU you analyze.

STEP 6.   PLOTTING OF SPUs OR SBUs ON A MULTICELLED, MULTIFACTORED MATRIX

You must now decide on the structure of the matrix you will use for your analysis. It can contain as few as four cells or an infinite number of cells, depending on two alternate trade-offs.

1.   Ease of analysis
2.   Sensitivity in your particular industry

The fewer the number of cells, the easier it will be to manipulate and develop strategies. On the other hand, some competitive environments are such that strategies are far more sensitive. In this case a more precise classification of position for each SPU or SBU can be obtained by increasing the number of cells to 9, 16, 25, and so forth. You can use any number as long as both horizontal and vertical axes have the same number of divisions. The example furnished (Figure 8.22) used a four-cell multifactored matrix.

Use Figure 8.23 and the value-weighted ranks calculated for each SPU to plot each SPU or SBU on this matrix. Thus for the previous example, which was a weighted rank for business strength of 3.95 and a weighted rank for market attractiveness of 3.40, the SPU was plotted where the x is on Figure 8.22. Note in the figure that market attractiveness increases from right to left and business strength increases along the vertical axis from the bottom of the figure to the top.

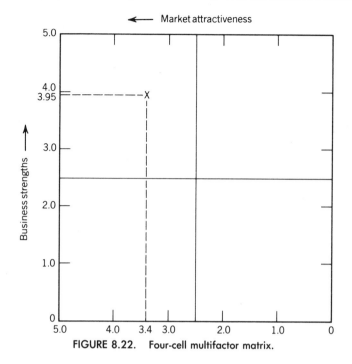

FIGURE 8.22.   Four-cell multifactor matrix.

STEP 7.   STRENGTHS, WEAKNESSES, OPPORTUNITIES, THREATS, AND SALES ANALYSIS

The strengths, weaknesses, opportunities, threats, and sales (SWOTS) analysis can be simply a listing of additional important factors that influence your strategic situation. They refer to the situation as it exists today and are simply a recapitulation of the environment you currently face due to competition and other environmental factors, as well as opportunities and threats you must consider for the future. Use the SWOTS analysis sheets in Figure 8.24 through 8.28 for this purpose.

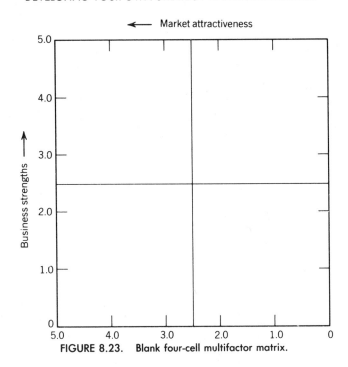

FIGURE 8.23.   Blank four-cell multifactor matrix.

STEP 8.   PLANNED STRATEGIC MOVES OF SPUs OR SBUs ON THE MULTICELLED, MULTIFACTOR ANALYSIS MATRIX

In order to plan strategic moves, it is helpful to know size of sales and share of the market. This can be accomplished as shown in Figure 8.29. Instead of merely placing an x at the position at which business strength and market attractiveness intersect on the matrix, a circle can be used, whose relative size indicates sales. Further, this circle can be shaded to show the relative share of the market that each SPU controls or dominates.

General strategic moves indicated by the position in the matrix have been discussed in Chapter 7. Those SPUs or SBUs moving to the far upper-left quadrant indicate the need for investment priority in order to maintain position, while those falling in the upper-right quadrant suggest a strategy of selective investment in order to repo-

SPU # _____ Date _____

Strengths _____

Weaknesses _____

Opportunities _____

Threats _____

Sales _____

FIGURE 8.24. SWOTS analysis sheet. (Copyright © 1983 by Dr. William A. Cohen.)

SPU # _____ Date _____

Strengths _____

Weaknesses _____

Opportunities _____

Threats _____

Sales _____

232

FIGURE 8.25. SWOTS analysis sheet. (Copyright © 1983 by Dr. William A. Cohen.)

SPU # _____ Date _____

Strengths _____

_____

_____

_____

Weaknesses _____

_____

_____

_____

Opportunities _____

_____

_____

Threats _____

_____

_____

Sales _____

_____

_____

233

FIGURE 8.26.   SWOTS analysis sheet. (Copyright © 1983 by Dr. William A. Cohen.)

SPU # _____ Date _____

Strengths _____

_____

_____

_____

_____

Weaknesses _____

_____

_____

_____

Opportunities _____

_____

_____

_____

Threats _____

_____

_____

_____

Sales _____

_____

_____

_____

234

FIGURE 8.27.   SWOTS analysis sheet. (Copyright © 1983 by Dr. William A. Cohen.)

SPU # _____   Date _____

Strengths _____

Weaknesses _____

Opportunities _____

Threats _____

Sales _____

FIGURE 8.28. SWOTS analysis sheet. (Copyright © 1983 by Dr. William A. Cohen.)

sition the SPU or to manage it for earnings. SPUs or SBUs falling in the lower-left quadrant are what are called "cash cows" in the Boston Consulting Group's matrix. Here we have, again, selected investment to move or to manage for earnings. Finally, SPUs or SBUs falling in the lower-right quadrant, known as "dogs" in the Boston Consulting Group's matrix, suggest a strategy of harvesting or divesting.

In all cases it will be noted that the strategic alternatives are to maintain a position, to change position, or to drop completely. Note

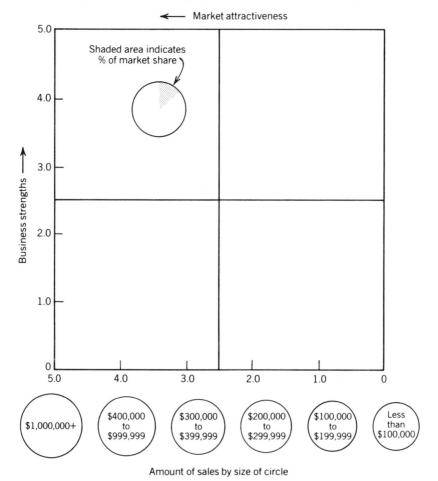

FIGURE 8.29.   Matrix showing sales and size or market for each SBU or SPU.

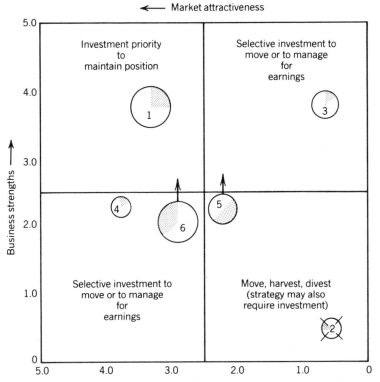

FIGURE 8.30. Planning strategic moves of SBUs on four-cell multifactor analysis matrix.
Strategic alternatives: (1) maintain position, (2) move, (3) drop.

that the suggestions made in the previous paragraph must not be
applied blindly, because every company situation is different. In
some cases, dogs must be maintained in order to support other
SPUs. In any case, each strategic alternative should be considered
for the SPU or SBU under analysis. Calculate each strategic move
and document it, as on Figure 8.30, using Figure 8.31.

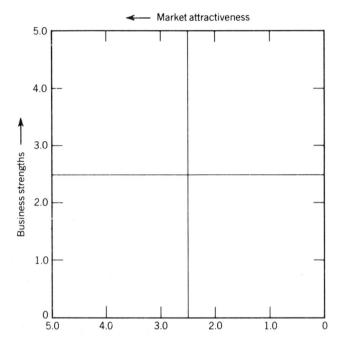

FIGURE 8.31.   Plan strategic moves using this form.

STEP 9. STRATEGY DEVELOPMENT FOR EACH SPU

Any decision for a strategic alternative must be based on what you are trying to achieve: your strategic objectives. A strategy simply consists of the strategic actions to achieve these objectives. To accomplish this, work with each SPU or SBU individually, but also consider the effect on other SPUs or SBUs that you have analyzed as a part of your corporate portfolio. Also consider the fit analysis, competitive profiles, SWOTS analysis sheets, and resources available to accomplish the action contemplated and the analyses you may have used earlier as a part of a life cycle analysis. Strategy development action forms, in Figures 8.32 through 8.36, can be utilized for this purpose. In addition to the listing of strategic actions, they permit documenting resources required to implement these strategies.

In this chapter we have discussed the methodology of developing your own structure for strategic analysis and the process that can be used to achieve the strategic objectives you have developed.

SPU # _____

List of
Strategic actions

Months after Strategy Initiation/$ Allocated

	1	2	3	4	5	6	7	8	9	10	11	Total $

240

Total $
Allocated

FIGURE 8.32. Strategy development actions. (Copyright © 1983 by Dr. William A. Cohen.)

SPU # _____ _____

Months after Strategy Initiation/$ Allocated

List of Strategic actions	1	2	3	4	5	6	7	8	9	10	11	Total $

Total $
Allocated

243

FIGURE 8.33. Strategy development actions. (Copyright © 1983 by Dr. William A. Cohen.)

SPU # _____

List of Strategic actions

Months after Strategy Initiation/$ Allocated

	1	2	3	4	5	6	7	8	9	10	11	Total $

Total $
Allocated

FIGURE 8.34. Strategy development actions. (Copyright © 1983 by Dr. William A. Cohen.)

SPU # _____

List of Strategic actions — Months after Strategy Initiation/$ Allocated

List of Strategic actions	1	2	3	4	5	6	7	8	9	10	11	Total $

Total $
Allocated

FIGURE 8.35.   Strategy development actions. (Copyright © 1983 by Dr. William A. Cohen.)

SPU # _____

List of Strategic actions	Months after Strategy Initiation / $ Allocated											
	1	2	3	4	5	6	7	8	9	10	11	Total $

Total $
Allocated

FIGURE 8.36. Strategy development actions. (Copyright © 1983 by Dr. William A. Cohen.)

9

DEVELOPING A MARKETING PLAN

A marketing plan is essential for efficient and effective marketing of any product or service or project in your corporation, and every corporate strategist should be able to develop a marketing plan that will ultimately lead to success. Seeking a project success without a marketing plan is much like trying to navigate a ship through rather perilous waters with the competition shooting at you and with neither a map nor a clear idea of your destination. Therefore, the time it takes to develop a marketing plan is well worthwhile and will allow you to visualize clearly both where you want your business to go and what you want it to accomplish. At the same time, a marketing plan maps out the important steps necessary to get from where you are now to where you want to be at the conclusion of the planning period. Further, you will have thought through how long it will take to get where you want to go and what resources in money and personnel will be needed and must be allocated from within your company. In fact, to obtain this allocation of resources, a competent and thoroughly thought-out plan is essential. Without a marketing plan, you will not even know whether you have reached your objectives or not!

WHAT A MARKETING PLAN WILL DO FOR YOU

A marketing plan accomplishes the following:

1. Acts as a road map
2. Assists you with management control
3. Helps you in briefing new employees and other personnel recently assigned to the project
4. Helps you in your briefings to higher management and in obtaining allocations of resources
5. Enables you to see problems and opportunities that may lie along the pathway to project success

A Marketing Plan as a Road Map

If you were traveling from point A to point B and you had never been to point B before, you would almost certainly consult a road map if you had any distance at all to travel. If you didn't use a map, you could drive around in circles for hours trying to locate point B, and if you couldn't ask anyone for directions, you probably would not get there. Many corporate executives attempt to do the same thing in the marketplace. The usual result is failure. However, with a marketing plan used as a road map, everything is made much simpler. Executives can follow a precise route from where they are presently to where they want to go. Of course, sometimes something occurs during the travel which is not foreseen on the map—perhaps the road is closed or blocked, requiring the driver to take a detour. Even when this happens, the map assists the driver by helping him or her choose the best alternative route to the destination. The marketing plan, or the corporate road map, works in the same way. A marketing plan, which documents and shows exactly how to reach carefully defined business goals, serves the same function as a road map for the driver of a car and will enable an executive to reach corporate goals much quicker and with much less effort and more efficient utilization of resources than would otherwise be possible.

Management Control

Previously I indicated that even the driver of a motor vehicle with a road map may find it necessary to take a detour because of unplanned circumstances. This may be because the road is being repaired or because the weather makes the most direct route to the destination impassable. In the same way, as you are in the process of starting up and implementing the project, you will encounter various problems that cannot be foreseen. In fact, it is almost certain that nothing will go exactly as planned. However, in thinking through your project and laying out a full and complete plan, you will be able to spot many potential problems ahead of time. Furthermore, inasmuch as you have a documented plan leading directly to the goals you have established, you will be able to see clearly the difference between what is happening during implementation and what you had planned to happen. This gives you control of the situation and lets you see more clearly the corrective action necessary to keep your project on the proper course to achieve the goals you have set.

A good analogy here is an aircraft flight. For almost every aircraft flight the pilot is required to file a flight plan that he or she has developed. This flight plan specifies all information, including course headings, distances, air and ground speed, fuel, time enroute, emergency airfields, and other factors, for the specific destination the pilot has decided on. Using the flight plan, the pilot can compare actual course and progress in the air with the course and progress planned before the flight. The pilot can analyze this information rapidly to make the best decisions in minimum time. So important is this aspect of management control in flight planning that for some military flights an air crew spends as much time planning the flight on the ground as it spends flying in the air.

The necessity for both a flight plan and a marketing plan can be illustrated by Clausewitz, the great German strategic thinker. According to Clausewitz, although detailed planning must always be done, plans never go exactly as foreseen after they were developed. The difference, according to Clausewitz, is called "battle friction." Battle friction is encountered by the pilot in the air and the driver on the ground in going from point A to point B. But the important point that Clausewitz makes and the reason that the flight planner, the driver, and the corporate strategist must develop good plans is that once the battle, the flight, or the trip or journey has started, little time may be available for decision making. A decision under high-density traffic in the air may sometimes need to be made within minutes or even seconds to avoid a catastrophe. In the same way, once the corporate strategist has developed the plan and its execution begins, the pressures on the firing line of the corporate battlefield deriving from competition and other environmental variables make it crucial to come up with good decisions fairly rapidly. A marketing plan therefore allows the corporate executive and strategist to think through most potential problem situations ahead of time, so that competent decisions can be made quickly when the plan is implemented under the pressures of the time and the competitive environment.

The marketing plan will give you management control over the particular project in your business just as a flight plan gives the pilot management control over the airplane and flight.

Briefing New Employees and Other Personnel

Many times you or the responsible executive will wish to inform other people regarding the project, its progress toward its goals and objectives, and the way you intend on reaching them. Such individuals may be new employees who have been recently hired and assigned to other projects having impact on or in support of your project, or they may be individuals assigned to the project itself. Having a ready reference does more than simply allow for easy briefing. It enables you to document and show the objectives that you have set and how and when the plan envisions reaching them. It will show them where they fit into the "big picture" and not only will assist in motivating them but also will help them to do a better job for you and for implementation of the plan. In addition, once you organize and document the material in a marketing plan, you have it for all time. You will not need to run around to assemble the information every time you wish to discuss or brief it to someone else.

Briefing Top Management and Obtaining Allocation of Resources

The corporate strategist must always keep in mind that resources for any organization are limited. This goes for a division of a large corporation, a small business, a Fortune 500 company, or even a country. No organization has unlimited resources. Therefore, projects must be allocated resources according to the overall benefit to the organization. When you develop a marketing plan, you will be able to demonstrate exactly how the money and resources will be used to reach the goals and objectives established. The marketing plan in itself is documented proof that every aspect of the situation has been thought through.

Many businesspersons prepare a business plan to help them obtain investment capital for their business. Sources of this capital frequently say that, without question, the success in obtaining capital is primarily due to the quality of the business plan prepared. What a business plan is to a small business, a marketing plan is to a larger one. In fact, a survey of top executives of several companies has indicated that the quality of the marketing plan can have the same effect in larger corporations. Success in obtaining resources and the green light to go ahead with the plan is frequently primarily dependent on the marketing plan prepared.

Seeing Problems and Opportunities

The requirement to sit down and think through a marketing plan will help you see all the problems and opportunities in any business situation. Thus it is not so important that a business situation has problems. This is always true. More important is the fact that these problems can be anticipated, and solutions worked out ahead of time. In this way you can develop your plans to take advantage of the opportunities, to solve the problems that arise, and to avoid potential threats or obstacles to achieving your objectives.

THE STRUCTURE OF THE MARKETING PLAN

A good marketing plan will contain a number of different sections. Marketing plans are situational, and additional sections can be added to those listed below or can be included as appendixes. But almost all marketing plans contain the following:

1. Executive summary
2. Table of contents
3. Background description of the business
4. Organization of company or project
5. Situation analysis
6. Problems and opportunities
7. Objectives
8. Marketing strategy
9. Marketing tactics
10. Budget
11. Financial plans
12. Strategy implementation time schedule

Let's look at each in turn.

Executive Summary

The executive summary is an overall view of your project and its potential, including what you want to do, how much money is needed for the project, how much money the project will make, and such financial measurements as return on investment. The executive summary is extremely important and should not be overlooked. As implied by its title, it is an overview or abstract of the entire plan. The target audience is the top-management executive. As this individual goes through your marketing plan, he or she will frequently skip over parts of the plan which are not of interest. Only certain sections will be read; most will only be scanned. However, the executive summary will always be read. Therefore, it is important that you present the essence of your plan as clearly and succinctly as possible. Using a few short paragraphs or a maximum of two or three pages, describe the thrust of what the plan purports to do, the objectives and goals to be achieved, and the overall strategy so that any reader can instantly understand what you are trying to do and how you propose to do it.

Table of Contents

You may wonder about the inclusion of the discussion of something as mundane as a table of contents under a subject as important as a marketing plan. However, you will find that the table of contents is extremely important. As indicated previously, most executives at the top levels of management will not read the entire plan in detail but, rather, will read only the executive summary and areas that are of particular interest to them. For example, a finance executive will surely read the finance section, while she or he may well skip over sections pertaining to product development, sales, or marketing. However, a marketing executive will certainly take particular note of what you have to say in these sections. It is not enough to ensure that every subject area pertaining to the project is covered in your plan. You have to make it as easy as possible for the executive who is looking for his or her topics of interest to find them quickly. If you do this through a table of contents, many executives will make a cursory attempt to locate the information they want. If they cannot do so, they will assume it is not there. This results in a negative impact on these executives from what might otherwise be a brilliant marketing plan. Therefore, do not neglect to include a thorough table of contents as part of your plan.

Background and Description of Project

In this paragraph you give the details of your project, including what it is, how it is going to be run, and, most importantly, why it will be successful. What differential advantage does it have over other similar projects either in your own company or the companies of your competition? This differential advantage is crucial. Without it there is no reason to invest in this project, since without a competitive advantage over your competition, you cannot win. Unless the project has advantages over other projects in your company, they should be funded, and not yours. The differential advantage should be clearly spelled out, be it a unique product, lower cost, better service, closer location to markets, unique expertise, and so forth.

Project Organization

In this section you should detail exactly how the project will be organized, including who will report to whom in collateral organizations. With certain projects you should even go to the extent of including a detailed résumé of the principal project leaders in an appendix. These should not be generalized to include all their experiences or background information that is not relevant but should zero in on experience, education, or background that specifically supports their assigned positions in the plan.

Situation Analysis

The situation analysis has several subsections, all of which are important and should be included and discussed as a part of your marketing plan. These should include demand for your product or service, target market, competition, unique advantages, legal retrictions if any, and any and all other situational variables that you feel are important to successful completion of the project.

Demand includes both the need for your project or service and the extent of this need. This need may be very basic if your product is a food staple. On the other hand, products or services may satisfy psychological needs that are not necessarily obvious. A brass case for business cards has been on the market for several years and is sometimes advertised in the *Wall Street Journal.* The brass case has sold for as much as $20 or more, although in recent years the price has been reduced as it has gone through its product life cycle. The initials of the purchaser are engraved free of charge. Now the question is, Is a brass case for business cards purchased primarily to protect business cards or to promote the status of the owner? Inasmuch as inexpensive plastic cases to protect business cards are frequently used as sales promotion giveaways and card cases are also frequently supplied free with the cards, chances are this product is purchased primarily to satisfy status needs. Whatever the needs satisfied by your product or service, they should be carefully considered and documented under this section. Indicate whether the product is a repeat product which will be purchased again and again by your customers, such as typewriter ribbon, or whether the product or service is a one-time need which is unlikely to be repeated, such as the purchase of a home. Also note whether the product or service is likely to continue to be sold over a long period of time or whether it is more likely to be a short-lived fad. Finally, what are the trends here? Is the demand for the product growing, leveling off, or declining?

The target market is the market that you intend to seek for your product or your service. Naturally, the larger the potential market, the better. But there are several different strategies you may follow. It might be advantageous to offer your product only to a certain segment of the total potential market. This is called a "strategy of market segmentation," and it offers a major advantage in certain situations, for you can concentrate all your resources on satisfying the specific needs of a certain segment of the market and can gear your promotional campaign to this segment. You will be stronger against this market segment than your competition will be if it spreads itself, its resources, and its promotional campaign across the total potential mass market. Because of this strategy and because of other possible strategies, which have been discussed in Chapter 2, you should note very carefully the market segments that make up the target market you intend to pursue, including the size of each market segment.

The importance of competition should never be underestimated. It is the only noncontrollable variable in your situation that will competitively react to your activities. Regardless of what product or service you offer, you will always have competition, even if the competition does not offer the exact same product or service. For example, home swimming pools may be indirect competition for health studios; however, they must be considered competition because the product or service fulfills the same need in your potential customers that your product or service fulfills. Perhaps you sell burglar alarms. Is your competition only other other firms selling burglar alarms? The answer is no. Other firms which fulfill the need for security must be considered competition. Such firms may offer iron bars to be installed over the windows, security guards, or watchdogs. All are indirect competition. Therefore, when you begin to analyze the competition for your product or service, be sure that you include all potential competitors, not just the direct competition of firms producing the identical product or service.

When you analyze your competition, you should also consider the fact that your competition will never remain static and will react to your marketing strategy if it proves effective. If you introduce a new product into the marketplace that competes with some other firm already there, you can be assured that if your product is successful, you will not be ignored. Your competition will then initiate an action in response in order to try to overcome your success. You might expect your competition to do something with the price of the product, to change the product, or to change its advertising. Therefore, you must, when you analyze your competition, think ahead as to what actions your competition might take, just as you would if you were in a chess game—only more thoroughly; not only because the stakes are higher but also because you will usually have more than one business opponent.

Your firm is not the same as any other firm. It is unique. So is your project. As pointed out earlier, you must sell this differential, or competitive, advantage. If you have no differential advantage, there is no reason to buy from you and you cannot win. In this section, emphasize the differential advantage from the point of view of your potential buyer. Some of these advantages have already been discussed, including specialized knowledge, lower prices, a totally unique product, additional services, and so forth. It is important to think through and write down these advantages in your marketing plan, so you will be certain not to overlook any and so you can exploit them to the maximum extent with the strategies you decide on. Remember, also, that although every single organization for any product or service has its advantages over competitors, if they are not identified in the marketing plan, they will probably not be exploited. And if they are not exploited, it is as if they did not exist.

Legal restrictions should always be noted in your marketing plan if they are applicable. They don't always exist, but if they do, you must consider them and note them down, not only so that they will not be overlooked but also so that others will know what they are and what their impact will be on other projects within the company. Every applicable restriction should be noted carefully, along with licenses and other legal obligations necessary for you to do business. You should do the research necessary to be absolutely certain that you meet your legal obligations. There is an additional advantage in documenting everything here: Sometimes someone going over your marketing plan will note something that you have forgotten and that in itself can save you a great deal of time, money, and allocation of important company resources, as well as your reputation as a corporate strategist.

Some years ago a company invested thousands of dollars in marketing to mix wine and fruit juice to produce a canned drink, not realizing that government tax made the cost of such a drink prohibitive unless the company itself manufactured the wine.

Other important situation variables should also be noted. These may be anything that you consider important to your business situation and to the success of your marketing plan. Let us say your product is seasonal and sold only in the summer or during Christmas holidays or during the football season. In such a case, there are special problems, including expensive overhead during the off-season, peak periods of sale, and so forth. Thus seasonality, in this case, would be an important situational variable.

Problems and Opportunities

Problems and opportunities are really different sides of the same coin. Many people make millions of dollars because when they note a problem, they also note within this problem a unique opportunity for success. Listerine is a mouthwash having a rather harsh taste. In the words of the advertisement of the competition, it tastes "mediciny." However, Listerine managed to make this problem an opportunity. The company realized that many consumers feel that if a mouthwash has a harsh taste, it must be harsher on germs, whereas if a mouthwash taste sweet or, in the words of a Listerine ad, tastes like "soda pop," it may not be killing germs nearly as well. Look for the opportunity in every problem that you find. And in this section specify both problems you have found and their solutions and any opportunities inherent in them that your company can take advantage of.

Objectives

Objectives should be stated explicitly. They may be defined by stating the volume to be sold in dollars or units, and they may also include financial measurements, such as return on investment or some other profitability measure. A complete list of such measurements is contained in Appendix II. If more than one objective is stated, be certain that the objectives do not conflict. For example, sometimes if a market share is specified as your objective, this can be reached only through a negative impact on short-term profitability. So if you specify more than one objective, check to be sure that one objective can be achieved only at the expense of another.

Marketing Strategy

Strategy for marketing your product should be stated as developed in previous chapters. What exactly are you going to do to reach your objectives? As noted in Chapter 2, strategy can frequently be described in terms of product, price, promotion, and distribution.

Marketing Tactics

Marketing tactics refer to how you will carry out the strategy, that is, the different tasks involved, including who will do them, what they will cost, and when they will be done. Marketing tactics can be described in the budget and the financial plans, as well as in the next section, Strategy Implementation Time Schedule.

Budget. As indicated previously, every single strategy costs resources. It is very important to indicate exactly what these resources are in hard dollar amounts. For this reason, it is essential to establish a budget for your total marketing plan for the project, including exactly how much each single task will cost and when these funds will be required. The "Strategy Implementation Time Schedule" section shows one way of describing the budget.

Financial plans. The financial-plan section should include not only the budget for the strategies and tactics required but also the projected income statement, as shown in Figure 9.1; a cash-flow projection as shown in Figure 9.2; and a balance sheet, as shown in Figure 9.3. Use of these forms is mandatory for many marketing plans. Financial plans give the entire financial picture for your project and will assist you not only with management control but also in allowing individuals who decide on the allocation of resources to your project or to other projects to have the complete financial picture.

Sometimes it is also useful to put a break-even analysis in this section. A "break-even analysis" is a method for evaluating relationships between sales revenues, fixed costs, and variable costs. The break-even point is the point at which the number of units sold

	Month 1	Month 2	Month 3	Month 4	Month 5	Month 6	Month 7	Month 8	Month 9	Month 10	Month 11	Month 12
Total net sales												
Cost of sales												
Gross Profit												
Controllable expenses Salaries												
Payroll taxes												
Security												
Advertising												
Automobile												
Dues and subscriptions												
Legal and accounting												
Office supplies												

Telephone	
Utilities	
Miscellaneous	
Total controllable expenses	
Fixed expenses Depreciation	
Insurance	
Rent	
Taxes and licenses	
Loan Payments	
Total fixed expenses	
Total Expenses	
Net Profit (Loss) **(before taxes)**	

FIGURE 9.1. Income statement for marketing plan.

265

	Start-up	Month 1	Month 2	Month 3	Month 4	Month 5	Month 6	Month 7	Month 8	Month 9	Month 10	Month 11	Month 12	Total
Cash (beginning of month)														
Cash on hand														
Cash in bank														
Cash in investments														
Total cash														
Income (during month)														
Cash sales														
Credit sales payments														
Investment income														
Loans														
Other cash income														
Total income														
Total Cash and Income														
Expenses (during month)														
Inventory or new material														

266

Wages							
Taxes							
Equipment expense							
Overhead							
Selling expense							
Transportation							
Loan repayment							
Other cash expenses							
Total Expenses							
Cash-Flow Excess (end of month)							
Cash-Flow Cumulative (monthly)							

FIGURE 9.2. Cash-flow projections for marketing plan.

_____ __ , 19__

	Year I	Year II
Current Assets		
Cash	$_____	$_____
Accounts receivable	_____	_____
Inventory	_____	_____
Fixed Assets		
Real estate	_____	_____
Fixtures and equipment	_____	_____
Vehicles	_____	_____
Other Assets		
License	_____	_____
Goodwill	_____	_____
Total Assets	$_____	$_____
Current Liabilities		
Notes payable (due within 1 year)	$_____	$_____
Accounts payable	_____	_____
Accrued expenses	_____	_____
Taxes owed	_____	_____
Long-Term Liabilities		
Notes payable (due after 1 year)	_____	_____
Other	_____	_____
Total Liabilities	$_____	$_____
Net Worth (Assets *minus* Liabilities)	$_____	$_____

Total Liabilities *plus* Net Worth should *equal* Assets

FIGURE 9.3.   Balance sheet for marketing plan.

covers all costs of developing, producing, and selling the product. Above this point you will make money, and below it you will lose money. It is one excellent measurement for determining the ultimate success of the project before you begin. In sum, the break-even analysis will tell you the following:

1. How many units you must sell in order to start making money
2. How much profit you will make at any given level of sales
3. How changing your price will affect profitability
4. How expense reductions at different levels of sales will affect profitability

To accomplish a break-even analysis, you must first separate the costs associated with your project into two categories: fixed costs and variable costs.

"Fixed costs" are those expenses associated with the project that you would have to pay whether you sold 1 unit or 10,000 units or, for that matter, whether you sold any units at all. For example, if you rented a building for use in your project and the owner of the building charged you a thousand dollars to rent the building for the period of the project, then this would be a fixed cost for that period. You would have to pay the thousand dollars whether or not you sold any products or many products. Research and development costs for a project or a product would also be considered a fixed cost, and this money would have to be paid whether or not you sold any product.

"Variable costs" vary directly with the number of units that you sell. If it costs you $1.80 to manufacture a unit, then that $1.80 is considered a variable cost. If postage for mailing your product to a customer is $1, then $1 is a variable cost. If you sell 10 units, then your postage cost is 10 times $1, or $10. If you sell 100 units, your total variable cost for postage would be 100 times $1, or $100.

It is difficult to decide whether to consider some costs fixed or to consider them variable, and very frequently there is no single right answer. You must make this decision either by yourself or with the help of corporate financial experts. As a general guide, if there is a direct relationship between cost and number of units sold, consider the cost variable. If you cannot find such a relationship, consider the cost fixed.

The total cost of your project will always equal the sum of the fixed costs plus the variable costs. Consider the following example for an item which you are going to sell for $10. How much profit would you make if you sold 1000 units?

Fixed Costs
——————

Utility expense at $100 per month for 36 months	= $3600
Telephone at $200 per year for 3 years	= 600
Product development cost	= 1000
Rental expense	= 2500
Total fixed costs =	$7700

Variable Costs
——————

Cost of product	= $1.00/unit
Cost of postage and packaging	= 0.50/unit
Cost of advertising	= 3.00/unit
Total variable costs =	$4.50/unit

To calculate break even, we start with an equation for profit. Total profit *equals* the number of units sold *multiplied* by the price at which we are selling them *less* the number of units sold *multiplied* by the total variable cost and that answer *minus* the total fixed cost. If P equals profit, p equals price, U equals the number of units sold, V equals variable costs, and F equals fixed costs, then our equation becomes:

$$P = (U \times p) - (U \times V) - F$$

Or we can simplify this to:

$$P = U(p - V) - F$$

Substituting the values given in our example, we have:

$$P = 1000(\$10.00 - \$4.50) - \$7700 =$$
$$\$5500 - \$7700 = -\$2200$$

What is the significance of a minus number? This means that instead of making a profit, we have lost money—$2200 to be exact. Now we want to know how many units we must sell in order to make money, or at what point we will stop losing money. This point at which we will either make money or lose money is called "break even." Beginning at this point we will show a profit. In order to calculate this, we use the break-even equation. And the break-even equation, using the same variables from above, is $P = U(p - V) - F$. At break even, profit by definition $= 0$. Thus, if we transpose terms and let $P = 0$, break even $= F/p - V$.

Since we know that F equals $7700, p equals $10, and V equals $4.50, break even equals:

$$\frac{\$7700}{\$10 - \$4.50} = 1400 \text{ units}$$

This means if we don't change price or reduce expenses in any way, we need to sell 1400 units of this product before we can start making any money. However, there is an easier way to calculate this. We can use the break-even chart shown in Figure 9.4. A break-even chart is a major advantage over the break-even and profit equation. It shows us graphically the relationship between profits and sales volume.

There are some limitations to break-even analysis:

1. Break-even analysis shows profit at various levels of sales but does not show profitability. Since there are always alternative uses

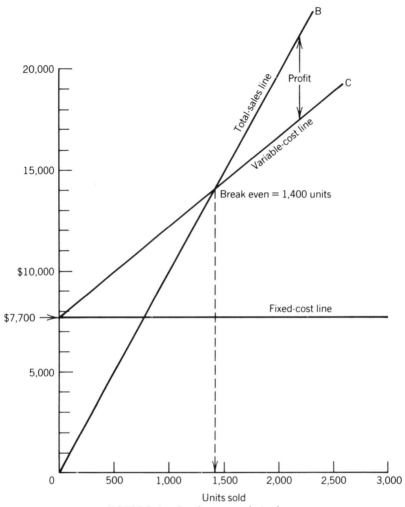

FIGURE 9.4.   Break-even analysis chart.

for your firm's financial resources, it is impossible to compare products for profitability solely on the basis of break even, yet profitability should be one of the major points of consideration. For a profitability comparison, you must use one of the financial ratio analyses.

2.   Break-even analyses do not allow you to examine cash flow. It is generally accepted that one appropriate way to compare invest-

ment or capital budgeting alternatives is to consider the value of cash flows over a period of time and to discount the cost of capital by an appropriate percentage. This cannot be done with break-even analyses either.

Strategy Implementation Time Schedule

The final section in your marketing plan should be a time schedule showing an overview of your strategy implementation and the time when each task will be completed. This is shown in Figure 9.5. The strategy implementation time schedule is extremely important, letting you know when you are supposed to do what, and it will greatly assist you in management control, as well as showing any reader of your marketing plan that you really know what you are doing.

Some general comments about writing a marketing plan follow:

1. *Establish Your Credibility.*   Remember that your firm and this project have unique advantages; if not, you should not proceed with the project. State these advantages clearly.

2. *Document Supporting Facts about New Concepts or Ideas.*   Remember that not everyone reading your marketing plan has your knowledge or experience. Therefore, new concepts or ideas should be carefully documented and described from established sources, such as those listed in Appendix I.

3. *Be Optimistic, But Be Truthful.*   There are always disadvantages or problems, but if you can anticipate them and indicate how you will overcome them, it will not only help in implementing the marketing plan at the appropriate time but will assist in convincing readers that your marketing plan can be implemented.

4. *Emphasize Your Uniqueness.*   You have something that is different in some way than what everyone else has. Play up this difference.

5. *Make Sure Your Marketing Plan Is Workable.*   It is essential to have a marketing plan, but it is useless if it is not workable. After you've gone through and completed the plan, be sure that the plan

Weeks after Project Initiation

Task	1	2	3	4	5	6	7	8	9	10	11	Total
Development and placement ads	$5,000	$5,000	$5,000	$5,000	$5,000	$5,000	$10,000	$10,000	$10,000	$10,000	$10,000	$80,000
Product manufacture, model I		$5,000	$7,500	$10,000	$10,000	$10,000						$42,500
Product manufacture, model II					$5,000	$5,000	$7,500	$10,000	$10,000	$10,000	$10,000	$57,500
Schedule promotional model II							$3,000	$3,000	$3,000	$3,000		$12,000
Running new contribution channel								$5,000	$5,000			$10,000
Phase-out promotion model I										$2,000	$2,000	$4,000
Monthly totals	$5,000	$10,000	$12,500	$15,000	$20,000	$20,000	$20,500	$28,000	$28,000	$25,000	$22,000	$206,000

Total for project strategy

FIGURE 9.5. Strategy implementation time schedule.

274

fits together and that each part is reasonable and can work. Be especially critical of the cash-flow and financial aspects, as well as the anticipated sales. One of the biggest problems of marketing plans is sales realism; that is, the strategist sometimes anticipates much higher sales than can realistically be expected. Analyze your plan by asking yourself what would happen if sales were 20, 30, 40, or even 50% less than you have forecast. Analyze your costs to make sure they are also realistic. Just as sales are frequently inflated during marketing planning, costs are sometimes deflated.

6. *Update Your Plan.* No marketing plan is "good forever." Further, the planning is never perfect, as you cannot foresee all circumstances that you will encounter at the start. Therefore, as the plan is implemented, it will have to be revised to be kept up to date. This is not to say that your plan has to be changed daily; however, you should be on top of conditions that are changing, and the plan should be adjusted accordingly as appropriate. To do this, you should first be alert to the changes that come about in your industry, market, customers, competition, technology, and so forth. Second, check your plan against these changes to make sure that the plan is still workable and to determine what revisions are necessary in your plan.

MARKETING PLAN DEVELOPMENT FORM

To assist you in developing your marketing plan, a special marketing plan development form has been put together in Figure 9.6. It begins by listing required information for your plan, including characteristics of customer identification; location; segments of market; growth trends; consumer attitudes and buying habits; size of market in dollars and numbers; needs of market; industry pricing; technological trends; threats and opportunities; distribution factors and structure; key success factors; identification of competing companies; size, trend, and share of market of each competitor; customers' perception of competition; comparison of competitive features; pricing in features; comparison of promotional distribution of competitor

Product _____

Required Information for Plan	How/Where Information to Be Obtained	Individual Responsible
Market Characteristics		
Customer identification and location		
Segments of market		
Growth trends		
Consumer attitudes and buying habits		
Size of market in dollars and numbers		
Needs of market		
Industry pricing		
Technological trends, threats, and opportunities		

Distribution factors and structure

Key success factors

Competition
Identification of competing companies

Size, trend, and share of market of each
competitor

Customers' perception of competition

Comparison of competitive products, pricing,
and features

FIGURE 9.6.   Marketing plan development form. (Copyright © 1983 by Dr. William A. Cohen.)

Product ___

Required Information for Plan	How/Where Information to Be Obtained	Individual Responsible
Comparison of competitive products, promotion and distribution		
Competitor strengths and weaknesses		
Competitors' strategies		
Manufacturing and Engineering Factors Processes and materials		
Environmental Climate Business, economic conditions		
Social factors		
Political factors		

FIGURE 9.6 (continued)

Governmental factors

Legal constraints

Internal Resources
Marketing

Engineering

Financial resources

FIGURE 9.6 (continued)

products; competitor strengths and weaknesses; competitor strategies; processes and materials; business and economic conditions; social factors; political factors; government factors; legal constraints; and internal resources for marketing, engineering, and financial resources. The form also has additional spaces for other information required to put your marketing plan together. Spaces are also allowed for listing how and where information is to be obtained and the name of an individual responsible for obtaining this information.

	Description of Strategy	Cost ($)
Product		
Price		
Distribution		
Promotion		

FIGURE 9.7. Strategy development form (functional approach). (Copyright © 1983 by Dr. William A. Cohen.)

To assist you in strategy development, the strategy development form using the functional approach (Figure 9.7) includes price promotion and distribution promotion aspects and asks you to write a description of the strategy and then to indicate an overall cost allocation for implementing it.

The marketing plan is one of the most powerful tools of the corporate strategist for planning. Literally billions of dollars have been made or lost through its use, misuse, or nonuse. Correctly put together, the marketing plan will guide your project from start-up to successful realization of your goals and objectives. It is totally worthy of your best efforts in putting it together.

SOURCES OF SECONDARY RESEARCH

Following are more than 100 sources based on bibliographies put together by Lloyd M. DeBoer, dean of the School of Business Administration at George Mason University, Fairfax, Virginia, and the Office of Management and Training of the SBA and published by the Small Business Administration as a part of two booklets, *Marketing Research Procedure* (SBB 9) and *National Directories for Use in Marketing* (SBB 13).

Preliminary Sources

This section lists a wider range of reference sources to help locate pertinent materials for specific data. It is a good idea to consult one or more of them before investing substantial time or effort in any kind of market analysis.

Basic Library Reference Sources (SBB-18). SBA. Free. Contains a section on marketing information and guides to research.

Bureau of the Census Catalog. Bureau of the Census, U.S. Department of Commerce. Quarterly, cumulative to annual, with monthly supplements. GPO. Part I lists all publications issued by the Bureau of the Census. Part II lists available data files, special tabulations, and other unpublished materials. Both indexed.

Bureau of the Census Guide to Programs and Publications, Subjects and Areas. Bureau of the Census, Department of Commerce, 1974. GPO. Stock Number 0324-00196. On charts, describes the statistical information available in Census Bureau publications since 1968; defines geographic areas covered, outlines programs and activities. Indexed.

Note: Census data are issued initially in separate, paperbound reports. Publication order forms are issued for reports as they become available and may be obtained from the Subscriber Service Section (Publications), Bureau of Census, Washington, D.C. 20233, or any U.S. Department of Commerce field office.

Director of Federal Statistics for Local Areas: A Guide to Sources. Bureau of Census, U.S. Department of Commerce. Gives detailed table-by-table descriptions of subjects for almost all types of areas smaller than states. Covers the whole range of local data—social, economic, technical—published by the U.S. government. Bibliography with names and addresses of source agencies. Appendixes. Indexed.

Industrial Market Information Guide. Regular monthly column appearing in every issue. Crain Communications, Inc., 740 North Rush St., Chicago, Ill. 60611. Lists, in 32 market categories, over 600 items of market data annually. Most items available from business publications, government agencies, and other publishers; some material for a limited period.

Measuring Markets: A Guide to the Use of Federal and State Statistical Data. Bureau of Domestic and International Business Administration, Department of Commerce. Revised periodically. Stock No. 003-025-00031. This is an excellent reference which not only describes federal and state government publications useful for measuring markets but also demonstrates the use of federal statistics in market measurement.

Statistical Abstract of the United States. Bureau of Census, Department of Commerce. Annual. GPO. This is the most comprehensive and authoritative data book on the social, economic, and governmental characteristics of the United States. Special features include sections on recent national trends and an appendix on statistical methodology and reliability. Indexed. Appendix IV, *Guide to Sources of Statistics,* is arranged alphabetically by major subjects listing government and private sources.

Statistics Sources: A Subject Guide to Data on Industrial, Business, Social, Educational, Financial, and Other Topics for the United States and Selected Foreign Countries. Gale Research Co., Book Tower, Detroit, Mich. 48226. Provides thousands of sources of statistics on about 12,000 subjects with 22,000 citations.

CONSUMER MARKET INFORMATION

This section lists references which provide information on products and services bought by individuals or households for home or personal use.

General Data

County and City Data Book. Bureau of Census, Department of Commerce. GPO. A total of 195 statistical items tabulated for the U.S., its regions, and each county and state; 190 items for each city; and 161 items for 277 Standard Metropolitan Statistical Areas. Information is derived from latest available censuses of population, housing, governments, mineral industries, agriculture, manufactures, retail and wholesale trade, and selected services. Also includes data on health, vital statistics, public assistance programs, bank deposits, vote cast for President, and crime.

Statistics for States and Metropolitan Areas. (A preprint from *County and City Data Book*). Bureau of Census, Department of Commerce. GPO. Presents data for 195 statistical items for the U.S., its regions, and each state, and 161 items for 277 Standard Metropolitan Statistical Areas.

Statistical Abstract of the United States. Bureau of Census, Department of Commerce. GPO. Includes many consumer market statistics such as income, employment, communications, retail and wholesale trade and services, housing, population characteristics by state and for large cities and standard metropolitan areas. Late editions carry new tables on such topics as gambling, daytime care for children, households with TV sets, federal R&D obligations for energy development, franchised businesses, among others.

A Guide to Consumer Markets. Annual. The Conference Board, Inc., Information Services, 845 Third Ave., New York, N.Y. 10022. Presents a detailed statistical profile of U.S. consumers and the consumer market. Contains data on population growth and mobility, employment, income, consumer spending patterns, production and sales, and prices.

E&P Market Guide. Published annually in fall. Editor & Publisher Company, 575 Lexington Ave., New York, N.Y. 10022. Tabulates current estimates of population, households, retail sales and for nine major sales classifications, income for states, counties, metropolitan areas, and 1500 daily newspaper markets. Also lists specific information on major manufacturing, retailing, and business firms, transportation and utilities, local newspapers, climate, and employment, for newspaper markets. Includes state maps.

S&MM's Survey of Buying Power. Revised annually in July. *Sales and Marketing Management,* 633 Third Ave., New York, N.Y. 10017. Information includes current estimates of population and households by income groups, total effective buying income, retail sales for major retail lines, and market quality indexes; given for all regions, states, counties, and metropolitan areas.

S&MM's Survey of Buying Power—Part II. Revised annually in October. *Sales and Marketing Management,* 633 Third Ave., New York, N.Y. 10017. Gives population, income, retail sales, and buying income figures for television and newspaper markets in the United States and Canada. The data for television markets outline the areas of dominant influence, while the newspaper markets information identifies both dominant and effective coverage areas.

Specific Data

Each of the reference sources listed above under "General Data" includes at least some *specific* market data. In addition, there are sources of data useful only for the appraisal and management of specific markets. Examples of some of these important market types are listed below.

Automotive Marketing Guide. *Motor Age,* Chilton Way, Radnor, Pa. 19089. Number and relative importance (shown as percentage of U.S. total) of automotive wholesalers, franchised car dealers, repair shops, and service stations for counties, marketing areas, and states.

The New Yorker Guide to Selective Marketing. Market Research Department, 25 West 43d St., New York, N.Y. 10036. Identifies and ranks markets for quality and premium-price products and services available in the United States. Includes maps and statistics for forty top-tier areas of best potential to sell premium-priced products. Gives statistics on high-income families, high-priced car registrations, expensive homes, and various retail sales indices for top forty and next twenty U.S. markets.

Survey of Industrial Purchasing Power. Revised annually in April. *Sales and Marketing Management,* 633 Third Ave., New York, N.Y. 10017. A comprehensive look at the nation's key industrial markets. Included are a sales road map for the industrial marketer, an evaluation of the top fifty manufacturing counties, and statistics showing manufacturing activity by state, county, and four-digit SIC code.

Sales and Marketing Management Survey of Selling Costs. Revised annually in February. *Sales and Marketing Management,* 633 Third Ave., New York, N.Y. 10017. Contains data on costs of sales meetings and sales training. Metro sales costs for major U.S. markets, compensation, sales-support activities, and transportation. There is also some cost information in the international area.

BUSINESS MARKET INFORMATION

This section lists references for all types of markets other than the consumer (individuals or household for personal use) markets. Some of the sources described in the "Consumer Market" sections of this *SBB* also provide data for *business* markets, such as commercial, farm, industrial, institutional, and federal and state governments.

General Data

County Business Patterns. Department of Commerce. Annual. GPO. Separate book for each state, District of Columbia, and a U.S. summary. Reports provide figures on first-quarter employment, first-quarter payroll, annual payroll, number of establishments and number of establishments by employment size class for some 700 different U.S. business and industries by each county in the United States.

County and City Data Book. Bureau of Census, Department of Commerce. GPO. Presents data on housing, population, income, local government financing, elections, agriculture, crime, for states, cities, counties, and 277 Standard Metropolitan Statistical Areas.

Statistics for State and Metropolitan Areas. (A reprint from *County and City Data Book,* 1977). Bureau of Census, Department of Commerce. GPO. Presents data for 195 statistical items for the U.S., its regions, and each state, and 161 items for 277 Standard Metropolitan Statistical Areas.

Statistical Abstract of the United States. Bureau of Census, Department of Commerce. Annual. GPO. Includes national and state data relating to business, industry, and institutional markets, as well as agriculture.

Specific Data

Automotive Marketing Guide. *Motor Age,* Chilton Way, Radnor, Pa. 19089. Number and relative importance (shown as a percentage of U.S. total) of automotive wholesalers, franchised car dealers, repair shops, and service stations for counties, marketing areas, and states.

Merchandising: Statistical Issue and Marketing Report. Annual. Billboard Publications, 1 Astor Plaza, New York, N.Y. 10036. Gives retail sales of major appliance types and number of appliance dealers by state and public utility service areas; also gives number of residential utility customers, and housing starts by state.

MAPS

This section lists (1) maps that serve merely as a base for market analysis by providing geographic information and (2) maps that themselves display marketing statistics. For ready reference, the maps are listed by publisher's name. Prices are shown when available.

American Map Company, Inc., 1926 Broadway, New York, N.Y. 10023. *Catalog of Cleartype and Colorprint Maps.* Free. The catalog describes the types of maps (including plastic-surfaced maps for crayon presentations and maps on steel to accommodate magnetic markers). Company publishes U.S. base maps for depicting sales, markets, territories, distribution, statistics, and traffic data; detailed state, county, zip codes and township maps; and several types of atlases for use in analyzing national markets.

Rand McNally & Company,   P.O. Box 7600, Chicago, Ill, 60680. Publishes a variety of maps and atlases. This publisher leases a *Commercial Atlas and Marketing Guide* which contains maps showing counties and cities, a road atlas, and statistical data on manufacturing, retail sales, and population. Standard metropolitan areas are shown. Includes a city index with information on transportation facilities, banks, and posted volume and an international section.

Sales Builders,   633 Third Ave., New York, N.Y. 10017. Publishes two sets of nine regional maps (11″ × 17″) which cover the 50 states and depict either retail sales or industrial sales information. Also publishes two 50-state wall maps (24½″ × 38″) which have county outlines and depict either the consumer or manufacturing data. For list of prices and order blank, write Sales Builders Division, *Sales and Marketing Management.*

U.S. Geological Survey,   Department of the Interior, Washington, D.C. 20402. Publishes a variety of maps that show state and city areas. The following maps and a list (free) of other available maps may be ordered from the Distribution Section, U.S. Geological Survey, 1200 South Eads St., Arlington, Va. 22202.

Map 2-A (54″ × 80″). Shows state and county boundaries and names. State capitals, and county seats in black, water features in blue.

Map 2-B (42″ × 65″). Same as above, without land-tint background.

Map 3-A (42″ × 65″). Shows state boundaries and names. State capitals and principal cities in black, water features in blue.

Map 5-A (24½″ × 38″). Shows state and county boundaries and names, water features in black.

Map 7-A (20″ × 30″). Shows state boundaries and principal cities in black, water features in blue.

Map 11-A (13½″ × 20″). Shows state boundaries and principal cities in black, water features in blue.

Map 16-A (9½″ × 13″). Shows state boundaries and principal cities in black, water features in blue.

Contour Map—Map 7-B (20″ × 30″). State boundaries and principal cities in black, water features in blue, contours in brown.

Outline Map—Map 5-D (24½″ × 38″). State boundaries and names only.

Physical Divisions Map—Map 7-C (28″ × 32″). Physical divisions are outlined in red on the base map. Subdivisions and characteristics of each division are listed on the margin.

LOCATING SOURCES OF NATIONAL LISTS

Other directories, new publications or revisions, may be located in one of the six following sources. Some of the selected directories, as well as the locating guides, are available for reference in public and university libraries.

1. *Mailing Lists.* A major use of directories is in the compilation of mailing lists. Attention, therefore, is directed to another SBA Bibliography (SBB 29), "National Mailing-List Houses," which includes a selected compilation of both general line and limited line mailing-list houses that are national in scope. Also, consult Klein's *Director of Mailing List Houses*—see listings under "Mailing-List Houses" for further description of these two publications.

2. *Trade Associations and National Organizations.* For those trades or industries where directories are not available, membership lists of trade associations, both national and local, or often useful. For names and addresses of trade associations, consult the following directory source—available at most business reference libraries: *Encyclopedia of Associations, Vol I., National Organizations of the United States,* Gale Research Co., Book Tower, Detroit, Mich. 48226. Published

annually. Lists trade, business, professional, labor, scientific, educational, fraternal, and social organizations of the United States, includes historical data.

3. *Business Periodicals.* Many business publications, particularly industrial magazines, develop comprehensive specialized directories of manufacturers in their respective fields. Names and addresses of business periodicals are listed (indexed by name of magazine and by business fields covered) in the *Business Publication Rates and Data* published monthly by Standard Rate and Data Service, 5201 Old Orchard Road, Skokie, Ill. 60077. Also, for listings of periodicals by subject index, consult the *Standard Periodical Directory*, and for a listing by geographical areas, refer to *Ayer Directory of Publications.* Most libraries have one or more of these directories for reference.

4. *American Directories.* Another source is *Guide to American Directories.* Published by B. Klein Publications, P.O. Box 8503, Coral Springs, Fla. 33065.

5. *F & S Index of Corporations and Industries.* It is available in most libraries. Indexes over 750 financial, trade, and business publications by corporate name and by SIC code. Published by Predicasts, Inc., 200 University Circle Research Center, 11001 Cedar Ave., Cleveland, Ohio 44106.

6. *The Public Affairs Information Service.* Available in many libraries, is published weekly, compiled five times a year, and put into an annual edition. This is a selective subject list of the latest books, government publications, reports, and periodical articles, relating to economic conditions, public conditions, public administration and international relations. Published by Public Affairs Information Service, Inc., 11 West 40th St., New York, N.Y. 10018.

DIRECTORIES

The selected national directories are listed under categories of specific business or general marketing areas in an alphabetical subject index.

When the type of directory is not easily found under the alphabetical listing of a general marketing category, such as "jewelry," look for a specific type of industry or outlet, for example, "department stores."

Apparel

Fur Source Directory, Classified. Annually in June. Alphabetical directory of fur manufacturers in New York city area classified by type of fur; names, addresses, and telephone numbers for each. Also, lists pelt dealers, fur cleaners, fur designers, resident buyers and brokers, and those engaged in fur repairing, processing, and remodeling. Fur Vogue Publishing Co., 127 West 30th St., New York, N.Y. 10001.

Hat Life Year Book (Men's). Annual. Includes classified list of manufacturers and wholesalers of men's headwear. Hat Life Year Book, 551 Summit Ave., Jersey City, N.J. 07306.

Knit Goods Trade, Davison's. Annual. Lists manufacturers of knitted products, manufacturers' agents, New York salesrooms, knit goods wholesalers, chain store organizations, department stores with names of buyers, discount chains, brokers and dealers, and rack jobbers. Davison Publishing Co., P.O. Drawer 477, Ridgewood, N.J. 07451.

Men's & Boys' Wear Buyers, Nation-Wide Directory of. (Exclusive of New York Metropolitan Area.) Annually in November. More than 20,000 buyers and merchandise managers for 5000 top department, family clothing, and men's and boys' wear specialty stores. Telephone number, buying office, and postal zip code given for each firm. Also available in individual state editions. The Salesman's Guide, Inc., 1140 Broadway, New York, N.Y. 10001. Also publishes *Metropolitan New York Directory of Men's and Boys' Wear Buyers.* Semiannually in May and November. (Lists same information for the metropolitan New York area as the nationwide directory.)

Teens' & Boys' Outfitter Directory. Semiannually in April and October. (Pocket size.) Lists manufacturers of all types of apparel for boys and students by category, including their New York City addresses and phone numbers; also lists resident buying firms for out-of-town stores, and all trade associations related to boys' wear. The Boys' Outfitter Co., Inc., 71 West 35th St., New York, N.Y. 10001.

Women's & Children's Wear & Accessories Buyers. National Directory of. (Exclusive of New York metropolitan area.) Annually in February. Lists more than 25,000 buyers and divisional merchandise managers for about 5,000 leading department, family clothing and specialty stores. Telephone number and mail zip code given for each store. Also available in individual state editions. The Salesman's Guide, Inc., 1140 Broadway, New York, N.Y. 10001.

Appliances, Household

National Buyer's Guide.   Annual. Lists manufacturers and distributors in home electronics, appliances, kitchens. Gives the products they handle, the territories they cover, and complete addresses for each distributor. Dealerscope, 115 Second Avenue, Waltham, Ma. 02154.

Arts and Antiques

American Art and Antique Dealers, Mastai's Classified, Directory of. Lists 20,000 art museums, with names of directories and curators; art and antique dealers; art galleries; coin, armor, tapestry and china dealers in the United States and Canada. Mastai Publishing Co., 21 E 57th St., New York, N.Y. 10022.

Automatic Merchandising (Vending)

NAMA Directory of Members.   Annually in July. Organized by state and by city, lists vending service company who are NAMA members. Gives mailing address, telephone number, and products vended. Also includes machine manufacturers and suppliers. National Automatic Merchandising Association, 7 South Dearborn St., Chicago, Ill. 60603.

Automotive

Automotive Affiliated Representatives, Membership Roster. Annual. Free to firms seeking representation. Alpha-geographical listing of about 400 member firms including name, address, telephone number, territories covered, and lines carried. Automotive Affiliated Representatives, 625 South Michigan Ave., Chicago, Ill. 60611.

Automotive Directory of Manufacturers and Their Sales Representatives, National. Annual. Alphabetical arrangement of manufacturers serving automotive replacement market. Where available, includes names and addresses of each manufacturers' representative showing territory covered. W. R. C. Smith Publishing Co., 1760 Peachtree Rd. N.W., Atlanta, Ga. 30357.

Automotive Warehouse Distributors Association Membership Directory. Annually. Includes listing of manufacturers, warehouse distributors, their products, personnel and territories. Automotive Warehouse Distributors Association, 1719 W. 91st Place, Kansas City, Mo. 64114.

Auto Trim Resource Directory. Nov. edition; annual issue of *Auto Trim News.* Alphabetical listing of name, address, and telephone number of auto trim resources and wholesalers who service auto trim shops. Has directory of product sources—listed by product supplied—with name and address of firm. Auto Trim News, 1623 Grand Ave., Baldwin, N.Y. 11510.

Credit and Sales Reference Directory. Three times annually. Available only to supplier-manufacturers on annual fee basis. Contains listings of 17,000 automotive distributors in the United States and Canada. Data include name and address of companies, and other pertinent information. Motor and Equipment Manufacturers Assn., MEMA Service Corp., 222 Cedar Lane, Teaneck, N.J. 07666.

Home Center, Hardware, Auto Supply Chains. Annually. Lists headquarter addresses, telephone numbers, number and types of stores and locations, annual sales volume, names of executives and buyers. Chain Store Guide Publications, 425 Park Ave., New York, N.Y. 10022.

Jobber Topics Automotive Aftermarket Directory. Annual. Lists 7000 automotive warehouse distributors automotive rebuilders, manufacturers agents, automotive jobbers, associations, and manufacturers. The Irving-Cloud Publishing Co., 7300 N. Cicero Ave., Lincolnwood, Chicago, Ill. 60646.

Aviation

World Aviation Directory. Published twice a year. Spring and fall. Gives administrative and operating personnel of airlines, aircraft, and engine manufacturers and component manufacturers and distributors, organizations, and schools. Indexed by companies, activities, products, and individuals. Ziff-Davis Aviation Division, 1156 15th St., N.W., Washington, D.C. 20005.

Bookstores

Book Trade Directory, American. Annual. Updated bimonthly. Lists retail and wholesale booksellers in the United States and Canada. Entries alphabetized by state (or province), and then by city and business name. Each listing gives address, telephone numbers, key personnel, types of books sold, subject specialties carried, sidelines and services offered and general characteristics. For wholesale entries give types of accounts, import-export information and territory limitations. Edited by the Jaques Cattell Press. R. R. Bowker Company, 1180 Avenue of the Americas, New York, N.Y. 10036.

Multiple Book Store Owners, Directory of. Annually. Lists over 1000 chains of book stores by state, city, and alphabetically by store within each city. Oldden Mercantile Corp., 560 Northern Blvd., Great Neck, N.Y. 11021.

Building Supplies

Building Supply News Buyers Guide. Annually. Classified directory of manufacturers of lumber, building materials, equipment, and supplies. Cahners Publishing Co., 5 S. Wabash Ave., Chicago, Ill. 60603.

Business Firms

Dun & Bradstreet Middle Market Directory. Annually in October. Lists about 31,000 businesses with net worth between $500,000 and $1,000,000. Arranged in three sections; alphabetically, geographically, and product classification. Gives business name, state of incorporation, address, telephone number, SIC numbers, function, sales volume, number of employees, and name of officers and directors. Marketing Services Division, Dun & Bradstreet, Inc., 99 Church St., New York, N.Y. 10007.

Dun & Bradstreet Million Dollar Directory. Annually in January. Lists about 46,000 businesses with a net worth of $1 million or more. Arranged in four sections; alphabetically, geographically, line of business, and officers and directors with the same information as detailed in the preceding entry. Marketing Services Division, Dun & Bradstreet, Inc., 99 Church St., New York, N.Y. 10007.

Buying Offices

Buying Offices and Accounts, Directory of. Annually in March. Approximately 230 New York, Chicago, Los Angeles, Dallas, and Miami Resident Buying Offices, Corporate Offices and Merchandise Brokers together with 11,000 accounts listed under its own Buying Office complete with local address and alphabetically by address and buying office. The Salesman's Guide, Inc., 1140 Broadway, New York, N.Y. 10001.

China and Glassware

American Glass Review. Glass factory directory issue. Annually. Issued as part of subscription (13th issue) to *American Glass Review.* Lists companies manufacturing flat glass, tableware glass and fiber glass, giving corporate and plant addresses, executives, type of equipment used. Ebel-Doctorow Publications, Inc., 1115 Clifton Ave., Clifton, N.J. 07013.

China Glass & Tableware Red Book Directory Issue. Annually. Issued as part of subscription (13th issue) to *China Glass & Tableware.* Lists about 1000 manufacturers, importers, and national distributors of china, glass, and other table appointments, giving corporate addresses and executives. Ebel-Doctorow Publications, Inc., 1115 Clifton Ave., Clifton, N.J. 07013.

City Directories Catalog

Municipal Year Book. Annual. Contains a review of municipal events of the years, analyses of city operations, and a directory of city officials in all the states. International City Management Association, 1140 Connecticut Ave., N.W., Washington, D.C. 20036.

College Stores

College Stores, Directory of. Published every two years. Lists about 3500 college stores, geographically with manager's name, kinds of goods sold, college name, number of students, whether men, women, or both, whether the store is college owned or privately owned. B. Klein Publications, P.O. Box 8503, Coral Springs, Fla. 33065.

Confectionery

Candy Buyers' Directory. Annually in January. Lists candy manufacturers; importers and U.S. representatives, and confectionery brokers. The Manufacturing Confectionery Publishing Co., 175 Rock Rd., Glen Rock, N.J. 07452.

Construction Equipment

Construction Equipment Buyer's Guide, AED Edition. Annual. Summer. Lists U.S. and Canadian construction equipment distributors and manufacturers; includes company names, names of key personnel, addresses, telephone numbers, branch locations, and lines handled or type of equipment produced. Associated Equipment Distributors, 615 West 22d St., Oak Brook, Ill. 60521.

Conventions and Trade Shows

Directory of Conventions. Annually in January, with July supplement. Contains about 21,000 cross-indexed listings of annual events, gives dates, locations, names, and addresses of executives in charge and type of group two years in advance. *Successful Meetings Magazine,* Directory Dept., 633 Third Ave., New York, N.Y. 10017.

Exhibits Schedule. Annually in January, with supplement in July. Lists over 10,000 exhibits, trade shows, expositions, and fairs held throughout the world with dates given two years in advance. Listings run according to industrial classification covering all industries and professions; full information on dates, city, sponsoring organization, number of exhibits, attendance, gives title and address of executive in charge. *Successful Meetings Magazine,* Directory Dept., 633 Third Ave., New York, N.Y. 10017.

Dental Supply

Dental Supply Houses, Hayes Directory of. Annually in August. Lists wholesalers of dental supplies and equipment with addresses, telephone numbers, financial standing and credit rating. Edward N. Hayes, Publisher, 4229 Birch St., Newport Beach, Calif. 92660.

Department Stores

Department Stores. Annually. Lists headquarters address and branch locations, telephone numbers, number of stores, resident buying office, names of executives and buyers for independent and chain operators. Chain Store Guide Publications, 425 Park Ave., New York, N.Y. 10022.

Sheldon's Retail. Annual. Lists 1700 large independent department stores, 446 large junior department store chains, 190 large independent and chain home-furnishing stores, 694 large independent women's specialty stores, and 270 large women's specialty store chains alphabetically by states and also major Canadian stores. Gives all department buyers with lines bought by each buyer, and addresses and telephone numbers of merchandise executives. Also gives all New York, Chicago, or Los Angeles buying offices, the number and locations of branch stores, and an index of all store/chain headquarters. Phelon, Sheldon & Marsar, Inc., 32 Union Sq., New York, N.Y. 10003.

Discount Stores

Discount Department Stores, Phelon's. Gives buying headquarters for about 2000 discount stores, chains, drug chains, catalog showrooms, major jobbers and wholesalers; lines of merchandise bought, buyers' names, leased departments, addresses of leasees, executives, number of stores, and price range. Includes leased department operators with lines and buyers' names. Phelon, Sheldon & Marsar, Inc., 32 Union Sq., New York, N.Y. 10003.

Discount Department Stores. Annually. Lists headquarters address, telephone number, location, square footage of each store, lines carried, leased operators, names of executives and buyers (includes Canada). Also special section on leased department operators. Chain Store Guide Publications, 425 Park Ave., New York, N.Y. 10022.

Drug Outlets—Retail and Wholesale

Drug Stores, Chain. Annually. Lists headquarters address, telephone numbers, number and location of units, names of executives and buyers, wholesale drug distributors (includes Canada). Chain Store Guide Publications, 425 Park Ave., New York, N.Y. 10022.

Druggists—Wholesale. Annually in March. Wholesale druggists in United States with full-line wholesalers specially indicated as taken from the *Hayes Druggist Directory.* Edward N. Hayes, Publisher, 4229 Birch St., Newport Beach, Calif. 92660.

Druggist Directory, Hayes. Annually in March. List all the retail druggists in the United States, giving addresses, financial standing, and credit rating. Also publishes regional editions for one or more states. Computerized mailing labels available. Edward N. Hayes, Publisher, 4229 Birch St., Newport Beach, Calif. 92660.

Drug Topics Buyers' Guide. Gives information on wholesale drug companies, chain drug stores headquarters, department stores maintaining toilet goods or drug departments, manufacturers' sales agents, and discount houses operating toilet goods, cosmetic, proprietary medicine, or prescription departments. Drug Topics, Medical Economics Company, Oradell, N.J. 07649.

National Wholesale Druggists' Association Membership and Executive Directory. Annually. Lists 800 American and foreign wholesalers and manufacturers of drugs and allied products. National Wholesale Druggists' Association, 670 White Plains Rd., Scarsdale, N.Y. 10583.

Electrical and Electronics

Electronic Industry Telephone Directory. Annual. Contains over 80,000 listings in White and Yellow Page sections. White Pages: name, address, and telephone number of manufacturers, representatives, distributors, government agencies, contracting agencies, and others. Yellow Pages: alphabetic listings by 600 basic product headings and 3000 subproduct headings. Harris Publishing Co., 2057-2 Aurora Rd., Twinsburg, Ohio 44087.

Electrical Wholesale Distributors, Directory of. Detailed information on almost 5000 listings, including name, address, telephone number, branch and affiliated houses, products handled, etc. Electrical Wholesaling. McGraw-Hill Publications Co., Dept. ECCC Services, 1221 Avenue of the Americas, New York, N.Y. 10020.

Who's Who in Electronics, including Electronic Representatives Directory. Annual. Postpaid. Detailed information (name, address, telephone number, products handled, territories, and so forth) on 7500 electronic manufacturers, 500 suppliers, 3500 independent sales representatives, and 2500 industrial electronic distributors and branch outlets. Purchasing index with 1600 product breakdowns for buyers and purchasing agents. Harris Publishing Co., 2057-2 Aurora Rd., Twinsburg, Ohio 44087.

Electrical Utilities

Electric Utilities, Electrical World Directory of. Annually in October. Complete listings of electric utilities (investor-owned, municipal, and government agencies in U.S. and Canada) giving their addresses and personnel, and selected data on operations. McGraw-Hill Publications Co., Inc., Directory of Electric Utilities, 1221 Avenue of the Americas, New York, N.Y. 10020.

Embroidery

Embroidery Directory. Annually in October–November. Alphabetical listing with addresses and telephone numbers of manufacturers, merchandisers, designers, cutters, bleacheries, yarn dealers, machine suppliers and other suppliers to the Schiffli lace and embroidery industry. Schiffli Lace and Embroidery Manufacturers Assn., Inc., 512 23d St., Union City, N.J. 07087.

Export and Import

American Register of Exporters and Importers. Annually. Includes over 30,000 importers and exporters and products handled. American Register of Exporters and Importers, Inc., 15 Park Row, New York, N.Y. 10038.

Canadian Trade Directory, Fraser's. Write directly for price. Contains more than 12,000 product classifications with over 400,000 listings from 38,000 Canadian companies. Also lists over 10,000 foreign companies who have Canadian representatives. Fraser's Trade Directories, 481 University Ave., Toronto M5W 1A4, Ontario, Canada.

Flooring

Flooring Directory. Annually in November. Reference to sources of supply, giving their products and brand names, leading distributors, manufacturers' representatives, and associations. Flooring Directory, Harcourt Brace Jovanovich Publications, 1 East First St., Duluth, Minn. 55802.

Food Dealers—Retail and Wholesale

Co-ops, Voluntary Chains and Wholesale Grocers. Annually. Lists headquarters address, telephone number, number of accounts served, all branch operations, executives, buyers, annual sales volume (includes Canada and special "rack merchandiser" section). Chain Store Guide Publications, 425 Park Ave., New York, N.Y. 10022.

Food Brokers Association, National Directory of Members. Annually in July. Free to business firms writing on their letterhead. Arranged by states and cities, lists member food brokers in the United States and Europe, giving names and addresses, products they handle, and services they perform. National Food Brokers Association, 1916 M St., N.W., Washington, D.C. 20036.

Food Service Distributors. Annually. Lists headquarters address, telephone number, number of accounts served, branch operations, executives, and buyers for distributors serving the restaurant and institutional market. Chain Store Guide Publications, 425 Park Ave., New York, N.Y. 10022.

Fresh Fruit and Vegetable Dealers, The Blue Book of Credit Book and Marketing Guide. Semiannually in April and October. (Kept up to date by weekly credit sheets and monthly supplements.) Lists shippers, buyers, jobbers, brokers, wholesale and retail grocers, importers and exporters in the United States and Canada that handle fresh fruits and vegetables in carlot and trucklot quantities. Also lists truckers, truck brokers of exempt perishables with "customs and rules" covering both produce trading and truck transportation. Produce Reporter Co., 315 West Wesley St., Wheaton, Ill. 60187.

Frozen Food Fact Book and Directory. Annual. Free to association members. Lists packers, distributors, suppliers, refrigerated warehouses, wholesalers, and brokers; includes names and addresses of each firm and their key officials. Contains statistical marketing data. National Frozen Food Association, Inc., P.O. Box 398, 1 Chocolate Ave., Hershey, Pa. 17033.

Grocery Register, Thomas'. Annual. Three volumes. Vol. 1 & 3 or Vol. 2 & 3. Volume 1: Lists supermarket chains, wholesalers, brokers, frozen food brokers, exporters, warehouses. Volume 2: Contains information on products and services; manufacturers, sources of supplies, importers. Volume 3: A–Z index of 56,000 companies. Also, a brand name—trademark index. Thomas Publishing Co., One Penn Plaza, New York, N.Y. 10001.

Quick Frozen Foods Directory of Wholesale Distributors. Biennially. Lists distributors of frozen foods. Quick Frozen Foods, P.O. Box 6128, Duluth, Minn. 55806.

Supermarket, Grocery & Convenience Store Chains. Annually. Lists headquarters address, telephone number, location and type of unit, annual sales volume, executive and buyers, cartographic display of 267 Standard Metropolitan Statistical Areas (includes

Canada). Chain Store Guide Publications, 425 Park Ave., New York, N.Y. 10022.

Tea and Coffee Buyers' Guide, Ukers' Internationa. Biennial. Includes revised and updated lists of participants in the tea and coffee and allied trades. The Tea and Coffee Trade Journal, 18-15 Francis Lewis Blvd., Whitestone, N.Y. 11357.

Gas Companies

Gas Companies, Brown's Directory of International. Annually in August. Includes information on every known gas utility company and holding company worldwide. Brown's Directory, Harcourt Brace Jovanovich Publications, 1 East First St., Duluth, Minn. 55802.

LP/Gas. Annually in March. Lists suppliers, supplies, and distributors. Harcourt Brace Jovanovich Publications, 1 East First St., Duluth, Minn. 55802.

Gift and Art

Gift and Decorative Accessory Buyers Directory. Annually in August. Included in subscription price of monthly magazine. *Gifts and Decorative Accessories.* Alphabetical listing of manufacturers, importers, jobbers, and representatives in the gift field. Listing of trade names, trademarks, brand names, and trade associations. Geyer-McAllister Publications, 51 Madison Ave., New York, N.Y. 10010.

Gift and Housewares Buyers, Nationwide Directory. Annually with semiannual supplement. For 4673 different types of retail firms lists store name, address, type of store, number of stores, names of president, merchandise managers, and buyers, and so forth, for giftwares and housewares. State editions also available. The Salesman's Guide, Inc., 1140 Broadway, New York, N.Y. 10001.

Gift & Tableware Reporter Directory Issue. Annual. Alphabetical listing by category of each (manufacturer, representative, importer, distributor, or jobber). Includes identification of trade names and trademarks, and statistics for imports, manufacturing, and retail sales. Gift & Tableware Reporter, 1 Astor Place, New York, N.Y. 10036.

Gift Shop Directory. Biennially. List 900 gift shops in the United States. Resourceful Research, Box 642, F.D.R. Station, New York, N.Y. 10022.

Hardware

Hardware Wholesalers Guide, National. Annual. Alphabetical listing of manufacturers of hardware and building supplies. Where available, includes names and addresses of each manufacturer's representative showing territory covered. W.R.C. Smith Publishing Co., 1760 Peachtree Rd. N.W., Atlanta, Ga. 30357.

Hardware Wholesalers, Verified List of. Lists distributors (wholesale general hardware houses and hardware chain stores) serving the United States and Canada. Also lists manufacturers' agents handling hardware and allied lines. Chilton Co., Chilton Way, Radnor, Pa. 19089.

Home Furnishings

The Antiques Dealer. Annual directory issue. Issued in September as part of subscription. Lists major wholesale sources by geographical section. Includes special listing for show managers, auctioneers, appraisers, reproductions, supplies, and services. Ebel-Doctorow Publications, Inc., 115 Clifton Ave., Clifton, N.J. 07013.

Home Lighting & Accessories Suppliers. Directory issues. Semiannual. Issue in March and October as part of subscription. Lists names and addresses of suppliers to the lamp and lighting industry. Ebel-Doctorow Publications, Inc., 1115 Clifton Ave., Clifton, N.J. 07013.

Interior Decorator's Handbook. Semiannually. To trade only. Published expressly for decorators and designers, interior decorating staff of department and furniture stores. Lists firms handling items used in interior decoration. Columbia Communications, Inc., 370 Lexington Ave., New York, N.Y. 10017.

Hospitals

American Hospital Association Guide to the Health Care Field. Annually in August. Lists registered hospitals, with selected data as well as listings of nursing homes, health related organizations, and professional schools. Includes international, national, regional, and state organizations and agencies. American Hospital Associations, 840 North Lake Shore Dr., Chicago, Ill. 60611.

Hotels and Motels

Hotel-Motel Guide and Travel Atlas, Leahy's. Annually. Lists more than 47,000 hotels and motels in the United States, Canada, and Mexico; includes room rates, number of rooms, and plan of operation. Also has extensive maps. American Hotel Register Co., 2775 Shermer Road, Northbrook, Ill. 60062.

Hotel Red Book. Annually in May. Lists hotels in the United States, Canada, Caribbean, Mexico, Central and South America. Includes a section covering Europe, Asia, and Africa. Gives detailed information for each hotel. American Hotel Association Directory Corporation, 888 Seventh Ave., New York, N.Y. 10019.

Hotels Systems, Directory of. Annually in July. Lists approximately 300 hotel systems in the Western Hemisphere, American Hotel Association Directory Corporation, 888 Seventh Ave., New York, N.Y. 10019.

Housewares

Housewares Reps Registry. Annually in May. (Included with subscription to *Housewares*.) Compilation of resources of the housewares trade, includes listing of their products, trade names, and a registry of manufacturers' representatives. Housewares Directory,

Harcourt Brace Jovanovich Publications, 1 East First St., Duluth, Minn. 55802.

Jewelry

The Jewelers Board of Trade Confidential Reference Book. Semiannually in March and September. Supplied only to members subscribing to the agency service. Write directly for prices. Lists manufacturers, importers, distributors, and retailers of jewelry; diamonds; precious, semiprecious, and imitation stones; watches; silverware; and kindred articles. Includes credit ratings. The Jewelers Board of Trade, 70 Catamore Blvd., East Providence, R.I. 02914.

Liquor

Wine and Spirits Wholesalers, Blue Book of. Annually in December. Lists names of member companies; includes parent house and branches, addresses, and names of managers. Also has register of suppliers, and give state liquor control administrators, national associations, and trade press directory. Wine and Spirits Wholesalers of America, Inc., 2033 M St., N.W., Suite 400, Washington, D.C. 20036.

Mailing-List Houses

Mailing List Houses, Directory of. Lists more than 3000 list firms, brokers, compilers, and firms offering their own lists for rent, includes the specialties of each firm. Arranged geographically. B. Klein Publications, P.O. Box 8503, Coral Springs, Fla. 33065.

National Mailing-List Houses. (Small Business Bibliography 29). Free. Lists selected national mailing-list houses; includes both general line and limited line houses. Small Business Administration, P.O. Box 15434, Ft. Worth, Tex. 76119.

Mail-Order Businesses

Mail Order Business Directory. Lists more than 6300 names or mail-order firms with buyers' names, and lines carried. Arranged geographically. B. Klein Publications, P.O. Box 8503, Coral Springs, Fla. 33065.

Manufacturers

MacRae's Blue Book. Annual. In five volumes: Volume 1—Corporate Index lists company names and addresses alphabetically, with 60,000 branch and/or sales office telephone numbers. Volumes 2, 3, and 4—companies listed by 40,000 product classifications. Volume 5—company product catalogs. MacRae's Blue Book, 100 Shore Drive, Hinsdale, Ill. 60521.

Manufacturers, Thomas' Register of American. Annual. In 14 volumes, Volume 1-7—products and services; suppliers of each product category grouped by state and city. Vols. 9-14—manufacturers' catalogs. Thomas Publishing Co., One Penn Plaza, New York, N.Y. 10001.

Manufacturers' Sales Representatives

Manufacturers & Agents National Association Directory of Members. Annually in July. Contains individual listings of manufacturers' agents throughout the United States, Canada, and several foreign countries. Listings cross-referenced by alphabetical, geographical, and product classification. Manufacturers' Agents National Association, P.O. Box 16878. Irvine, Calif. 92713.

Mass Merchandisers

Major Mass Market Merchandisers, Nationwide Directory of. (Exclusive of New York metropolitan area). Annually. Lists men's, women's, and children's wear buyers who buy for over 175,000 units—top discount, variety, supermarket, and drug chains; factory outlet stores; leased department operators. The Salesman's Guide, Inc., 1140 Broadway, New York, N.Y. 10001.

Mass Retailing Merchandiser Buyers Directory.   Annually. Lists 7000 manufacturers, mass retail chains, manufacturers' representatives, jobbers, and wholesalers serving the mass-retailing field. Merchandiser Publishing Co., Inc., 222 West Adams, Chicago, Ill. 60606.

Metalworking

Metalworking Directory, Dun & Bradstreet.   Annually in May. Published in one national and five sectional editions. Retail price available upon request. Lists about 44,000 metalworking and metal-producing plants with twenty or more production employees. Arranged in four sections: geographically, line of business, alphabetically, and statistical courts summary. Marketing Services Division, Dun & Bradstreet, Inc., 99 Church St., New York, N.Y. 10007.

Military Market

Buyers' Guide.   Annually. Listings grouped by systems served of suppliers names and addresses, military representatives, and civilian brokerage firms that specialize in serving military stores are given. Military Market, 475 School St., S.W., Washington, D.C. 20024.

Nonfood Products

Non-Food Buyers, National Directory Of.   Annually. Alpha-geographical listing of 9000 buyers of nonfood merchandise for over 336,000 outlets. United Publishing Co., 1372 Peachtree St., N.E., Atlanta, Ga. 30309.

Paper Products

Sources of Supply Buyers' Guide. Lists mills and converters of paper, film, foil and allied products, and paper merchants in the United States alphabetically with addresses, principal personnel, and products manufactured. Also lists trade associations, brand names, and manufacturers' representatives. Advertisers and Publishers Service, Inc., P.O. Drawer 795, 300 N. Prospect Ave., Park Ridge, Ill. 60068.

Physicians and Medical Supply Houses

Medical Directory, American. Volumes 1–4 gives complete information about all physicians in the United States and possessions—alphabetical and geographical listings. Volume 5— Directory of Women Physicians. American Medical Associations, 535 North Dearborn St., Chicago, Ill. 60610.

Physician and Hospital Supply Houses, Hayes' Directory of. Annually in August. Listings of 1850 U.S. wholesalers doing business in physician, hospital, and surgical supplies and equipment; includes addresses, telephone numbers, financial standing, and credit ratings. Edward N. Hayes, Publisher, 4229 Birch St., Newport Beach, Calif. 92660.

Plumbing

Manufacturers' Representatives, Directory of. Annually as a special section of the February issue of *The Wholesaler* magazine. Write directly for subscription price. Lists representatives of manufacturers selling plumbing, heating and cooling equipment, components, tools and related products, to this industry through wholesaler channels with detailed information on each. Scott Periodicals Corp., 135 Addison Avenue, Elmhurst, Ill. 60126.

Premium Sources

Premium and Incentive Buyers, Directory of.   Annual in September. Lists over 16,000 executives for 12,000 firms with title, telephone number, address, and merchandise executive desires to buy in the premium, incentive, and travel fields. The Salesman's Guide, 1140 Broadway, New York, N.Y. 10001.

Incentive Marketing/Incorporating Incentive Travel: Supply Sources Directory.   Annual in January. Contains classified directory of suppliers, and list of manufacturers' representatives serving the premium field. Also, lists associations and clubs, and trade shows. Incentive Marketing, 633 Third Ave., New York, N.Y. 10017.

Purchasing, Government

U.S. Government Purchasing and Sales Directory.   Booklet by Small Business Administration. Designed to help small business receive an equitable share of government contracts. Lists types of purchases for both military and civilian needs, catalogs procurement offices by state. Lists SBA regional and branch offices. Order from Superintendent of Documents, U.S. Government Printing Office, Washington, D.C. 20402.

Refrigeration and Air-Conditioning

Air Conditioning, Heating & Refrigeration News.   Special issue. Lists alphabetically and by products, the names of refrigeration, heating and air-conditioning manufacturers, trade names, wholesalers, and associations in the United States. Business News Publishing Co., P.O. Box 2600, Troy, Mich. 48084.

Air-Conditioning & Refrigeration Wholesalers Directory.   Annually. Lists alphabetically 950 member air-conditioning and refrigeration wholesalers with their addresses, telephone numbers, and official representatives by region, state, and city. Air-conditioning and Refrigeration Wholesalers, 22371 Newman Ave., Dearborn, Mich. 48124.

Restaurants

Restaurant Operators. (Chain.) Annually. Lists headquarters address, telephone number, number and location of units, trade names used, whether unit is company-operated or franchised, executives and buyers, annual sales volume for chains of restaurants, cafeterias, drive-ins, hotel and motel food operators, industrial caterers, and so forth. Chain Store Guide Publications, 425 Park Ave., New York, N.Y. 10022.

Roofing and Siding

RSI Trade Directory. Annually in April. With subscription to *Roof Siding and Insulation,* monthly. Has listing guide to products and equipment manufacturers, jobbers and distributors, and associations in the roofing, siding, and home improvement industries. RSI Directory, Harcourt Brace Jovanovich Publications, 1 East First St., Duluth, Minn. 55802.

Selling, Direct

Direct Selling Companies, A Supplier's Guide to. Information supplied by member companies of the Direct Selling Association includes names of contact persons, company product line, method of distribution, and so forth. Direct Selling Association, 1730 M Street, N.W., Washington, D.C. 20036.

Direct Selling Directory. Annually in February issue of *Specialty Salesman and Business Opportunities Magazine.* Alphabetical listing of name and address under product and service classifications of specialty sales firms and their products. Specialty Salesmen, 307 North Michigan Ave., Chicago, Ill. 60601.

Who's Who in Direct Selling. Membership roster of the Direct Selling Association. No charge for single copies. Active members classified by type of product or service. Alphabetical listing gives name, address, and telephone of firm, along with managing official. Direct Selling Association, 1730 M Street, N.W., Washington, D.C. 20036.

Shoes

Chain Shoe Stores Directory.   Lists chain shoe stores at their headquarters including officers, buyers, lines carried, trading names of stores, number of operating units. The Rumpf Publishing Co., Div. of Nickerson & Collins Co., 1800 Oakton St., Des Plaines, Ill. 60018.

Shopping Centers

Shopping Centers in the United States and Canada, Directory of.   Annual. Alphabetical listing of 16,000 American and Canadian shopping centers, location, owner-developer, manager, physical plant (number of stores, square feet), and leasing agent. National Research Bureau, Inc., 424 North Third St., Burlington, Iowa 52601.

Specialty Stores

Women's Specialty Stores, Phelon's.   Lists over 18,000 women's apparel and accessory shops with store headquarters name and address, number of shops operated, New York City buying headquarters or representatives, lines of merchandise bought and sold, name of principal and buyers, store size, and price range. Phelon, Sheldon, & Marsar, Inc., 32 Union Sq., New York, N.Y. 10003.

Sporting Goods

Sporting Goods Buyers, Nationwide Directory of.   Including semiannual supplements. Lists over 4500 top retail stores (23 different types) with names of buyers and executives, for all types of sporting goods, athletic apparel and footwear, hunting and fishing, and outdoor equipment. The Salesman's Guide, Inc., 1140 Broadway, New York, N.Y. 10001.

The Sporting Goods Register. (Including jobbers, manufacturers' representatives, and importers). Annual. Geographical listing of firms (name, address, buyers, types of goods sold, and so forth) doing wholesale business in sporting goods merchandise and equipment. Similar data for Canadian firms. Alphabetical grouping of manufacturers' representatives and importers. The Sporting Goods Dealer, 1212 North Lindbergh Blvd., St. Louis, Mo. 63132.

The Sporting Goods Dealer's Directory. Annual. Lists about 5000 manufacturers and suppliers. Also includes names of manufacturers agents, wholesalers, and sporting goods associations and governing bodies of sports. The Sporting Goods Dealer, 1212 North Lindbergh Blvd., St. Louis, Mo. 63132.

Stationers

Wholesale Stationers' Association Membership Roster. Annually. Alphabetical listing by company of over 300 wholesaler companies. Wholesale Stationers Assn., 3166 Des Plaines Ave., Des Plaines, Ill. 60018.

Textiles

Textile Blue Book, Davison's. Annual. Contains over 18,000 separate company listings (name, address, and so forth) for United States and Canada. Firms included are cotton, wool, synthetic, mills, knitting mills, cordage, twine, and duck manufacturers, dry goods commission merchants, converters, yarn dealers, cordage manufacturers' agents, wool dealers and merchants, cotton merchants, exporter, brokers, and others. Davison Publishing Co., P.O. Drawer 477, Ridgewood, N.J. 07451.

Toys and Novelties

Toys, Hobbies & Crafts Directory. Annually in June. Lists manufacturers, products, trade names, suppliers to manufacturers,
supplier products, character licensors, manufacturers' representatives, toy trade associations, and trade show managements. Toys
Directory, Harcourt Brace Jovanovich Publications, 1 East First
St., Duluth, Minn. 55802.

Wholesalers and Manufacturers, Directory of. Contains information
on wholesalers, manufacturers, manufacturers' representatives of
toys, games, hobby, art, school, party, and office supply products.
Toy Wholesalers' Association of America, 1514 Elmwood Ave.,
Evanston, Ill. 60201.

Trailer Parks

*Campground Directory, Woodall's North American Canadian Edi-
tion.* Annually. Lists and star-rates public and private camp-
grounds in North American continent alphabetically by town
with location and description of facilities. Also lists more than
1000 RV service locations. Regional editions available. Woodall
Publishing Company, 500 Hyachinth Place, Highland Park, Ill.
60035.

Trucking

*Trinc's Blue Book of the Trucking Industry and Trinc's Five Year Red
Book.* Retail price upon request. Together these two directories
furnish comprehensive statistics on the trucking industry and individual truckers represented by about 3500 Class I and Class II
U.S. motor carriers of property. TRINC Transportation Consultants, P.O. Box 23091, Washington, D.C. 20024.

Variety Stores

General Merchandise, Variety and Junior Department Stores. Annually.
Lists headquarters address, telephone number, number of units

and locations, executives and buyers (includes Canada). Chain
Store Guide Publications, 425 Park Ave., New York, N.Y. 10022.

Warehouses

Distribution Services, Guide to. Annually in July. Lists leading public warehouses in U.S. and Canada, as well as major truck lines,
airlines, steamship lines, liquid and dry bulk terminals, material
handling equipment suppliers, ports of the world and railroad
piggyback services and routes. Distribution Magazine, Chilton
Way, Radnor, Pa. 19089.

Public Refrigerated Warehouses, Directory of. Annually. Free to con-
cerns in perishable food business. Geographical listing of over 750
public refrigerated warehouse members. International Associations of Refrigerated Warehouses, 7315 Wisconsin Ave., N.W.,
Washington, D.C. 20014.

OTHER IMPORTANT DIRECTORIES

The following business directories are helpful to those persons doing
marketing research. Most of these directories are available for reference at the larger libraries. For additional listings, consult the *Guide
to American Directories* at local libraries.

*AUBER Bibliography of Publications of University Bureaus of Business
and Economic Research.* Lists studies published by Bureaus of Business and Economic Research affiliated with American colleges
and universities. Done for the Association for University Bureaus
of Business and Economic Research. Issued annually. Previous
volumes available. Bureau of Business Research, College of Business and Economics, West Virginia University, Morgantown,
W.Va. 26506.

*Bradford's Directory of Marketing Research Agencies and Management
Consultants in the United States and the World.* Gives names and ad-
dresses of over 350 marketing research agencies in the United
States, Canada, and abroad. Lists service offered by agency, along

with other pertinent data, such as date established, names of principal officers, and size of staff. Bradford's Directory of Marketing Research Agencies, P.O. Box 276, Department B-15, Fairfax, VA 22030.

Consultants and Consulting Organizations Directory.   Contains 5041 entries. Guides reader to right organization for a given consulting assignment. Entries include names, addresses, phone numbers, and data on services performed. Gale Research Company, Book Tower, Detroit, Mich. 48226.

Research Centers Directory.   Palmer, Archie M., editor. Lists more than 5500 nonprofit research organizations. Descriptive information provided for each center, including address, telephone number, name of director, data on staff, funds, publications, and a statement concerning its principal fields of research. Has special indexes. Gale Research Company, Book Tower, Detroit, Mich. 48226.

MacRae's Blue Book—Materials, Equipment, Supplies, Components.   Annual. In five volumes: Vol. 1 is an index by corporations; Vols. 2–4 are a classification by products showing under each classification manufacturers of that item; Vol. 5 contains company catalogs. MacRae's Blue Book Company, 100 Shore Drive, Hinsdale, Ill. 60521.

Thomas' Grocery Register.   Annual. Lists wholesale grocers; chain store organizations; voluntary buying groups; food brokers; exporters and importers of food products; frozen food brokers; distributors and related products distributed through grocery chains. Thomas Publishing Company, One Penn Plaza, New York, N.Y. 10001.

Thomas' Register of American Manufacturers.   Annual. In 14 volumes. Vols. 1–7 contain manufacturers arranged geographically under each product, and capitalization or size rating for each manufacturer, Vol. 7 lists brands names and their owners; Vol. 8 lists company addresses, phone numbers, and local offices; Vols. 9–14 contain company catalogs. Thomas Publishing Company, One Penn Plaza, New York, N.Y. 10001.

OTHER SOURCES

U.S. Small Business Administration, Washington, D.C. 20416. SBA issues a wide range of management and technical publications designed to help owner-managers and prospective owners of small business. (For general information about SBA, its policies, and assistance programs, ask for *SBA—What It Is*, free on request to nearest SBA office.) Listings of currenty available publications (free and for sale) may be requested from SBA, P.O. Box 15434, Ft. Worth, Tx. 76119, or any of SBA's field offices. Ask for: *SBA 115—Free Management Assistance Publications* and *SBA 115B—For-Sale Booklets*. The lists are free and may be used for ordering the particular series listed, either the free series from SBA, or the for-sale series from the Superintendent of Documents (GPO).

Small Business Bibliography. (8- to 12-page-pamphlet.) Each title in this series deals with a specific kind of business or business function, giving reference sources. It consists of an introduction that gives a description of the operation, listing of references applicable to the subject covered. Free.

> *Statistics and Maps for National Market Analysis* (SBB 12)
> *National Directories for Use in Marketing* (SBB 13)
> *Basic Library Reference Sources* (SBB 18)
> *Advertising-Retail Store* (SBB 20)

Management Aids for Small Manufacturers (4- to 8-page leaflet.) Each title in this series discusses a specific management practice to help the owner-manager of small manufacturing firms with their management problems. Free.

> *Using Census Data in Small Plant Marketing* (MA 187)
> *Locating or Relocating Your Business* (MA 201)
> *Finding a New Product for Your Company* (MA 216)

Small Marketers Aid. (4- to 8-page leaflet.) Each title in this series gives guidance on a specific subject for owners of small retail, wholesale, and service business. Free.

Measuring the Results of Advertising (SMA 121)

Factors in Considering a Shopping Center Location (SMA 143)

Using a Traffic Study to Select a Retail Site (SMA 152)

Using Census Data to Select a Store Site (SMA 154)

Advertising Guidelines for Small Retail Firms (SMA 160)

Small Business Management Series. Each booklet in this series discusses in depth the application of a specific management practice. The series covers a wide range of small business subjects. Prices vary. GPO.

Office of Management and Budget, Executive Office Building, Washington, D.C. 20503.

Standard Industrial Classification Manual. GPO. Gives the definitions of the classifications of industrial establishments by the type of activity in which each is engaged and the resulting Industrial Classification Code. Very useful in classifying data collected from industrial firms so its classification is comparable to data reported by government sources.

Bureau of the Census, Commerce Department, Suitland, MD 20233. Request list of publications from the Census Bureau. Publication order forms are issued for reports as they become available.

Census of Business: Retail-Area Statistics—U.S. Summary. GPO. Final figures from the Census of Retail Trade, includes statistical totals for each region, state, city and standard metropolitan area—tabulated by type of establishment.

County Business Patterns. GPO. A series of publications presenting first-quarter employment and payroll statistics, by county and by industry. Separate reports issued for each of the fifty states, the District of Columbia, Puerto Rico, and outlying areas of the United States.

County and City Data Book. VGTB. GPO. Contains data for 50 states, 3141 counties or county equivalents, 243 SMSAs, 840 cities of 25,000 inhabitants or more, among others.

Directory of Federal Statistics for Local Areas, A Guide to Sources. GPO. Guide to local area socioeconomic data contained in 182 publications of 33 federal agencies.

Directory of Federal Statistics of States, A guide to Sources. GPO. Guide to state socioeconomic data contained in more than 750 publications of federal agencies.

Directory of Non-Federal Statistics for State and Local Areas. GPO. Guide to nonfederal sources of current statistics on social, political, and economic subjects for fifty states, the District of Columbia, Guam, Puerto Rico, and the Virgin Islands.

Standard Metropolitan Statistical Areas. GPO. Gives the criteria followed in establishing Standard Metropolitan Statistical Areas. Changes issued periodically as amendments.

Department of Commerce, Domestic and International Business Administration, Washington, D.C. 20230.

Measuring Markets: A Guide to the Use of Federal and State Statistical Data. GPO. Presents features and measurements of markets, types of useful data published by federal and state governments, case examples of market measurement by use of government data, and bibliographies.

IMPORTANT FINANCIAL RATIOS

Measures of Liquidity

Liquidity is the ability to use the money available in your business. In general, the more liquid, the better the state of financial health. However, this is a bit oversimplified as I will show you later. The ratios intended to measure liquidity in your business will tell you whether you have enough cash on hand plus assets that can be readily turned into cash to pay debts that may fall due during any given period. They will also tell you about how quickly they can be turned into cash.

The Current Ratio

The current ratio is possibly the best-known measure of financial health. It answers this question: Does your business have sufficient current assets to meet current debts with a margin of safety for possible losses due to uncollectible accounts receivable and other factors?

The current ratio is computed by using information on your balance sheet. You simply divide current assets by current liabilities. For example, if we consider the sample balance sheet in Figure 1,

Balance Sheet		December 31, 19—
Current assets:		
Cash	$ 35,000.00	
Accounts receivable	55,000.00	
Inventory	60,000.00	
Temporary investments	3,000.00	
Prepaid expenses	2,000.00	
Total current assets		$155,000.00
Fixed assets:		
Machinery and equipment	$ 35,000.00	
Buildings	42,000.00	
Land	40,000.00	
Total fixed assets		117,000.00
Other assets:		
None		
Total other assets		0
Total assets		$272,000.00
Current liabilities:		
Accounts payable	$ 36,000.00	
Notes payable	44,000.00	
Current portion of long-term notes	4,000.00	
Interest payable	1,000.00	
Taxes payable	3,000.00	
Accrued payroll	2,000.00	
Total current liabilities		$ 90,000.00
Long-term liabilities:		
Notes payable	$ 25,000.00	
Total long-term liabilities		$ 25,000.00
Equity:		
Owner's equity	$115,000.00	
Total equity		$115,000.00
Total liabilities and equity		$272,000.00

FIGURE 1.   Sample balance sheet for the XYZ Company.

current assets are $155,000 and current liabilities are $90,000; $155,000 divided by $90,000 equals a current ratio of 1.7.

Now you may ask: Is this a good current ratio or is it not? You cannot determine this from the numerical value of 1.7 by itself, even though there is a popular rule of thumb which says that a current ratio of at least two to one is okay. The current ratio very much depends on your business and the specific characteristics of your current assets and liabilities. However, one major indication is a comparison with other companies in your industry. I'll give you sources for this information in the section "Sources of Ratio Analyses from All Industries."

If after analysis and comparison you decide that your current ratio is too low, you may be able to raise it by the following actions:

1. Increase your current assets by new equity contributions.
2. Try converting noncurrent assets into current assets.
3. Pay some of your debts.
4. Increase your current assets from loans or other types of borrowing which have a maturity of at least a year in the future.
5. Put some of the profits back into the business.

The Acid Test, or "Quick," Ratio

The acid test, or "quick," ratio is also an outstanding measurement of liquidity. You calculate this ratio as follows: cash plus government securities plus receivables divided by current liabilities.

The company shown in Figure 1 has no government securities. Therefore, the numerator of this figure becomes $35,000 cash plus $55,000 in accounts receivable, or $90,000. This is divided by current liabilities on the same balance sheet of $90,000 to result in an acid test ratio of 1.0.

The quick ratio concentrates on really liquid assets whose values are definite and well known. Therefore, the quick ratio will answer this question: If all your sales revenue disappears tomorrow, can you meet current obligations with your cash or quick funds on hand? Uusually an acid test ratio of approximately 1.0 is considered satisfactory. However, you must also make this decision conditional on the following:

1.   There should be nothing in the offing to slow up the collection of your accounts receivable.

2.   The receipt of accounts receivable collections should not trail the due schedule for paying your current liabilities. In checking out this timing, you should consider payment of your creditors sufficiently early to take advantage of any discounts which are offered.

If these two conditions are not met, then you will need an acid test ratio higher than 1.0. However, it is erroneous to believe that either the current or the acid test ratio should always be as high as possible. Only those from whom you have borrowed money would say this is so. Naturally, they are interested in the greatest possible safety of their loan. However, you do not want to have large sums of money lying idle and not earning you additional profits. If you do have idle cash balances and receivables and inventories which are out of proportion to your needs, you should reduce them. The key here is to be conservative enough to keep a safety pad and yet bold enough to take advantage of the fact that you have these resources which can be used to earn additional profits for you. Before you make this decision as to the right amount of liquidity, you should consider the two ratios discussed next, average collection period and inventory turnover.

Average Collection Period

The average collection period is the number of days that sales are tied up in accounts receivable. This number can be calculated by using your profit and loss statement or income statement as shown in Figure 2. First, take your net sales which in Figure 2 are $1,035,000, and divide this figure by the days in your accounting period, or 365. This equals $2836, the average sales per day in the accounting period. Next, take your accounts receivable which you obtain from

Income Statement		For the year ended December 31, 19—
Sales or revenue:		$1,040,000.00
Less returns and allowances		5,000.00
Net sales		$1,035,000.00
Cost of sales:		
Beginning inventory, Jan 1, 19—		250,000.00
Merchandise purchases	500,000.00	
Cost of goods available for sale		750,000.00
Less ending inventory, Dec 31, 19—		225,000.00
Total cost of goods sold		525,000.00
Gross profit		$ 510,000.00
Operating expenses:		
Selling and general and administrative		
Salaries and wages		180,000.00
Advertising		200,000.00
Rent		10,000.00
Utilities		5,000.00
Other expenses		10,000.00
Total operating expenses		405,000.00
Total operating income		$ 105,000.00
Other revenue and expenses		0
Pretax income:		$ 105,000.00
Taxes on income		50,000.00
Income after taxes but before extraordinary gain or loss		$ 55,000.00
Extraordinary gain or loss		0
Net income (or loss)		$ 55,000.00

FIGURE 2.   Sample income statement for the XYZ Company.

the balance sheet, Figure 1. Accounts receivable are $55,000. Divide $55,000 by the figure you just calculated ($2836); $55,000 divided by $2836 equals 19. This is the average number of days sales are tied up in receivables. It is also your average collection period.

This tells you how promptly your accounts are being collected considering whatever credit terms you are extending. It tells you two other things: (1) the quality of your accounts and notes receivable, that is, whether you are really getting paid rapidly or not, and (2) how good a job your credit department is doing in collecting these accounts.

Now the question is, Is the figure of 19 days good or not good? There is a rule of thumb that says the average collection period should not exceed one and one-third times the credit terms offered. Therefore, if your company offers 30 days to pay and the average collection period is only 19 days, you are doing very well. On the other hand, anything in excess of 40 days ($1\frac{1}{3} \times 30 = 40$) would show that you may have a problem.

Inventory Turnover

Inventory turnover will show you how rapidly your merchandise is moving. It will also show you how much capital you had tied up in inventory to support the level of your company's operations for the period that you are analyzing. To calculate inventory turnover, simply divide the cost of goods sold that you obtain from your income statement, Figure 2, by your average inventory. According to Figure 2, your income profit and loss statement, the cost of goods sold equals $525,000. You cannot calculate your average inventory from Figure 1. You only know that for the period for which the inventory is stated, it equals $60,000. Let's assume that the previous balance sheet indicated that your inventory was $50,000. Then the average inventory for the 2 periods would be $60,000 plus $50,000 divided by 2, or $55,000. Now, let's see what inventory turnover is: Cost of goods sold again was $525,000 divided by $55,000 equals 9.5.

This means that you turned your inventory 9.5 times during the year. Put another way, through your business operations you used up merchandise which total 9.5 times the average inventory investment. Under most circumstances, the higher the turnover of inventory, the better, because it means that you are able to operate with a relatively small sum of money invested in this inventory. Another implication is that your inventory is the right inventory. That is, it is salable and has not been in stock too long. But, even here, you must consider that too high a figure may be a sign of a problem. Very high inventory may mean that you have inventory shortages, and inventory shortages soon lead to customer dissatisfaction and may mean a loss of customers to the competition in the long run.

Is 9.5 a satisfactory inventory turnover or not? Again, the desirable rate depends on your business, your industry, your method of valuing inventories, and numerous other factors that are unique to your situation. And, once again, it is helpful to study and compare your turnover rate with that of similar businesses of your size in your industry. Once you have been working and operating for some time, past experiences with inventory turnover will indicate what is good and what is not with less reliance on inventory comparisons.

Very frequently it is helpful to analyze not just your total inventory but specific inventory turnover for different products or even groups of products or product lines. This will show you which items are doing well and which are not. You may also prepare turnover analyses for much more frequent periods than a year. Even monthly or weekly periods may be necessary or required for perishable items or items that become obsolete very quickly. Thus you will know to reorder those items which are truly "hot" items early and in plenty of time, and you will also know which items you should not order and which items you must order before their value goes down to a point where you can no longer sell them.

PROFITABILITY MEASURES

Measures of profitability are essential in your business if you are to know how much money you are making, whether you are making as much as you can, or whether you are making money at all. There are several different ratios which will assist you in determining this. These are the asset earning power, return on owner's equity, net profit on sales, investment turnover, and, finally, return on investment (ROI).

Asset Earning Power

Asset earning power is determined by the ratio of earnings before interest and taxes to total assets. From the income statement in Figure

2 we can see that total operating profit or income is $105,000. Total assets from the balance sheet, Figure 1, are $272,000. Therefore, $105,000 divided by $272,000 equals 0.39, or 39%.

Return on the Owner's Equity

Return on the owner's equity shows the return that you received in exchange for your investment in your business. To compute this ratio you will usually use the average equity for twelve months, if it is available, or, if not, the average of figures from two different balance sheets, your latest and the one prior. Return on the owner's equity equals net profit divided by equity. Net profit from Figure 2 is $55,000. Equity from Figure 1 is $115,000. Assuming the equity from the period before is also $115,000, we will use this as an average. Therefore, return on the owner's equity equals $55,000 divided by $115,000, which equals 0.48, or 48%.

You can calculate a similar ratio by using tangible net worth in lieu of equity. Tangible net worth equals equity less any intangible assets, such as patents and goodwill. If no intangible assets exist, then, of course, the two will be equal.

Net Profit on Sales

The net profit on sales ratio measures the difference between what you take in and what you spend in the process of doing business. Again, net profit was determined to be $55,000. Net sales from Figure 2 are $1,035,000. Therefore, net profit on sales equals 0.053, or 5.3%.

This means that for every dollar of sales the company has made a profit of 5.3¢.

The net profit on sales ratio depends mainly on these two factors: (1) operating costs and (2) pricing policies. Therefore, if this figure goes down, it could be because you have lowered prices or it could be because costs have been increasing at the same time that prices have remained stable.

Again, this ratio should be compared with figures from other similar businesses, and you should consider trends over a period of time. It is also useful to compare net profit on sales ratios for individual products to show which products or product lines should be given additional emphasis and which should be eliminated.

Investment Turnover

This ratio is annual net sales to total assets. In this case, net sales of $1,035,000, divided by total assets of $272,000 from Figure 1, equals 3.8.

Again, investment turnover should be compared and watched for trends.

Return on Investment (ROI)

There are several different ways of calculating return on investment. It is a very useful method of measuring profitability. One simple way is simply to take net profit and divide it by total assets. In this case, the net profit equals $55,000. Total assets are $272,000. Therefore, $55,000 divided by $272,000 equals 0.20, or 20%.

It is desirable here to have the highest net profit for the smallest amount of total assets invested. You can use this rate of return on investment for intercompany and interindustry comparisons, as well as pricing costs, inventory and investment decisions, and many other measurements of efficiency and profitability. However you use it, always be sure that you are consistent in making your comparisons; that is, be sure that you use the same definitions of net profit and assets invested.

Here are some additional measures of profitability using ROI:

1. *Rate of earnings on total capital employed equals net income plus interest and taxes divided by total liabilities and capital.* This ratio serves as an index of productivity of capital as well as a measure of earning power in operating efficiency.

2. *Rate of earnings on invested capital equals net income plus income taxes divided by proprietary equity and fixed liabilities.* This ratio is used

as a measure of earning power of the borrowed invested capital.

3. *Rate of earnings on proprietary equity equals net income divided by total capital including surplus reserves.*   This ratio is used as a measure of the yield on the owner's investment.

4. *Rate of earnings on stock equity equals net income divided by total capital including surplus reserves.*   This ratio is used as a measure of the attractiveness of common stock as an investment.

5. *Rate of dividends on common stock equity equals common stock dividends divided by common stock equity.*   This ratio is used to indicate the desirability of common stock as a source of income.

6. *Rate of dividends on common stock equity equals common stock dividend per share divided by market value per share of common stock.*   This ratio is used as a measure of the current yield on investment in a particular stock.

SOURCES OF RATIO ANALYSES FROM ALL INDUSTRIES

In order to be able to compare your business with other businesses in your industry, it is necessary to obtain pertinent data on other businesses. Here are different sources for such information:

1. Dun & Bradstreet, Inc., Business Information Systems, 99 Church St., New York, NY 10007. This firm publishes key business ratios in 125 lines annually. Legal copies can be obtained free on request.

2. Accounting Corporation of America, 1929 First Ave., San Diego, CA 92101. This organization publishes *Parameter of Small Businesses* which classifies its operating ratios for various industry groups on the basis of gross volume.

3. National Cash Register Co., Marketing Services Department, Dayton, OH 45409. This firm publishes *Expenses in Retail Businesses* which examines the cost of operations in over fifty kinds of businesses obtained from primary sources, most of which are trade associations.

4. Robert Morris Associates, Philadelphia National Bank Building, Philadelphia, PA 19107. Robert Morris has developed and published ratio studies for over 225 lines of business.

5. The Small Business Administration. The SBA has a new series of reports which provide expenses as a percentage of sales for many industries. While the reports do not provide strict ratio information, a comparison of percentage expenses will be very useful for your financial management.

6. Trade Associations. Many national trade associations publish ratio studies, including the following:

Air-Conditioning & Refrigeration Wholesalers, 22371 Newman Avenue, Dearborn, MI 48124

Air Transport Association of America, 1000 Connecticut Avenue NW, Washington, DC 20036

American Bankers Association, 90 Park Avenue, New York, NY 10016

American Book Publishers Council, One Park Avenue, New York, NY 10016

American Booksellers Association, 175 Fifth Avenue, New York, NY 10010

American Carpet Institute, 350 Fifth Avenue, New York, NY 10001

American Electric Association, 16223 Meyers Street, Detroit, MI 48235

American Institute of Laundering, Doris and Chicago Avenues, Joliet, IL 60433

American Institute of Supply Associations, 1505 22d Street NW, Washington, DC 20037

American Meat Institute, 59 East Van Buren Street, Chicago, IL 60605

American Paper Institute, 260 Madison Avenue, New York, NY 10016

American Society of Association Executives, 2000 K Street, NW, Washington, DC 20006

American Supply Association, 221 North LaSalle Street, Chicago, IL 60601

Automotive Service Industry Association, 230 North Michigan Avenue, Chicago, IL 60601

Bowling Proprietors' Association of America, Inc., West Higgins Road, Hoffman Estates, IL 60172

Florists' Telegraph Delivery Association, 900 West Lafayette Boulevard, Detroit MI 48226

Food Service Equipment Industry, Inc., 332 South Michigan Avenue, Chicago, IL 60604

Laundry and Cleaners Allied Trades Association, 1180 Raymond Boulevard, Newark, NJ 07102

Material Handling Equipment Distributors Association, 20 North Wacker Drive, Chicago, IL 60616

Mechanical Contractors Association of America, 666 Third Avenue, Suite 1464, New York, NY 10017

Menswear Retailers of America, 390 National Press Building, Washington, DC 20004

Motor and Equipment Manufacturers Association, 250 West 57th Street, New York, NY 10019

National-American Wholesale Lumber Association, 180 Madison Avenue, New York, NY 10016

National Appliance and Radio-TV Dealers Association, 1319 Merchandise Mart, Chicago, IL 60654

National Association of Accountants, 525 Park Avenue, New York, NY 10022

National Association of Building Owners and Managers, 134 South LaSalle Street, Chicago, IL 60603

National Association of Electrical Distributors, 600 Madison Avenue, New York, NY 10022

National Association of Food Chains, 1725 Eye Street, NW, Washington, DC 20006

National Association of Furniture Manufacturers, 666 North Lake Shore Drive, Chicago, IL 60611

National Association of Insurance Agents, 96 Fulton Street, New York, NY 10038

National Association of Music Merchants, Inc., 222 West Adams Street, Chicago, IL 60606

National Association of Plastic Distributors, 2217 Tribune Tower, Chicago, IL 60611

National Association of Retail Grocers of the United States, 360 North Michigan Avenue, Chicago, IL 60601

National Association of Textile and Apparel Wholesalers, 350 Fifth Avenue, New York, NY 10001

National Association of Tobacco Distributors, 360 Lexington Avenue, New York, NY 10017

National Automatic Merchandising Association, Seven South Dearborn Street, Chicago, IL 60603

National Beer Wholesalers' Association of America, 6310 North Cicero Avenue, Chicago, IL 60646

National Builders' Hardware Association, 1290 Avenue of the Americas, New York, NY 10019

National Electrical Contractors Association, 1200 18th Street, NW, Washington, DC 20036

National Electrical Manufacturers Association, 155 East 44th Street, New York, NY 10017

National Farm and Power Equipment Dealers Association, 2340 Hampton Avenue, St. Louis, MO 63130

National Home Furnishing Association, 1150 Merchandise Mart, Chicago, IL 60654

National Kitchen Cabinet Association, 918 Commonwealth Building, 674 South 4th Street, Louisville, KY 40204

National Lumber and Building Material Dealers Association, Ring Building, Washington, DC 20036

National Machine Tool Builders Association, 2071 East 102d Street, Cleveland, OH 44106

National Office Products Association, Investment Building, 1511 K Street, NW, Washington, DC 20015

National Oil Jobbers Council, 1001 Connecticut Avenue, NW, Washington, DC 20036

National Paper Box Manufacturers Association, 121 North Bread Street, Suite 910, Philadelphia, PA 19107

National Paper Trade Association, 220 East 42d Street, New York, NY 10017

National Parking Association, 1101 17th Street, NW, Washington, DC 20036

National Restaurant Association, 1530 North Lake Shore Drive, Chicago, IL 60610

National Retail Furniture Association, 1150 Merchandise Mart Plaza, Chicago, IL 60654

National Retail Hardware Association, 964 North Pennsylvania Avenue, Indianapolis, IN 46204

National Retail Merchants Association, 100 West 31st Street, New York, NY 10001

National Shoe Retailers Association, 200 Madison Avenue, New York, NY 10016

National Sporting Goods Association, 23 East Jackson Boulevard, Chicago, IL 60604

National Stationery and Office Equipment Association, Investment Building, 1511 K Street, NW, Washington, DC 20005

National Tire Dealers and Retreaders Association, 1343 L Street, NW, Washington, DC 20005

National Wholesale Druggists' Association, 220 East 42d Street, New York, NY 10017

National Wholesale Hardware Association, 1900 Arch Street, Philadelphia, PA 19103

National Wholesale Jewelers Association, 1900 Arch Street, Philadelphia, PA 19103

North American Heating & Airconditioning Wholesalers Association, 1200 West 5th Avenue, Columbus, OH 43212

Optical Wholesalers Association, 222 West Adams Street, Chicago, IL 60606

Paint and Wallpaper Association of America, 7935 Clayton Road, St. Louis, MO 63117

Petroleum Equipment Institute, 525 Dowell Building, Tulsa, OK 74114

Printing Industries of America, 711 14th Street, NW, Washington, DC 20005

Robert Morris Association, Philadelphia National Bank Building, Philadelphia, PA 19107

Scientific Apparatus Makers Associates, 20 North Wacker Drive, Chicago, IL 60606

Shoe Service Institute of America, 222 West Adams Street, Chicago, IL 60606

Super Market Institute, Inc., 200 East Ontario Street, Chicago, IL 60611

United Fresh Fruit and Vegetable Association, 777 14th Street, NW, Washington, DC 20005

United States Wholesale Grocers' Association, 1511 K Street, NW, Washington, DC 20005

Urban Land Institute, 1200 18th Street, NW, Washington, DC 20036

Wine and Spirits Wholesalers of America, 319 North Fourth Street, St. Louis, MO 63102

MARKETING PLAN FOR "LIMIT"—DISPOSABLE ALCOHOL TESTING UNIT

Developed
by

SCOTT GILMOUR
STEVEN LUBEGA
ANDREW SMITH
MATT SMITH

TABLE OF CONTENTS

I. EXECUTIVE SUMMARY

This report presents a detailed marketing plan for introducing a disposable alcohol testing unit (DATU) into the Los Angeles and Orange counties consumer market.

On the basis of information we gathered during the course of our research, we determined that there is a considerable need for this product and a large potential demand. The number of drunk-driving arrests in Los Angeles and Orange counties last year was 106,585, while the number of drunk-driving occurrences exceeded some 213,000,000. Following a detailed analysis of our target market, we projected the sale of over 205,000 units, totaling some $197,-000 in sales, with profits exceeding $50,000.

Our marketing strategy consists of repositioning a product designed for law enforcement use and promoting it in the consumer market. Market penetration pricing of $1.69 will be used for initial introduction, distributed through existing channels, utilizing agent middlemen and wholesale distributors of sundry items within liquor stores. The product will be sold through grocery and liquor stores, with the primary promotional emphasis on point-of-purchase displays. Planned date of introduction is to begin in May 1983.

II. INTRODUCTION

In 1978, there were 51,500 traffic fatalities on the nation's highways, 50% or some 26,300 of which were caused by drunk drivers. In addition, more Americans died at the hands of drunk drivers during the past two years than were killed in Vietnam during the entire U.S. involvement.[13]

Recent studies by such groups as the National Highway Traffic Safety Administration (NHTSA), the Gallup Poll, and others indicate that 6 out of every 100 (6%) cars you pass on the highway may be operated by a drunk driver, increasing to 10 out of every 100 (10%) on the weekends.[13]

In an effort to reduce these unacceptable figures, a number of interest groups have sprung up across the country, such as MADD (Mothers Against Drunk Drivers), and have begun a concerted effort to pass tougher drinking and driving laws. Already twenty-seven state legislators this year have passed their own versions of "the toughest drunk driving law in the country," while twenty other states have raised the legal drinking age.[13]

Clearly, the need exists to find a solution to this problem. For our marketing plan we are proposing a unique approach to this situation. The solution we are offering is a disposable "go–no go" alcohol breath analyzer, a low-cost, inexpensive one-time-use product that can determine whether a person is legally intoxicated. "Anti-drunk driving crusaders hope that breath-testing devices will become as much a fixture on the social scene as the shaker and stirrer."[13]

The purpose of this "Marketing Plan Report" is to present a viable means of marketing such a product to the general consumer in an effort to reduce the number of alcohol-related accidents that occur on the nation's highways.

III. SITUATIONAL ANALYSIS

Market Characteristics

Because the product we are proposing to market is unique, the characteristics of our market are not as clear as we would like. The information we came across in our research effort, however, has presented us with some very useful data.

To begin, motor vehicle accidents represent the nation's single greatest killer of people in the under-forty age group, the highest rate occurring between the ages of sixteen and twenty-four. Of all causes of death in all age groups, automobile deaths rank fourth after heart disease, cancer, and strokes. Add to that information that 50% of all traffic accidents are caused by drunken drivers, and you begin to see the potential market for such a product as ours.

The number of people arrested in the Los Angeles–Orange County area last year for drunk driving was 106,585.[12] Add to that knowledge that only an estimated 1 drunk driver out of 2000 is actually caught and arrested, and you really begin to see the potential number of prospects for our breath analyzer.[3]

The Los Angeles marketing area is one of the largest and most powerful markets in the United States, accounting for at least 40% of the population, households, effective buying income, and retail sales of the entire state of California.

In 1978, there were some 9 million people living within this area, equating to some 3.5 million households. According to a *Los Angeles Times* market research "Consumer Trend Analysis" on beer, wine, and distilled spirits, more than half of all Los Angeles households reported purchasing at least one type of alcoholic beverage in the preceding thirty days. Figure 1 illustrates the purchase incidence of any alcoholic beverage during the prior thirty-day periods. Overall, the incidence of purchase was generally higher for beer than for wine or distilled spirits.

Family income is an important determinant of beverage purchase and thus would be of concern to us as well. Alcoholic beverage purchases are more prominent in higher-income households. In 1977, 39.6% of all Los Angeles households earnings incomes of $25,000 or more annually purchased an alcoholic beverage within the preceding thirty-day period.

Equally important is the fact that fully 47.9% of the households

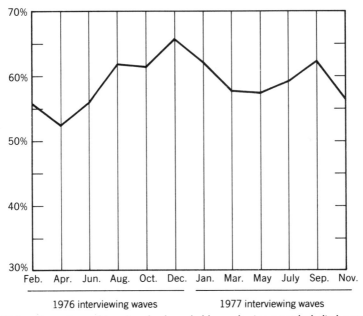

FIGURE 1.   Percentage of Los Angeles households purchasing any alcoholic beverage in last thirty days.

where the age of the household head was under forty accounted for 64.3% of the beer purchases, 56.2% of the wine purchases, and 50.4% of the distilled spirits purchases.

Households in which the head has had some college education or more dominated total expenditures for alcoholic beverages. The 59.1% of all Los Angeles households where this was the case was responsible for 59.5% of the beer purchases, 80.3% of the wine purchases, and 73.1% of the distilled spirits purchases.

Finally, households headed by someone in a professional or managerial position were the primary contributors to total expenditures on alcoholic beverages. These two occupational groups made up 38.1% of all Los Angeles households and were responsible for purchasing 39.7% of the beer sold, 56.7% of the wine sold, and 50.8% of the distilled spirits sold.

Examination of purchase patterns to determine where purchases of alcoholic beverages were made, by type of store, found that the majority of purchases were made at grocery stores, followed by liquor stores, drug stores, discount stores, department stores, and others. The following chart breaks down the specific place of purchase by beverage type:

	Beer, %	Wine, %	Distilled Spirits, %
Grocery store	61.5	60.0	40.9
Liquor store	36.6	37.8	54.5
Drug store	1.2	1.9	2.7
Discount store	2.1	0.9	3.1
Department store	0.7	0.9	0.8
Other	2.8	5.9	2.7
Don't know	—	0.3	1.6

The vast majority of households indicated the male household head was the primary decision maker and purchaser of alcoholic beverages, responsible for 62.5% of the beer purchases, 52.2% of the wine purchases, and 61.5% of the distilled spirits purchases.

Among households purchasing an alcoholic beverage in the preceding thirty-day period, about 7 out of 10 reported serving each type once a week or more, with beer (72.7%) being more likely to be served on a daily basis than either wine (69.7%) or distilled spirits (68.4%). Almost two-thirds (65.1%) of all Los Angeles households reported serving an alcoholic beverage within the preceding thirty-day period, with beer (47%) and wine (45%) being the most popular. More than 13% of these households serve them on a daily basis.

One study concluded that adults in the Los Angeles marketing area are more likely than the average U.S. adult to consume most types of alcoholic beverages and the tendency to consume increases with socioeconomic level: "In this higher-than-average liquor-drinking market, marketers who zero in on Los Angeles adults in the higher-demographic groups are getting the best possible target audience for their products."

Key Success Factors

1. *Limited Competition.* No known competitors exist in the Southern California test market who:

   Distribute a similar product at a low price level, therefore creating a price advantage

   Distribute a disposable device, therefore creating a product portability advantage

2. *Legal Climate.* Currently the trend is heading toward stricter penalties for driving while intoxicated.

   The trend has clearly provided penalties of increasing severity over time (see legal appendix).

3. *Ease of Operation.* The DATU is relatively small, "pocket-sized" (Figure 2).

   The usage procedure is simple (i.e., blow breath sample into tube and compare color change to calibration on instrument).

4. *Price versus Value.* DATU provides relatively inexpensive protection to drivers who are under the influence of alcohol to some degree.

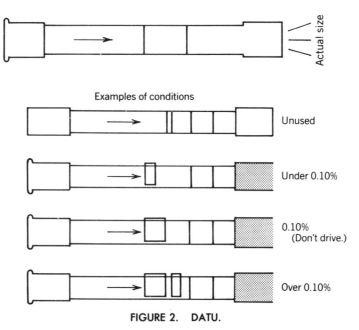

FIGURE 2.   DATU.

Value exists in that DATU is significantly less expensive than the potentially negative outcomes of driving while intoxicated including:

a.   Loss of license
b.   Legal fine
c.   Loss of life

Price has been designed to be within affordable reach of target market (i.e., under $3).

Competition and Product Comparisons

To date there are no manufacturers who have distributed a DATU to the consumer market. There are three manufacturers in the United States who produce breath–alcohol testing equipment: C.M.I. Incorporated, Minturn, Colorado; Intoximeter Incorporated, St. Louis, Missouri; and Smith and Wesson General Ordinance Equipment Company, Springfield, Massachusetts.

Their major marketing emphasis is toward the law enforcement agencies throughout the United States and abroad. The equipment they produce is used to gain evidential-quality results as to a suspect's breath–alcohol count. The results are used as evidence in the conviction of an intoxicated individual.

These products are very expensive, ranging in price from $300 to over $3500. Their ownership by the general public for self-testing is nonexistent, due to the prohibitive pricing. The competition posed by these manufacturers should be considered potential, rather than direct. Their present market emphasis is due to the expense of their current product line and lack of familiarity with the public consumer market.

The exception to the expensive product lines produced by these manufacturers is the Alcolyser PST (preliminary screening device) produced by Intoximeter Incorporated (Figure 3). This device is used by mobile highway patrol and sheriff units throughout the United States. Approximately 1.5 million of these units have been sold to this market. The PST is a disposable, one-time-use device that is portable and reasonably accurate for its intended use. The law enforcement agencies use this device in the field instead of the manual dexterity manipulations to determine a person's ability to drive. The sales of the PST have increased steadily as its application qualities have been recognized. Eventually, the subjective judgment call will be replaced by the PST or a similar product.

In Europe, a similar product has been successfully introduced to the consumer market, with sales of approximately 12 million units. Europe's generally harsher penalties for driving under the influence of alcohol have greatly increased the need for this type of product. For example, in Switzerland the penalty for drunk driving is the loss of one's driver's license for five years. Our current laws and penalties are not nearly as severe but are moving in that general direction.

The Alcolyser PST meets our product specifications and will be used for the initial introduction to the consumer market. We are repositioning this existing product for use by the general consumer.

Basically, any one of the manufacturers could produce a DATU

Description	The "Alcolyser" is a simple, portable, scientific device for measuring the alcohol content of blood via expired breath. The indication of the Alcolyser detector tube is based on Widmark's reaction principle, with the alcohol in expired breath reacting with the yellow crystals and turning them green.
	For the test, expired air (mixture of tidal and alveolar air) is blown through the tube into a plastic bag in approximately 20 seconds. The "Alcolyser" will indicate an absolute quantity of alcohol of as little as 5 mg. or an alcohol concentration in blood of 0.3 promille. (30 mg. of alcohol per 100 ml. of blood.)
	The length of the green stain in the tube is proportional to the blood alcohol concentration. When the green stain extends to the red mark at the center of the tube, then the alcohol level in the blood corresponds to the prescribed limit as indicated on the box label.
Calibration	The Alcolyser detector tubes have been calibrated against direct blood alcohol analysis employing a gas chromatograph with a flame ionization detector.
	The prescribed legal limits of alcohol in the blood vary from one country to another. The ALCO-LYSER range consists of the following calibrated detector tubes:
	ALCOLYSER 50, 80, 100, 125 and
	150 mg./100 ml. blood.
Precautions	It is important to allow at least fifteen minutes to elapse after taking alcoholic drink in order to allow mouth alcohol to disappear. Smoking should be avoided prior to breath test.
Estimation of blood alcohol level	The basis of the determination of blood alcohol via expired breath relies on the established ratio[2] between the alcohol content of blood to that of breath (2,100 to 1). Provided the breath test is carried out in accordance with the manufacturers instructions this ratio holds true.
Correlation results	The results given in Table 1 were carried out at Indiana Toxicology, Department of Police Administration, University of Indiana, Illinois, U.S.A.

FIGURE 3.   Alcolyser PST Preliminary Screening Test.

	BLOOD	ALCO-LYSER	BREATH-ALYSER	BLOOD	ALCO-LYSER	BREATH-ALYSER
	.09	.09	.07	.07	.08	.08
	.06	.08	.07	.04	.04	.03
TABLE 1	.05	.07	.05	.03	.04	.04
	.07	.08	.08	.09	.10	.09
	.11	.12	.12	.06	.08	.06
	.08	.09	.08	.07	.10	.09
	.08	.09	.08	.14	.12	.16
	.07	.08	.07	.07	.09	.09
	.08	.09	.07	.10	.10	.12
	.10	.10	.10	.03	.04	.02

Alcolyser screening test calibrated for 0.10%

Summary of Results

(i) Within the limits of accuracy of alcohol detector tubes results show that there is a good correlation between the "Alcolyser" detector tube and direct blood alcohol estimations.[4]

(ii) When the blood alcohol concentration is at the prescribed limit the "Alcolyser" gives a reliability of over 90%.

(iii) When the blood alcohol level is above the prescribed limit, then the reliability of the "Alcolyser" approaches 100%.

(iv) When the blood alcohol level is below the limit, reliability is of the order of 90% (just below the limit) but approaching 100% when the alcohol level is signficantly below the limit.

When used in accordance with the Manufacturer's instructions the "Alcolyser" can provide a rapid and reliable guide to the alcohol level of the blood.

References

1. Ducie, W. L. and Jones, T. P. Means for detecting breath-alcohol, Pat. No. 1,143,818.
2. Harger, et al. Journal of Biological Chemistry, 1950, 18B, 197.
3. Curry, et al. The Analyst, November, 1966, 91, 742.
4. Jones, T. P. Alcohol and Traffic Safety, 5th International Conference, Freiburg, 1969.

FIGURE 3. (continued)

because the technology is simple and the capital equipment costs are relatively low. Our competitive edge is our expertise in the consumer market and their lack of interest in selling to this market.

Technology

The technology upon which the DATU is based is incredibly simple. It is based primarily upon the scientific principle that deep lung breath and blood alcohol are related in a definite and predictable way.

The DATU is comprised of a glass tube containing potassium dichromate crystals and a catalyst which maximizes the presence of the dichromate ions. We aim to maximize the concentration of the dichromate ion because when one breathes over the crystals, the moisture in the breath dissolves them, at which point both chromate and dichromate ions exist. The dichromate ion, however, has a higher oxidation potential (E^o = 1.33 volts) than the chromate ion (E^o = −0.13 volts).

E^o represents an oxidation potential measured in volts. More oxidation takes place if the change in energy is greater.

When alcohol is introduced into the DATU, the dichromate ion oxidizes the alcohol (C_2H_5OH). The resultant products are chromic ions (responsbile for the change in color). The equation below shows the reaction if a catalyst like sulfuric acid (H_2SO_4) was used.[5]

		Alcohol	Chromic sulfate	Acetaldehyde
$K_2Cr_2O_7$	+ 3 C_2H_5OH −	$Cr_2(SO_4)_3$	+ 3 CH_3CHO	

Potassium dichromate +	4 H_2SO_4 +	K_2SO_4	+	7 H_2O
	Sulfuric acid	Potassium sulfate		Water

Legal Environment

The legal environment relating to the sale and consumption of alcoholic beverages in California is to be a crucial variable in our marketing strategy. In fact, the whole raison d'être for our product is embodied in the realization that drinking and driving will in all probability lead to injury of some sort. The recognition of this fact by the law and the consequent penalties are the two factors that make our market viable.

Legally, a person is deemed intoxicated (in California) when their blood alcohol reaches 0.10%. It is well recognized, however, that functions critical in driving coordination are impaired quite a bit before the 0.10% level. Because "driving under the influence" (DUI) is rightly presumed to represent unreasonable risk both to the driver and to others who may be using the roads, penalties for doing so are becoming stiffer and stiffer. In addition, under California's "implied consent law" (see appendix), the relevant authorities can require any driver using the highways to submit to an alcohol test (blood, breath, or urine).

If the criminal liability of being intoxicated is frightening, the civil liability is equally so, if not more so. While criminal liability may mean up to three months in jail and $500 in fines, civil liability could easily expose an individual to personal financial ruin.

Under civil liability, specifically under the tort liability of "negligence," tort-feasor may literally have his or her pants sued off. Prior to 1971, for instance, "a commercial vendor of alcoholic beverages could not be held liable to a *third party* injured by an individual who became intoxicated as the result of the negligent serving of alcoholic beverages."[4]

In June 1971, the California Supreme Court handed down *Vesley v. Sager,* 5 Cal. 3d 153, 95 Cal. Rptr. 623; which opened up the door of so-called third-party liability. With the decision in Vesley the then-reigning theories which had barred liability (theories relating to proximate and superseding causation) went out the door.[4]

It is well recognized, therefore, that one can be held liable for harm caused to another through an intermediate party—a kind of vicarious liability.

Section 430 of the American Restatement of Law on Torts states that there has to be an adequate causal relationship between the person harmed and the individual who causes the harm (the actor).

Additionally, it must be shown that the actor's conduct was negligent before liability can attach:

> The actor's conduct, to be negligent toward another, must involve an unreasonable risk of: (1) causing harm to a class of persons of which the other [plaintiff] is a member and (2) subjecting the other to the hazard from which the harm results.[1]

Section 431 holds that the actor's negligent conduct is a legal cause for harm if it was a substantial factor in bringing about the harm and if "there is no rule of law relieving the actor from liability because of the manner in which his negligence has resulted in harm."[1]

In Section 432, we find that even if there were some other factor operating at the same time as the actor's negligence, which factor in itself would cause the ensuing harm, the actor may not thereby be relieved of substantially causing the harm.[1]

Section 435 establishes that foreseeability of the harm is immaterial. In other words, once it has been decided that the actor was negligent, it becomes immaterial whether or not the person actually or reasonably should have foreseen that harm would result from the action so long as the conduct was a substantial cause of the harm.[1]

Section 437 states that once it has been established that the actor's negligence is a substantial factor in bringing about harm, it is immaterial, too, that the actor "exercised reasonable care to prevent harm from taking effect." The actor continues to be liable for ensuing harm.[1]

What constitutes negligent conduct? According to the restatement:

> In order that either an act or a failure to act may be negligent, the one essential factor is that the actor realizes or should realize that the act or the failure to act involves an *unreasonable risk of harm* to an interest of another, which is protected against unintended invasion.[1] [*Emphasis added.*]

It seems apparent, therefore, that the legal environment within which we will implement our marketing strategy is ripe for our expolitation.

Social Environment

With regard to the social environment surrounding our breath analyzer and its use to reduce the number of drunk drivers, there is a good deal of activity going on.

At least two major organizations have been formed within the past three years in an effort to provide a vent for public outcry. The persons responsible for founding these organizations, MADD (Mothers Against Drunk Driving) and RID (Remove Intoxicated Drivers), lost loved ones because of alcohol-related accidents. In addition, some twenty-seven states have passed or put into effect tougher drinking and driving laws this year alone, while twenty other states have actually raised the legal-drinking age.

In a recent survey, published in the September 1982 edition of *Glamour* magazine, 60% of the respondents said they thought the drinking age should be raised to twenty-one in all states. In addition, 69% said they would not feel safe driving if they had been drinking or riding with a driver who had been. When asked what they would do if they had planned to drive home with someone who had had too much to drink, 7% said they would refuse to go, 61% said they would insist that someone else drive, and 26% said they would call a taxi or go with someone else.

When asked if they thought police should have the right to give breath tests, 89% said yes. Finally, 53% of the respondents said that drivers who are arrested for drunk driving should have their license revoked for six months to a year, and 89% said that all learning drivers should be required to attend classes about the danger of drunk driving.

Problems and Opportunities

1. *Market Characteristics*
   Problem. The actual product demand is unknown.
   Opportunities. The geographic area targeted (Los Angeles and Orange counties) is densely populated. Forty percent of Cali-

fornia's population resides here, allowing ease of covering target market.[7]

The average alcohol consumption in this area exceeds the national average.[7] This, combined with the fact that freeways are the major source of transportation, creates a large potential for driving while intoxicated.

Existing distribution channels are available through sales representatives who handle liquor and sundry items.

2. *Competition*
    Problem. The technology is simple and easily duplicated.
    Opportunities. Being the first in the market maximizes the chance to become the market leader.

    The consumer market is currently ignored by the competition.

3. *Product Comparisons*
    Problem. DATU is designed for one-time usage, as compared with multiple usage of competitors' higher-priced units.
    Opportunities. The device is small and portable, as compared with other similar units.

    Disposability, as compared with multiple usage of competitors' products, creates convenience.

    DATU is relatively inexpensive, being priced well under competitors' units.

4. *Manufacturing and Technical Factors*
    Problem. DATU has a limited shelf life of approximately six months due to perishability of chemicals employed.
    Opportunities. The simple technology will allow eventual "in-house" manufacturing.

5. *Environmental Climate*

   Problem. Psychographics with respect to target market attitudes toward admittance of being under the influence of alcohol are unknown. (Will potentially intoxicated drivers react defensively to being told they are "drunk"?)

   Opportunities. There is a trend toward stricter drinking and driving laws (see legal appendix).

   The trend has also shown increasing mobilization of action groups (e.g., MADD, or Mothers Against Drunk Drivers).

   The "innkeepers law" is most likely to be reenacted (allows control of patrons' alcohol consumption by placing responsibility on innkeeper for results of drunk drivers' actions).

6. *Internal Resources*

   Problem. DATU requires $30,000 in start-up and introduction costs.

   Opportunities. The existing product manufactured by Intoximeter, Incorporated, meets the need.

   The relatively low cost of the project has a high expected return.

IV. MARKETING OBJECTIVES

Target Market

On the basis of the information presented in our "Situational Analysis," we identified the following target market segment as potential product users:

Males who are members of households where household income exceeds $25,000 annually, are in the twenty-one- to forty-year-old age group, have had at least some college education, and are employed in professional or managerial positions.

In addition, the ideal purchaser would shop frequently at grocery stores and could be either male or female as the split between sex in purchasing alcoholic beverages in such markets is almost even.

Target Volume in Dollars and/or Units

Once again, on the basis of the information presented in our "Situational Analysis," we are projecting the sale of approximately 205,000 units. Arriving at this number involved a complicated and detailed assimilation of data as the following presentation shows:

Percent of households earning $25,000 or more	40.6%
Percent of households less than 40 years of age	47.9%
Percent of households having some college education or more	59.1%
Percent of households where household head is employed in a professional or managerial position	38.1%
Average households in one or more groups	46.4%
Estimated percent of households falling in all categories (as agreed to by L.A. Times Marketing Research Department)	40.0%
Percent of households in all categories (target market)	18.6%
Number of households in market	× 3,417,000
Number of households in target market	635,500
Percent of driving households[2]	× 66.4%
Number of driving households in target market	421,980
Estimated percent of social drinkers who drive while intoxicated[4]	× 15.0%

Number of drinking-driving households in target market	63,297
Average number of occurrences of driving while intoxicated per year[3]	× 65
Number of occurrences of driving while intoxicated by target market, last year	4,114,310
Projected market share captured	× 5%
Projected unit sales	205,700
Unit sales price	0.96¢
Projected total annual sales	$ 196,800

1. $\dfrac{6{,}250{,}600 \text{ drinking drivers in L.A.-Orange counties}}{9{,}410{,}366 \text{ residents L.A.-Orange counties}} = 66.4\%$

2.
106,585	Drunk-driving arrests
× 2,000	Estimated number of individuals not arrested per every individual arrested[3]
213,200,000	Drunk-driving occurrences in L.A.-Orange counties per year
÷ 1,562,650	Drivers who drink and drive (6,250,600 drivers × 25% estimate[3]
136.39	Number of times each person was driving while intoxicated
× 50%	Estimated split of drunk-driving occurrence between "problem drinkers" and "social drinkers"[3]
68.2%	Rounded to 65

It should be noted that the 5% figure for our projected captured share of the market was our best estimate based on the information we came across during the course of our research, as well as our knowledge of market conditions (including input from the manufacturer, a prospective wholesale-distributor for sundry items in liquor stores, and other individuals involved in marketing this product in another area of the country).

Profit Analysis

	Unit Cost, $	Total, $
Projected sales (205,000 units)		$198,850
Less:		
Variable Costs		
Alcolyser	0.40	82,000
Packaging	0.065	13,325
Labor	0.02	4,100
Promotion	0.08	16,400
Shipping	0.04	10,000
Total variable costs		125,825
Fixed Costs		
General and administrative	0.10	$ 20,500
Total fixed and variable costs		$146,325
Net profit after year one before taxes		$ 50,475

Percent Profit

$$\$50,475 \div \$198,850 = \quad 25.4\%$$

Break-Even Analysis

$$1x = 0.605x + 20,500$$

Approximately 51,900 units

$36,589

V. STRATEGY

The marketing strategy for the DATU is to introduce the product in an area that is densely populated and has a specified demographic makeup: Los Angeles and Orange counties were chosen on the basis of the large number of drivers and other factors already noted in our "Situational Analysis."

Product Strategy

The keystones of our product strategy are based on the following: simplicity, quality, and convenience. The product is extremely simple—both in conception and in use. We believe that to appeal to the average consumer who merely wants to discover the "risk factor" after a few beers, the product has to be simple. The device should be psychologically comforting and not elicit aversion, which it is likely to do if it were complicated.

We believe, and our research confirms, that most people are more interested in knowing whether or not they should drive (go–no go) than in knowing the actual level of their blood alcohol. In fact, our research indicates that knowing the actual level of blood alcohol is psychologically discomforting because it causes apprehension about the physiological effects of the alcohol. We do not want to turn our potential customers off. Neither do we want to scare them away from drinking altogether, for it is from the drinking population that we draw our market.

The simplicity of our product is embodied in one word: *packaging.* Our packaging will carry our message of simplicity par excellence. Thus packaging will fulfill the fundamental marketing concepts of containment and promotion.[14] Packaging is especially crucial for us since we are marketing the DATU as a convenience item. As is noted by authorities in the field: "Packaging is usually a more critical element for convenience goods than for shopping or specialty goods."[14]

The second keystone of our product strategy, *quality,* is ensured through the confidence we have in the technology behind the DATU. Quality will become an increasingly important element as sales pick up, because good quality will ensure user-oriented promotion for us through word-of-mouth recommendation.

The third keystone, *convenience,* is reflected by the disposable nature of the DATU. The device will be a one-use item procured at a relative giveaway price. It will be small enough to put in one's pocket, glove compartment, or briefcase and will be easily disposed of once used. There will be no clumsy meters to unsecure and no bags to save. Our product strategy can, therefore, be summarized by the following diagram:

Key Elements	*How Achieved*
Simplicity ⟶	Packaging/technology
Quality ⟶	Technology
Convenience ⟶	Disposability

Pricing Strategy

Our pricing strategy will complement our product strategy. We want to enter our selected market and achieve maximum level of penetration. We shall, therefore, use a price-penetration strategy: Enter the desired market at a low price and market the DATU as a convenience item.

Promotional Strategy

Our promotional strategy will be to achieve maximum reach with our message with minimum resource outlay. This strategy is dictated by the limited resources we have on hand. Fortunately, we believe the DATU lends itself to the use of just such a strategy.

The message content of our pitch will be unambiguous. The DATU is designed to give a drinking driver a quick-decision criterion. *The actual decision made must be the driver's.* It will be necessary to embody this in our promotional messages to guard against possible legal liability.

The promotional message will also bring to bear on the driver the possible legal consequences of *not knowing whether he or she has reached the 0.10% blood alcohol level.* Thus we will aid the driver in making a "safe" decision. Note should be taken, however, that our message will not be designed to *discourage* the driver from the consumption of alcohol. In fact, our message will be designed to *encourage* the *responsible* consumption of alcoholic beverages.

Because of the minimum outlay approach, we will not advertise via television or print, at the outset. The details of implementation of this strategy are enumerated under "Promotional Tactics."

Distribution Strategy

Since the DATU is to be marketed as a convenience item, its distribution is a crucial element. Again we will aim for reach and penetration.

The ultimate consumer of the DATU will be most effectively

reached through the retail supermarket and retail liquor stores. Our strategy will be to use a bichanneled approach, on the one hand distributing through wholesale distributors and on the other through agent middlemen.

The distribution channel is presented in Figure 4.

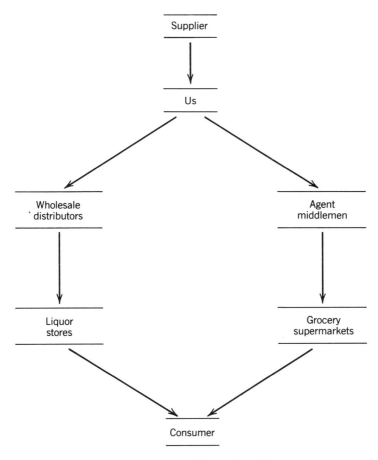

FIGURE 4.   Distribution channel.

Marketing Strategy—A Recoup and a Projection

The entire strategy is product-driven. We believe we have found an unexploited niche in the universe of drinking drivers. Our product is going to satisfy the need which has already been created by stiff legal and social consequences of driving under the influence of alcohol. We see an even rougher horizon: the consequences are to get even tougher.

In the future, we see our sales generated from desire by consumers to know their alcohol level for three reasons:

1. Criminal liability (DUI).
2. Liability of commercial vendors who negligently serve alcohol
3. Liability of hosts (in private homes) who negligently serve alcohol

We see a time when insurance companies may actively get in on the market to cover "liquor liability." At present, there are some "general liability comprehensive policies," but many of them exclude liability for harm caused by liquor consumption.[4] We also see insurance companies requiring policyholders to keep a kit of breath-analysis devices. In future, therefore, we see a potential for marketing to large institutional buyers—whereupon product changes might be necessary.

As far as our present legal liability is concerned, for harm caused by a drunken driver who may use our product, the following is our strategy:

To negate the legally implied warranty of fitness of the DATU for a particular purpose, we will have clear and unambiguous language stating our nonliability except for the ordinary purpose for which the DATU is intended.[6]

The express warranties we make will be in boldfaced, clear, and unambiguous language.[6]

We are not liable under present product liability theories for harm caused by our products unless the products were defective.[6]

VI. TACTICS

Product

1. Arrange a contractual supply agreement for a minimum of one year with Intoximeter, Incorporated. This will be done now (December 1982) and purchase will begin in March 1983.
2. Obtain support from consumer awareness groups (MADD, RID, and CHP) in January 1983. The cost is zero.
3. Purchase DATU in an initial quantity of 30,000 units from Intoximeter, Incorporated, at a cost of $0.40 per unit, in March 1983.

Promotion

1. Produce point-of-purchase display board in January 1983 (Figure 5).
2. Package DATU in shrink to fit material onto cardboard backing which will hang on display board (see Figures 6 and 7 for illustration). Will occur in March 1983.
3. Contact television, radio, and newspapers in May 1983 for creation of public information news segments. (ABC and CBS television have already shown interest).
4. During DATU introduction in May 1983, employ information leaflets at point of purchase.
5. Use the name "Limit" as trademark of DATU, implying the function of the device (i.e., a person has reached his or her alcohol limit).

Price

1. "Limit" will be priced at $1.69 each (see Figure 8 for pricing breakdown).

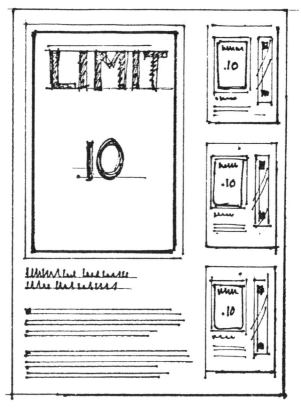

FIGURE 5.   Point of purchase display.

Distribution

1. Distribute "Limit" in Los Angeles and Orange counties in May 1983.
2. Use brokers who distribute alcohol-related products for grocery, drug, and discount stores. This will begin in March 1983, with "Limit" being introduced to retailers for May 1983 delivery. The brokers are paid 25% of the wholesale price.
3. Use sundry-item wholesale distributors for liquor store penetration. These will be paid 25% of the wholesale price, and the timing is identical to item 2 above.

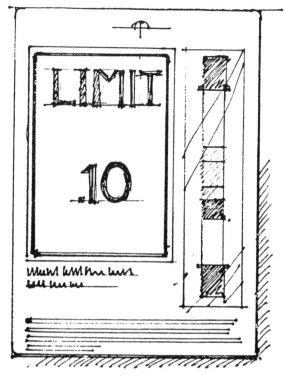

FIGURE 6.   Hang card.

VII. REFERENCES

1. *American Law Institute Restatement of the Law,* 2nd Torts Edition, Vol. 2 (St. Paul, Minn.: American Law Institute Publishers).
2. *Glamour,* "This Is What You Thought About . . . Raising the Drinking Age." September, 1982.
3. J. Linda Mood, "Driving Drunk." *Car & Driver,* September, 1982.
4. *Insurance Company of North America vs. Aaron Shanedling et al.;* 2nd Civil Suit #51790, Court of Appeal of the State of California, 2nd Appellate District (mimeograph).
5. Interview with William Kalema, Ph.D. (chemical engineering), California Institute of Technology, 1983.
6. Len Young Smith and G. Gale Roberson, *Business Law,* 4th ed. (St. Paul, Minn.: West Publishing Co., 1977).
7. *Los Angeles Times Marketing Research.* "Beer/Wine/Champagne/Distilled Spirits Consumer Trend Analysis," 1979.
8. J. Marks, "Drinking and Driving: A Ticket to Disaster." *Teen,* May, 1982.

9. Interview with Bud Miller, National Highway Traffic Safety Administration, San Francisco, Calif., November, 1982.
10. *National Underwriter*, "Joint Action Needed [Editorial Comment]," October 31, 1981.
11. Annmarie B. Piontek, "Drunk Driver: Challenge to Industry." *National Underwriter*, Sept. 12, 1980.
12. Interview with Charlotte Rae, State of California Criminal Statistic Program: Uniform Crime Reporting Unit, Sacramento, Calif., November, 1982.
13. M. Starr, "The War against Drunk Driving." *Newsweek*, Sept. 13, 1982.
14. Stewart H. Rewoldt, James D. Scott, and Martin R. Warshaw, *Introduction to Marketing Management* (Homewood, Ill: Richard D. Irwin, Inc., 1981).

LEGAL APPENDIX

§ 13353. Chemical Blood, Breath, or Urine Tests

(a) Any person who drives a motor vehicle upon a highway shall be deemed to have given his consent to a chemical test of his blood,

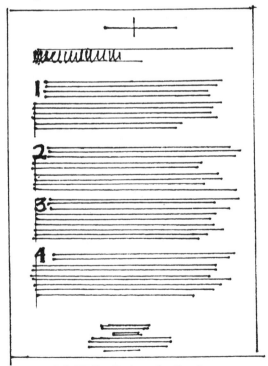

FIGURE 7.   Back card—directions.

Variable Costs		Unit
Alcolyser		$0.40
Packaging		0.065
Labor		0.02
Promotion		0.08
Shipping and handling		0.04
		$0.605
Fixed Cost		
General and administrative		0.10
Total cost		$0.705
List Price		$1.69
Less: Retailer margin 40%		0.48
Wholesaler margin	25%	0.24
		0.97
Total cost		0.705
Profit		$0.265
Percent profit		27.3%
Actual profit due to round-off		
Error		25.4%

FIGURE 8. Pricing in the consumer market (based on 10,000-unit production runs).

breath or urine for the purpose of determining the alcoholic content of his blood if lawfully arrested for any offense allegedly committed while the person was driving a motor vehicle under the influence of intoxicating liquor. The test shall be incidental to a lawful arrest and administration at the direction of a peace officer having reasonable cause to believe such person was driving a motor vehicle upon a highway while under the influence of intoxicating liquor. Such person shall be told that his failure to submit to or complete such a chemical test will result in the suspension of his privilege to operate a motor vehicle for a period of six months.

The person arrested shall have the choice of whether the test shall be of his blood, breath or urine, and he shall be advised by the officer that he has such choice. If the person arrested either is incapable, or states that he is incapable, of completing any chosen test, he shall then have the choice of submitting to and completing any of the remaining tests or test, and he shall be advised by the officer that he has such choice.

Such person shall also be advised by the officer that he does not have the right to have an attorney present before stating whether he will submit to a test, before deciding which test to take, or during administration of the test chosen.

Any person who is dead, unconscious, or otherwise in a condition rendering him incapable of refusal shall be deemed not to have withdrawn his consent and such tests may be administered whether or not such person is told that his failure to submit to or complete the test will result in the suspension of his privilege to operate a motor vehicle.

(b) If any such person refuses the officer's request to submit to, or fails to complete, a chemical test, the department, upon receipt of the officer's sworn statement that he had reasonable cause to believe such person had been driving a motor vehicle upon a highway while under the influence of intoxicating liquor and that the person had refused to submit to, or failed to complete, the test after being requested by the officer, shall suspend his privilege to operate a motor vehicle for a period of six months. No such suspension shall become effective until 10 days after the giving of written notice thereof, as provided for in subdivision (c).

(c) The department shall immediately notify such person in writing of the action taken and upon his request in writing and within 15 days from the date of receipt of such request shall afford him an opportunity for a hearing in the same manner and under the same conditions as provided in Article 3 (commencing with Section 14100) of Chapter 3 of this division. For the purposes of this section the scope of the hearing shall cover the issues of whether the peace officer had reasonable cause to believe the person had been driving a motor vehicle upon a highway while under the influence of intoxicating liquor, whether the person was placed under arrest, whether he refused to submit to, or failed to complete, the test after being requested by a peace officer, and whether, except for the persons described in paragraph (a) above who are incapable of refusing, he had been told that his driving privilege would be suspended if he refused to submit to, or failed to complete, the test.

An application for a hearing made by the affected person within 10 days of receiving notice of the department's action shall operate to stay the suspension by the department for a period of 15 days during which time the department must afford a hearing. If the department fails to afford a hearing within 15 days, the suspension shall not take place until such time as the person is granted a hearing and is notified of the department's action as hereinafter provided. However, if the affected person requests that the hearing be continued to a date beyond the 15-day period, the suspension shall become effective immediately upon receipt of the department's notice that said request for continuance has been granted.

If the department determines upon a hearing of the matter to suspend the affected person's privilege to operate a motor vehicle, the suspension herein provided shall not become effective until five days after receipt by said person of the department's notification of such suspension.

(d) Any person who is afflicted with hemophilia shall be exempt from the blood test required by this section.

(e) Any person who is afflicted with a heart condition and is using an anticoagulant under the direction of a physician and surgeon shall be exempt from the blood test required by this section.

(f) A person lawfully arrested by any offense allegedly committed while the person was driving a motor vehicle under the influence of intoxicating liquor may request the arresting officer to have a chemical test made of the arrested person's blood, breath or urine for the purpose of determining the alcoholic content of such person's blood, and, if so requested, the arresting officer shall have the test performed.

Legislative History:
1. Added by Stats 1st Ex Sess 1966 ch 138 § 1.
2. Amended by Stats 1969 ch 1438 § 1, adding "and he shall be advised by the officer that he has such choice" in the second paragraph of subd (a).
3. Amended by Stats 1970 ch 733 § 2.
4. Amended by Stats 1970 ch 1103 § 2, adding (1) "or complete" after "submit to" in the first and fourth paragraph of subd (a); (2) the second sentence of the second paragraph of subd (a); (3) the third paragraph of subd (a); (4) "or fails to complete," in subd (b), and (5) "or failed to complete," wherever it appears in subds (b) and (c).

Former § 13353, relating to the beginning of suspension (based on former Veh C § 307 subd (b)), was enacted Stats 1959 ch 3 and repealed by Stats 1959 c 1996 § 18.4.

Collateral References:
  Cal Jur 2d Automobiles § 372, Criminal Law § 118, Evidence § 396, Searches and Seizures § 46, Witnesses § 29.

§ 23126. Driving While Intoxicated; Presumption

(a) Upon the trial of any criminal action, or preliminary proceeding in a criminal action, arising out of acts alleged to have been committed by any person while driving a vehicle while under the influence of intoxicating liquor, the amount of alcohol in the person's blood at the time of the test as shown by chemical analysis of his blood, breath, or urine shall give rise to the following presumptions affecting the burden of proof:

(1) If there was at that time less than 0.05 percent by weight of alcohol in the person's blood, it shall be presumed that the person was not under the influnce of intoxicating liquor at the time of the alleged offense.

(2) If there was at that time 0.05 percent or more but less than 0.10 percent by weight of alcohol in the person's blood, such fact shall not give rise to any presumption that the person was or was not under the influence of intoxicating liquor, but such fact may be considered with other competent evidence in determining whether the person was under the influence of intoxicating liquor at the time of the alleged offense.

(3) If there was at that time 0.10 percent or more by weight of alcohol in the person's blood, it shall be presumed that the person was under the influence of intoxicating liquor at the time of the alleged offense.

(b) Percent by weight of alcohol in the blood shall be based upon grams of alcohol per 100 milliliters of blood.

(c) The foregoing provisions shall not be construed as limiting the introduction of any other competent evidence bearing upon the question whether the person was under the influence of intoxicating liquor at the time of the alleged offense.

Legislative History:
  Added by Stats 1969 ch 231 § 1.

INDEX

371